Early Childhood Education

Sara Miller McCune founded SAGE Publishing in 1965 to support the dissemination of usable knowledge and educate a global community. SAGE publishes more than 1000 journals and over 800 new books each year, spanning a wide range of subject areas. Our growing selection of library products includes archives, data, case studies and video. SAGE remains majority owned by our founder and after her lifetime will become owned by a charitable trust that secures the company's continued independence.

Los Angeles | London | New Delhi | Singapore | Washington DC | Melbourne

Early Childhood Education

Current realities and future priorities

Edited by

Cathy Nutbrown

100 YEARS 1923 - 2023
Early Education
The British Association for Early Childhood Education

Los Angeles | London | New Delhi
Singapore | Washington DC | Melbourne

SAGE

Los Angeles | London | New Delhi
Singapore | Washington DC | Melbourne

SAGE Publications Ltd
1 Oliver's Yard
55 City Road
London EC1Y 1SP

SAGE Publications Inc.
2455 Teller Road
Thousand Oaks, California 91320

SAGE Publications India Pvt Ltd
B 1/I 1 Mohan Cooperative Industrial Area
Mathura Road
New Delhi 110 044

SAGE Publications Asia-Pacific Pte Ltd
3 Church Street
#10-04 Samsung Hub
Singapore 049483

Editor: Delayna Spencer
Editorial assistant: Bali Birch-Lee
Production editor: Nicola Marshall
Copyeditor: Sharon Cawood
Proofreader: Sarah Cooke
Marketing manager: Lorna Patkai
Cover design: Wendy Scott
Typeset by: C&M Digitals (P) Ltd, Chennai, India
Printed in the UK

Library of Congress Control Number: 2022942315

British Library Cataloguing in Publication data

A catalogue record for this book is available from the British Library

ISBN 978-1-5296-0007-0
ISBN 978-1-5296-0006-3 (pbk)

At SAGE we take sustainability seriously. Most of our products are printed in the UK using responsibly sourced papers and boards. When we print overseas we ensure sustainable papers are used as measured by the PREPS grading system. We undertake an annual audit to monitor our sustainability.

CONTENTS

ACRONYMS

ALN	Additional learning needs
AOLE	Areas of learning and experience
ASD	Autistic spectrum disorder
CC	Children's Centres
CEL	Characteristics of effective learning
CoP	Community of Practice
CPD	Continuing professional development
DES	Department of Education and Science
DfE	Department for Education
EAL	English as an additional language
ECE	Early childhood education
ECEC	Early childhood education and care
EHCP	Education health and care plan
ELC	Early learning and childcare
ELG	Early learning goals
EYC	Early Years Coalition
EYE	Early years education
EYFS	Early Years Foundation Stage
EYFSP	Early Years Foundation Stage Profile
EYPS	Early Years Professional Status
EYTS	Early Years Teacher Status
GLD	Good level of development
GLF	Graduate Leader Fund
HLE	Home learning environment
HR	Human Resources
IDP	Individual development plan
ITE	Initial Teacher Education
MBC	Metropolitan Borough Council
MNS	Maintained Nursery School
NIFS	Northern Ireland Foundation Stage

NPQEL	National Professional Qualification in Executive Leadership
NPQH	National Professional Qualification in Headship
OAP	Observation, assessment and planning
OFSTED	Office for Standards in Education
PCP	Person-centred planning
PVI	Private, Voluntary, Independent settings
QTS	Qualified Teacher Status
RCT	Randomised control trial
REAL	Raising Early Achievement in Literacy
SENCo	Special educational needs coordinator
SEND	Special educational needs and disabilities
SEN/D	Special educational needs and/or disabilities
SIG	Special interest groups
SNP	Scottish National Party
TA	Teaching assistant
UNCRC	United Nations Convention on the Rights of the Child
UNSDGs	United Nations Sustainable Development Goals

ABOUT THE EDITOR AND CONTRIBUTORS

EDITOR

Cathy Nutbrown is President of Early Education and Professor of Education in the School of Education at the University of Sheffield. Her research on work with parents to support young children's literacy development has won an ESRC Award for Research with Outstanding Impact on Society. Cathy chaired the Nutbrown Review of the Early Years Workforce (DfE, 2012) and, in 2013 received the Nursery World Lifetime Achievement Award. Her some 150 publications, include *Early Literacy Work with Families* (with Hannon and Morgan, Sage, 2005), *Early Childhood Educational Research* (Sage, 2019), *Threads of Thinking* (Sage, 2011) and *Home Learning Environments for Young Children* (with Clough, Davies and Hannon, Sage, 2022).

CONTRIBUTORS

Helen Adams has worked as a teacher and leader throughout Nursery and Primary phases, working in small rural schools, larger primary schools in areas of high deprivation and a forces school in Germany. Since 2009, Helen has been Headteacher of Truro Nursery School, Cornwall. Helen promotes the role of the reflective practitioner and sees research and development as critical to ensuring the best start for all children.

Sue Allingham has been a teacher, a Senior Early Years Lead in a primary school, an LA Lead Teacher and an LA Early Years Adviser. Having gained an MA and a Doctorate in Early Childhood Education from the University of Sheffield, Sue is now an independent consultant, author and trainer. She is Consultant Editor of EYE (Early Years Educator) and author of *Transitions in the Early Years* and *Emotional Literacy in the Early Years* (Practical Pre-School Books).

Nathan Archer is Director of the International Montessori Institute at Leeds Beckett University. Initially trained as a Montessori teacher, Nathan has worked in the public, private and voluntary sectors of early childhood education in practice, policy and research. He completed a PhD at the University of Sheffield in 2020, exploring the agency and activism of early years educators.

Lisa Barnes is a Quality Improvement Education Officer for the City of Edinburgh Council. She qualified as a primary teacher with an early years specialism at the Institute of Education, University of London. Having worked as a teacher in Tower Hamlets where the nursery was at the heart of the school, she went on to become a nursery teacher and worked in further and higher education. Lisa was Headteacher of a nursery school in Midlothian for eight years, adopting a values-based, person-centred approach, and drawing deeply on the work of Froebel, McMillan and Isaacs.

Fifi Benham is an early years educator who has been working in pre-schools for nearly six years, been a SENCO for three years and became a pre-school deputy manager in 2020. Fifi started a blog (Early years activity) during lockdown about inclusion and activism in early years and, through that, has been engaging with a range of practitioners online who are also keen to keep pushing the sector forwards.

Jacqueline Bremner holds a BA in Childhood Practice and has worked in early years settings for some 20 years. She is presently an Early Years Excellence and Equity Practitioner in an urban setting, supporting parents and children, focusing particularly on language and communication. She has a special interest in young children's learning in outdoor environments.

Nicola Brinning is Headteacher at Grangetown Nursery School, Cardiff, and has worked in the teaching profession for over 16 years, mostly in Wales and also in Valencia, Spain. Nicola is a passionate early years practitioner, committed to providing quality experiential learning, in an environment that reflects the diverse nature of its community. Celebrating inclusive settings, where autonomous, confident, resilient learners thrive, is at the core of her work. Nicola received the SEN Teacher of the Year Award in 2015. Nicola is inspired daily by the creativity of the community she serves and the commitment of her team.

Verity Campbell-Barr is Associate Professor in Early Childhood Studies and Associate Head of Research at the University of Plymouth Institute of Education. Verity has over 15 years of experience in researching early childhood education and care services. Her research centres on the quality of early childhood services, particularly the early childhood workforce. She has co-led two European projects on what the concept of child-centredness means for quality pedagogic interactions in early years services. Verity has undertaken international research on workforce knowledge, skills and attitudes and an analysis of early childhood degrees in England. Her extensive publications include *Professional Knowledge and Skills in the Early Years* (Sage, 2019).

Sally Cave is the head teacher of Guildford Nursery School and Family Centre, Surrey. She believes that it is important to build positive relationships based on trust and respect with children, families and educators; and that we all need to feel we belong and that we are valued for who we are, just as we are. She believes that without significant relationships, there can be no significant learning. Froebelian principles guide her work with children, parents and staff.

Becky Cook has worked with and for young children for 22 years. She is Executive Headteacher for Pre-Schools at Waterton Academy Trust and Chair of the Board of Trustees of Early Education. Her particular interests in work with young children are developing relationships with children and their families, and establishing inclusive early years settings at the heart of the communities they serve.

Kierna Corr is a nursery teacher at Windmill Integrated Primary School, Dungannon, Northern Ireland. She has built a reputation as a risk-taking, pioneering early years teacher, and is known for her internationally popular blog: *No Such Thing as Bad Weather*. Beginning with a 'blank canvas' and since 2006, Kierna has transformed her own class's outdoor play space into a haven of exploration, challenge and generosity – of resources, time and attitude. The nursery at Windmill has been visited by teachers and pedagogues from the UK, Europe and beyond, and Kierna's authoritative voice is regularly called upon to contribute to or comment on outdoor issues.

Lesley Curtis OBE is the Headteacher and Head of Centre of Everton Nursery School and Family Centre, Liverpool, and has undertaken the role for 23 years. Lesley leads and manages a team in developing high-quality, innovative, multi-agency, centre-based provision. The Nursery School and Children's Centre provide opportunities to share high-quality early years educational practice with colleagues locally, regionally, nationally and internationally. Hence, Lesley has contributed to the boards of local early years groups and Headteacher organisations, locally and nationally. Lesley was awarded an OBE in 2015 for services to education.

Aline-Wendy Dunlop is Emeritus Professor at the University of Strathclyde in Glasgow and has been a member of Early Education since 1971. After initial teacher education, she gained the PG Froebel Certificate at Moray House, specialising in infant and nursery teaching. She went on to teach at the Moray House Nursery School, where the design of the building and the surrounding garden inspired a Froebelian approach. Following a long early years focused career in nurseries, community, schools, further and higher education, she continues to play and learn with her grandchildren.

Alison Featherbe is an independent early years consultant and trainer. Alison has had a long career in the early years sector. She has been a private nanny, teaching assistant in a special school, childminder, nursery practitioner, crèche manager, early years teacher,

EYFS lead and pre-school SEN advisor and an LA early years development officer. Alison currently mentors early years teacher students at the University of Brighton and the University of Sussex. Alison is a SchemaPlay trainer, is NSPCC trained and received the Nursery World Trainer of the Year Award in 2021.

Jan Georgeson is Associate Professor of Education at the Plymouth Institute of Education and has a professional background as teacher of young children with special educational needs. She has also worked as a Portage worker supporting parents and carers of children showing developmental delay. Jan has written extensively on early years topics and carried out national and international research into professional development for early years practitioners and support for families of young children at risk of learning delay.

Emma Gordon is the manager of an early years setting in Aberdeen, which remained open throughout the pandemic. She has worked in the sector for 12 years and is currently working towards an MEd Early Years Pedagogue. Emma has a particular interest in under 2s: how they learn and the role of practitioners in supporting this. With a passion for life, Emma is also a qualified snowboard instructor and loves being outdoors!

Elizabeth Henderson holds a doctorate in education and has, for the last 42 years, worked in all sectors of education from nursery to university. As an innovator in the early years field, she developed an outdoor Community of Practice for ELC professionals in Aberdeen called WIGLS, and founded Nature Nurture, the first outdoor project in Scotland for children under 3 from complex backgrounds. Elizabeth's innovative academic research and writing include the first book in the early years field to use autoethnography. At the age of 3, she fell in love with flowers, precipitating a lifelong love of nature.

Julia Henderson has worked in early years education for 25 years. Now a nursery school principal, she has also worked in a range of educational settings. Her career began in Foundation Stage in inner-city Leicester and later, Nottingham. In 2007, she relocated to Northern Ireland where she worked in curriculum advisory and school development within early years. In 2010, she returned to a school setting with a teaching principal role in a nursery school. She has also actively forged professional networks among educational professionals and is dedicated to developing early years pedagogy.

Louise Kay is a lecturer in Education at the University of Sheffield, School of Education where she teaches undergraduate, Masters and Doctoral students. She has a particular interest in curricular and assessment policy frameworks and how these impact on teachers and children. Her current research includes the collaborative project 'Learning-rich leadership for quality improvement in early education', which focuses on ECE leadership in Australia and England.

Louise Lloyd-Evans is the owner of Young Friends Kindergarten in Hove, East Sussex, and founder of Young Friends Tribe, formerly SNAP – Sustainable Nurseries Against Plastic. She passionately believes that all nurseries should become sustainable, and in teaching the next generation to look after our planet, the nursery offers all children a wealth of experiences which promote sustainable citizenship. Louise and her team have received many Nursery World awards: Early Years Professional of the Year, Enabling Environments, Manager of the Year, Highly Commended Nursery of the Year, and Eco Early Years Award, and many other awards for their website, food and recycling.

Stella Louis, Ph.D. is an early years consultant working with individual nursery settings, parents, nursery schools, local authorities, government departments and charities. She provides training and consultancy with Early Education, running courses on observations, schemas and race, equality, equity, diversity and unconscious bias, and is also a consultant to the Froebel Trust. Her Publications include *Understanding Schemas in Young Children: Again! Again!* (Bloomsbury), *How to Use Work Group Supervision to Improve Early Years Practice* (Routledge), *Let's Talk about Race* (Nursery World), *Observing Young Children: A Froebelian Approach* (Froebel Trust), *Unconscious Bias in the Observation, Assessment and Planning Process* (Foundation Stage Forum, with Betteridge) and *Let's Talk about Bias in the Early Years* (FAMLY, with Betteridge).

Maggie MacDonald has worked in early years for more than 30 years, in voluntary, private, and local authority settings. She holds an HNC in Childcare and Education. Maggie has developed her early years practice through Wee Green Spaces and WIGLS (Working in Green Local Spaces) training, so she can pass on her love of learning in the outdoors, while supporting the well-being of all.

Helen McKinnon has worked in early years education in Scotland for over 22 years and currently holds the position of Senior Early Years Practitioner. Helen is committed to improving outdoor learning experiences for children, combined with an ever-deepening understanding of the far-ranging benefits. In 2020, Helen and her team were presented with an Aberdeen ELC Academy award in recognition of the significant improvement to their setting's outdoor environment.

Myra McRobbie is Chair of the Aberdeen branch of Early Education, and Early Years Project Officer for Aberdeenshire Council. She qualified with the Scottish Nursery Nurse Board in 1986 and graduated in 2011 from Aberdeen University with a BA in Early Childhood Studies. She has worked in a social work day care centre, and as a childminder, a playgroup manager and in a local authority early years setting.

Nazma Meah is an early years teacher with a BA (Hons) Early Years. She has worked in ECEC for some 20 years and has five children. She owns and manages pre-schools and nurseries in deprived and disadvantaged areas, and is passionate about working to ensure high-quality provision for young children with special educational needs and disabilities, and developing inclusive approaches to work with all children and their families.

Beatrice Merrick has been Chief Executive of Early Education since 2013, leading its work on campaigning for every child's right to the best start in life, and promoting high-quality professional development for practitioners. She chaired the Early Years Coalition which produced the 'Birth to 5 Matters' non-statutory guidance in 2021. She had previously spent over 20 years working on the internationalisation of higher education.

Helen Moylett is an independent early years consultant and a vice president of Early Education. She has worked as a teacher, an adviser, Head of the Early Years Centre and a lecturer at Manchester Metropolitan University. She worked on the DfE (2004–2011) National Strategies, developing the EYFS, and leading the Every Child a Talker programme. She was an expert adviser to the *Tickell EYFS Review* and co-authored *Development Matters* (Early Education, 2012). Helen's many publications include *Characteristics of Effective Early Learning: Helping young children become learners for life* (2nd edn, OUP, 2022). She received the 2019 Nursery World Lifetime Achievement Award.

Emma Short started her teaching career in London as a reception and nursery class teacher, before moving to The International Schools, in Prague then Rome. In 2005, Emma became a Children's Centre Teacher based in Penzance, Cornwall supporting local settings to develop their ethos and pedagogy. Emma became head teacher of Camborne Nursery School, Cornwall in 2011 where parental participation and outdoor provision are of particular interest.

Nancy Stewart, MEd., is an independent consultant and writer with experience across many early years sectors and settings; teaching and leading teams working with children aged 2–7, and their families. In the National Strategies team, as Senior Early Years Adviser for Every Child a Talker, she provided advice on the 2012 EYFS review. Nancy also led development of 'Birth to 5 Matters' (EYC, 2021). Her many publications include *Development Matters* (with Moylett; Early Education, 2012) and *How Children Learn: The characteristics of effective early learning* (Early Education, 2016). She is also a vice president of Early Education.

Kathy Sylva OBE is Professor of Educational Psychology in the Department of Education, University of Oxford. She conducts large-scale studies on the effects of early education/care on children's development and has led RCTs evaluating parent interventions. She has been specialist adviser to Parliamentary Select Committees, Ofsted, the Early Intervention Foundation and the Education Endowment Foundation. She is a Fellow of the British Academy and of the Academy of Social Sciences, and received the Nisbett Award from the British Educational Research Association. She is a vice president of Early Education and was awarded an OBE for services to children and families in 2008.

Shaddai Tembo PhD, is a lecturer in Early Childhood Studies (UK and China) at Bath Spa University and an associate lecturer at the Open University. He has been a trustee for Early Education and is a trustee for the Fatherhood Institute. Shaddai is also an independent writer and speaker through Critical Early Years.

Jessica Travers is the Phase Leader of Early Years Foundation Stage at Wigfield Primary School, London, following two years as Assistant EYFS Phase Leader. Having been a primary school teacher for 11 years in the Royal Borough of Greenwich, Jessica has taught in nursery and Reception classes. She has led developments in adventure learning, geography and history and is a trained Forest School teacher.

Sasha Tregenza is a sessional lecturer at Truro College, Cornwall and a doctoral teaching and research assistant at the University of Plymouth, Institute of Education. She worked within the early childhood sector for over 12 years, in roles including early years teacher, deputy manager and SENDco support. Sasha has EYPS, QTS and an M.Ed., and is currently completing her Doctorate in Education, focusing on how young children's views of learning may enhance ECEC practice.

Kate Ullman has taught in special schools for children with complex needs since 1997, after completing her degree and PGCE. At Mill Ford Special School, Plymouth, she has focused on the early years stage, applying an 'EYFS ethos' across Key Stage 1. Kate is particularly interested in supporting parents and families, coordinating a 'Family Project' whereby parents work alongside professionals in developing children's play, social interaction and communication skills, and receiving support to understand the sensory needs of their children.

Elizabeth Wood is Professor of Education at the University of Sheffield. Her research interests include play in early childhood, specifically children's social relationships, how they exercise choice and agency, the meaning of freedom, and the relationship between play and learning. Her work with Liz Chesworth focuses on children's interests in multi-diverse pre-school and school settings. She has collaborated with colleagues in Sheffield (England) and Melbourne (Australia) on comparative research into educational leadership in early childhood. Elizabeth is also interested in policy analysis and critique, and has worked with Louise Kay on the il(logic) of policy discourses, and their power effects.

David Yates is an early years practitioner and teacher. He is secretary of the Early Education South Yorkshire branch. After qualifying, he became Early Years Professional/Senior Early Years Practitioner in a Children's Centre nursery in a culturally diverse community in Sheffield, where most families used EAL. He has led practice with children from birth to 5+. With an MA in Early Childhood Studies and a Level 5 qualification in Leadership, he now leads the nursery unit in a primary school. His interests include following children's interests and fascinations, emergent mark-making and writing, outdoor play, supporting children's transition from FS1 to FS2, and developing close, trusting relationships with children and their families.

ABOUT EARLY EDUCATION

Early Education was founded in 1923 as the Nursery School Association. In 1972, it became the British Association for Early Childhood Education and later, for short, Early Education.

Throughout its history, Early Education has had two main aims. First, it campaigns publicly for universal access to high-quality nursery education, especially for the most disadvantaged children and families. Second, it brings together those working with young children for professional learning and mutual support.

Early Education has established its place nationally as the foremost source of expertise on early years pedagogy, for instance developing guidance including *Development Matters* (DfE, 2020) and *Birth to 5 Matters* (Early Years Coalition, 2021). Our Associates are early years experts who are commissioned through us by national and local government, schools and settings to provide training and consultancy. They also contribute to our open programme of continuing professional development, publications and online resources – available to all early years practitioners – nationally and internationally.

Early Education campaigns on issues that affect the quality and availability of early childhood education. For example, our flagship campaign for a long-term sustainable funding solution for maintained nursery schools reflects a continued belief that early years provision should be led by highly qualified staff, including teachers, with specialist early years expertise and in an environment designed for the needs of young children. We are committed to the principle that early years education should be levelled up to this same high quality everywhere, not levelled down reduce costs, and therefore there should be maintained nursery schools in every area of disadvantage to guarantee children the best start in life – especially those who most need it.

Early Education's local branches are at the core of grass-roots membership activity. Run by committees of volunteers, they provide a forum for practitioners to come together in locations around the UK. Their focus is primarily to support practitioners' continuing professional development, with campaigning activity when local early years provision is threatened by changing local or national policies or funding cuts.

Membership is open to anyone studying or working in the early years in the UK and beyond: students and apprentices, childminders, early years practitioners, teachers, leaders and managers, Headteachers, lecturers, consultants and local authority advisers. Organisational members include private, voluntary and independent settings, nursery, infant and primary schools, colleges, universities and local authorities. Find out more and become part of the Early Education community at www.early-education.org.uk.

ONLINE RESOURCES

The Early Education website, **https://early-education.org.uk/centenary-book**, provides further information and resources related to each chapter. Dedicated pages for each chapter include:

- chapter overview
- chapter objectives
- supplementary material
- links to related continuing professional development
- further reading.

INTRODUCTION

This book, published to mark the 100th anniversary of Early Education, discusses key issues in early childhood education (ECE) around the UK. Chapters are written by many members of Early Education, both well-known leaders and leading, innovative practitioners whose research and practice spans England, Northern Ireland, Scotland and Wales.

Policy and practice vary across the UK, yet what unites those working in ECE, in all parts of the country, is a commitment to shared values of high-quality pedagogy in all settings, equity for all children and their families, and a vision of strong professionalism and leadership across the field.

Three overarching themes run throughout the book:

Children: their rights, play, settings, learning experiences, their families and their relationships and interactions with practitioners;

Equality: for all children, their families and their practitioners – including the attitudes, skills and knowledge needed to identify and tackle discrimination and inequity in all their forms;

Practitioners: their skills, knowledge and understanding stemming from high-quality initial and ongoing qualifications, leadership skills suited to ECE teams, settings and services, leadership of play-based pedagogy, and the importance and impact of their work.

The chapters recognise the historical legacies of ECE, discuss present policies and practices, anticipate the future and pose questions. We conclude with an *Agenda for the Future of Early Childhood Education* which will inform Early Education's agenda for action as we move forward, building on a hundred years of campaigning and professional support for high-quality early childhood education for all young children.

Where we refer to 'parents', we intend this to include all those in a parenting role, unless we specifically state otherwise. Names of parents, practitioners, carers and children are usually pseudonyms. Some case studies are anonymous, others are identified; we thank all who have shared their practice, and the chapter authors for their contributions.

1

THE CENTRALITY OF PLAY IN EARLY CHILDHOOD

NANCY STEWART, KIERNA CORR AND JULIA HENDERSON

CHAPTER OBJECTIVES

- To evidence play as central to child development
- To demonstrate uneven policy support for play pedagogy around the UK
- To exemplify strong and developing play practice
- To argue for an intentional focus to ensure and support play, alongside knowledgeable and sensitive adults, as a right.

CHAPTER OVERVIEW

Play is a fundamental in childhood, and enshrined as a right within the United Nations (1989) *Convention on the Rights of the Child*. Although children play in different ways depending on cultural and environmental contexts, playing is a universal part of development and learning which helps children's successful growth into complex and capable human beings. Today's children are growing up in times of uncertainty and rapid change; extensive opportunities to play are crucial for them to develop flexible minds, creativity, the ability to work with others and the resilience to manage future challenges. This chapter first considers the meaning of play and its centrality in early childhood development. With examples of children's play, we examine the policy contexts of play in early years settings across the nations of the UK. Finally, we suggest some necessary conditions to secure play as a right for all young children.

INTRODUCTION

Children need play and, alongside family life, ECE constitutes a significant part of many children's lived experience. So, play within ECE settings is crucial.

Play belongs to children – arising from their own motivations and bringing enjoyment and satisfaction. To rehearse the benefits of play can seem almost churlish; children play for its own sake and play needs no justification. Yet, to offer the best conditions for children to flourish, educators must understand the unique and powerful contribution of play to children's development.

Defining play is complex, since play appears in many different guises in different types of activity – such as physical, fantasy and exploratory play. One all-encompassing definition focuses on *the player*. Play is distinguished by the central agency of the child who freely chooses to play, what it is about, what to use, how to use it, whether to play with others, and how long to play. So, a child whose own motivation and ideas lead them to build a tower with bricks is playing, whereas a child who has been told to build a brick tower is not. Alongside the child's agency, play which supports development and learning has been described as being joyful, meaningful, actively engaging, iterative and socially interactive (Zosh et al., 2017).

MESSAGES FROM RESEARCH

'Play is the "rocket fuel" of child development' (Brodin et al., 2018: 2), and the benefits of play include all the interconnected areas of child development (Gleave and Cole-Hamilton, 2012). Children's physical health and well-being grow in active play, as they are motivated to move and challenge themselves in developing strength, balance and coordination, while sensory neural networks form (Ginsburg, 2007). Emotional well-being grows as children engage in open-ended activity, free from external pressures, spurred on by intrinsic curiosity and enjoyment. Social development is enhanced as children learn how to engage with others, sharing interests and ideas, negotiating and understanding the perspectives of others (Berk et al., 2006). Communication and language development are well supported through rich meaningful exchanges and experiences which build vocabulary and stretch children's ability to express their thoughts (Hà, 2022).

Well-resourced play environments offer children opportunities to develop knowledge and understanding across various domains of learning, including community, technology, the natural world, the creative arts, literacy, science and mathematics. Play experiences in these areas can lead to deep, embedded learning because meaningful content is encountered with high levels of motivation and enjoyment (Hirsh-Pasek, 2009).

Crucially, play is where children develop attitudes, approaches and skills which foster a strong capacity to learn (Whitebread, 2015). In play, children make choices, follow intrinsic motivation, try out ideas, develop and test theories, explore and take risks. They learn by trial and error, with failure becoming a chance to try again. They find and set challenges, are motivated to persist when they encounter frustration, enjoy their own achievements, think imaginatively, make connections between experiences, and solve problems – all attributes of independent, emotionally and cognitively self-regulated learners.

The early years are crucial for the development of self-regulation, increasingly identified as underlying children's ongoing learning capacities (McClelland et al., 2013). Self-regulation includes elements of executive function: the abilities to defer gratification, control impulses and direct one's attention – all experienced and practised in play (Berk et al., 2006). Children decide their own rules in play, being motivated to follow them consistently to sustain the play they have created.

Where play and children's agency are prioritised in ECE settings, children have been found to benefit into adulthood in terms of education, careers, social adjustment and health, compared to children in settings where directed academic foci were prioritised over play, where any early advantages waned (Chambers et al., 2010).

Developmental benefits arise from different types of play (Whitebread et al., 2012), as Table 1.1 summarises. Ensuring that children are offered play experiences across all types of play, with appropriate levels of potential and challenge as they move through their early years, is an important responsibility for educators.

Table 1.1 Developmental benefits arising from different types of play

Type of play	Examples	Supports development of:
Physical play	active exercise play	whole body and hand–eye co-ordination, strength, endurance
	rough-and-tumble play	emotional and social skills
	fine-motor play	concentration, perseverance
Play with objects	'sensori-motor' exploratory play and construction play	thinking, reasoning, problem-solving, goal-setting and monitoring, perseverance, positive attitude toward challenge
Symbolic play	with spoken language, reading, writing, number, drawing, music, etc.	expression, reflection on experiences, ideas, emotions, language development, early literacy, mathematics
Pretence/socio-dramatic play	small-world play and role play, alone and with others	narrative skills, deductive reasoning, social responsibility, self-regulation
Games with rules	including child-devised rules	social skills: sharing, taking turns, understanding others' perspectives

Children have a right to play freely throughout early childhood. While early years curricula specify learning objectives, play, by its nature, is unpredictable and responsive to children's own purposes. Tension or uncertainty can arise, when contrasting *free play* with activity planned and *controlled by adults*. Zosh et al. (2018) suggest a *play continuum*, with play without adult involvement at one end, moving into a subtle, negotiated space, described as *guided play* where the adult has a significant role in preparing and continually refreshing an environment that invites exploration, offers open-ended challenge and provides children with space, time and resources to use flexibly. The adult partner also has a critical role in the midst of children's play, observing to see if they might usefully add, join in or interact to extend the child's challenge and thinking. Through back-and-forth exchanges, adults respect the child as the leading partner while sensitively offering expertise. Moving further along the continuum in guided play, the adult may initiate a specific activity with a particular objective, while ensuring that there is room for the child to make choices, and responding flexibly depending on the children's input and ideas. At the opposite pole from *free play* lies *direct teaching* where children have no agency and instead fulfil predetermined outcomes – they are instructed receivers, even if doing 'child-friendly' activities. *Child-led play*, supported by adults, has been found to benefit language, cognitive development and emotional regulation (Goble and Pianta, 2017; Zosh et al., 2017), with *guided play* equally or more effective than *direct teaching* (Skene et al., 2022).

Play outdoors contributes to physical and mental health as well as learning, being beneficial also for children who need additional support. For example, one child with additional needs struggled in the pre-school setting to settle to calm activities or play indoors. He often stacked toys, chairs, knocked towers down and climbed furniture. Outdoors one day he spent over half an hour carefully picking tiny berries and collecting them in a bucket, showing enough fine motor control to remove each berry without squashing it and using the language he had to mimic counting as he placed each one in the bucket. His perseverance in this self-chosen task showed the value of the opportunity to explore freely.

Outdoor play, especially in natural environments, gives children a sense of personal freedom, supporting well-being, emotional resilience and cognitive functioning. Outdoor learning in nature can boost confidence, social skills, communication, motivation, physical skills, knowledge and understanding (Gill, 2014). Having regular opportunities to play freely in nature during childhood increases the likelihood of enjoying nature across the life course (Pretty et al., 2009) (see Chapters 4 and 5).

PLAY AND EDUCATIONAL POLICY ACROSS THE UK

Early childhood educators practise in accordance with their own professional knowledge and understanding, within their policy and regulation contexts which can have marked effects on the environments, interactions, and experiences offered to children. Policy and official guidance in relation to play vary widely across the nations of the UK.

Scotland demonstrates a unified and thoughtful commitment to play. Care and education from birth to five are covered in national practice guidance (Education Scotland, 2020a), which foregrounds the importance of play, the outdoors and playful pedagogy. In 2022 the Scottish Government adopted 'Resolution 24', potentially paving the way for a kindergarten stage from birth to six, building on the existing Early Level (Curriculum Review Group, 2004), and further sanctioning play-based learning. Scotland's curriculum is learner-centred, aiming to foster confident individuals, effective contributors, successful learners and responsible citizens. Play engenders these characteristics (Education Scotland, 2020a, 2020b) (see chapters 5 and 7).

Wales adopts a similarly broad focus on developing learners, rather than instilling specific knowledge, with a strong emphasis on play, including outdoor play. The Curriculum for Wales 2022 (Welsh Government, 2020) aims for all children to develop as ambitious, capable learners; enterprising, creative contributors; ethical, informed citizens; and healthy, confident individuals. Through the Foundation Phase, ages 3–6, 'Children learn through first-hand experiential activities with the serious business of "play" providing the vehicle'; play features throughout guidance on curricular objectives, but for 5–6-year-olds, play in literacy and mathematics is reduced (Welsh Government, 2015).

For non-maintained publicly funded nurseries, Welsh guidance (Welsh Government, 2022) highlights play, play-based learning, being outdoors, authentic and purposeful learning, and physical literacy. Rather than subject areas, Wales outlines 'developmental pathways': Belonging, Communication, Exploration, Physical Development, Well-being, which 'represent a child's right to experience an environment where play is valued for itself and as part of learning' (p. 26).

England focuses on a narrow vision of the purpose of education for children aged birth to 5. The Early Years Foundation Stage (EYFS) (DfE, 2021a) aims 'to ensure that children learn and develop well and are kept healthy and safe' (5), with an emphasis on children being 'ready for Year 1' (7). Play features minimally in the educational programmes of required 'activities and experiences'. The EYFS does not *require* a particular pedagogical approach, acknowledging that play is essential, including children leading their own play and 'taking part in play which is guided by adults'. However, adult-led teaching increases for 4–5-year-olds to 'help children prepare for Year 1' (16). Child-led play is sacrificed to this early ascendancy of adult-identified curricular objectives. The dominance of structured teaching is heightened by the Ofsted inspection framework (Ofsted, 2019), which centralises attention on the curriculum, constructed according to adult consideration of what children should know and remember. The strong Ofsted influence favours a precisely structured curriculum from a child's first entry to an ECE setting, with planned progression towards curriculum subjects in Year 1. Such top-down curricular pressure limits the potential to follow children's own curiosities and motivations in play, squeezing out any priority for the power of play to develop children's fundamental personal capacities.

In Northern Ireland, the stated vision focuses on raising standards for all and closing the performance gap (DENI, 2013: 16–17). Early years policy on play falls somewhere between those previously described; as in England, policy is based on academic goals rather than wider development. Recognition of 'the importance of play in its own right, and as a pedagogical tool' (18) is stronger in relation to the pre-school year than from school entry at age 4, where focus on academic goals is perhaps driven by a culture of preparation for academic selection at the end of the primary phase. For the non-statutory pre-school year, guidance (DENI, 2018) calls for children to be offered 'a rich variety of challenging play activities and other experiences in a stimulating environment' (5), with frequent reference to play throughout the curricular areas and inclusion of guidance on adult interaction in play. The guidance allows flexibility, with no formal expectations in curricular areas.

The Northern Ireland Foundation Stage curriculum covers the first two years in primary school (age 4–6 years), and describes play as an appropriate transition into school. Children are gradually introduced to more formal learning, particularly in literacy and numeracy. While there is little discussion of play, references to 'well-planned and challenging play', with adults expected to 'ensure challenge within play activities, altering these in the light of the children's responses', raise questions regarding understanding of the nature of children's agency in play. In case study 1.1, we see 2-year-old Sara's agency as her play is fuelled by lived experiences.

CASE STUDY 1.1: SARA'S CHINESE RESTAURANT

Julia Henderson, Head, Mossley Nursery School, Newtownabbey, Northern Ireland

Within the nursery, a planning-in-the-moment approach supports incorporating children's interests and experiences (Ephgrave, 2018). When one child told us about preparing for Chinese New Year at home, we involved the children in setting up Chinese restaurant role play. Most children in the class are age 4, but some are 2 years old. Another child, Sara (2), said her mummy and daddy have Chinese food, and talked about being in a restaurant, referring to herself in the role play as the 'restaurant lady'. Wearing a dress-up tabard in Chinese fabric and holding a notebook and pen, Sara asked each child and the teacher at the table: 'What you want?' As each person ordered their food, she made a left-to-right zigzag line on her notebook, (using a tripod grip); a separate line for each person at the table. Chat about the menu continued, with the teacher asking if anyone had tried the food listed.

Robert asked Sara if his food was ready, saying he had to 'go back to work'. Sara had moved to the cooker, fully engaged in adding plastic food and wool noodles to the wok – mixing, stirring and negotiating resources with other children in the kitchen. She served the food, placing a plate in front of each person at the table. 'Robert, that's your spicy one, and that's your chicken. Do you want a drink?' She provided cups and poured from the jasmine teapot, then wrote in her notebook, highly focused on making clear emergent writing patterns. A minute later, Robert said, 'I have to go back to my work now, here's my money'. Sara said, 'That's 1, 2, 3, 4, 5 dollars', holding out her hand for money which she put in the till and giving some coins to Robert, saying: 'Here's your money back'. She then returned the plates to the dresser in the kitchen.

Although two years younger than the children she was playing with, Sara had evidently benefited from high-quality play and interaction at home. She used her experience of visiting a restaurant, showed experience of cooking, and knew writing had purpose. Her number conservation was emerging, she communicated effectively, understood the use of money and adopted a role. Sara confidently brought her real-life experiences and 'funds of knowledge' (Amanti et al., 1992) to her pretend play. The teacher reflected that skilled and effective adult interactions would help Sara build on this while in nursery, noting that assumptions based on children's ages should never be made.

As Head of Nursery in a nursery unit attached to a Northern Ireland primary school, Kierna Corr's understanding of outdoor play was first challenged by visits to a Norwegian kindergarten in 2006 and 2008. She then transformed play practice in her setting, sharing her approach to support other educators in developing their practice (case study 1.2).

CASE STUDY 1.2: DEVELOPING APPROACHES TO OUTDOOR PLAY

Kierna Corr, Head of Nursery, Windmill Integrated Primary School, Belfast

In the Norwegian kindergarten, the 5–6 year olds were based outdoors all year round – starting and ending each day in a wooden hut but otherwise in the woods with staff. The 2–5 year olds were based in a traditional building and, despite rain and cold, they were outdoors much more than in my setting.

Observing the play, I found myself asking, 'Are they allowed to do that? Should they be up there? Can they do that?' The staff explained 'if they can get up, they can get down', and when adults help or lift children up onto structures, that is when they get stuck. Staff talked children down from heights, but never 'rescued' them.

The kindergarten staff seemed less involved in the children's play than I expected, though they were skilful observers of play, ready to step in if needed or to add an item to help extend the play. This was quite different from my approach – at one point, I was asked to come out of the sand box and leave the children to play on their own!

(Continued)

The children never seemed at a loss for what to do with the resources, which mainly consisted of natural objects – sticks, logs, sand, mud and water. I saw 'loose parts' in action for the first time. Young children were confident around fires and responsible for their own safety, going as far away as they wished while still being able to see an adult.

I returned to my setting enthused and determined, together with the nursery assistant, to try to introduce what I had learned in Norway. Deciding to go outside every day, we invested in waterproof clothing for staff and children. Initially, we took equipment and furniture outdoors, until we were confident to allow the children to explore the outdoor space as it was, with a bark-chipped area, willow dens, and logs, tyres and crates zoning the small outside space.

Thirteen years on, we embrace risky play, allowing children time to develop their play throughout the day, usually going inside only for snack, dinner and story. Visits to Sweden, Finland and Iceland have further influenced our practice. We adopt an unhurried pace with staggered snack and dinners, so that children have a choice about when they leave their play. Play ebbs and flows through the five-hour day, with minimal interruptions. Our wooded area within school grounds now offers a more natural learning environment, giving children an appreciation of nature in different weather conditions. In any typical outdoor day, the children have freedom to develop deep, sustained play scenarios, and are happy and engaged.

Exchanging experiences across settings and sharing professional learning are crucial for the vibrant development of play pedagogy. Visiting settings with well-established play-oriented practice is part of professional development. Full-time teaching head Julia Henderson describes the wealth of support practitioners derived from a connected community of early years professionals (case study 1.3, see also Chapter 5).

CASE STUDY 1.3: PASSING IT ON – LEARNING IN A COMMUNITY OF PROFESSIONALS

Julia Henderson, Head, Mossley Nursery School, Newtownabbey, Northern Ireland

Our team reflected that play in the extensive outdoor area focused heavily on physical skills and vigorous play which, though important for overall development, confined adult roles to supervising and monitoring safety. We needed to develop more varied outdoor experiences, with opportunities for imaginative, exploratory and creative play.

I visited Kierna's nursery and saw how, in a relatively small area, all the children were fully engaged, occupying all available space, independently creating their own play and investigating all resources – mostly loose parts. The children were suitably dressed for the outdoors, unconcerned with weather and mess.

Adults were present and watching, not merely supervising; poised to engage where required or invited, they did not interfere with the play, while children engaged in everything in the area, in groups or independently.

Inspiration from Kierna's practice has led to a markedly improved quality of play within our setting. We saw that outdoor provision was successful because staff invested in the experience: outdoor clothing for all, zoned areas, loose parts for exploratory play, and a culture of trust and risk-benefit with the children. We decided to develop our practice to incorporate these approaches. Over time, we modified our nursery's approach to suit the outdoor space; defining areas for bark and stones, and introducing resources of loose parts and real objects, had a huge and immediate impact on the play. Children are drawn to investigating pipes, crates, logs, weather and natural phenomena. The development of our Forest School comes next.

Kierna's and Julia's experiences show how the sharing and development of play practices through visits (international and local) is an essential part of CPD which benefits educators who seek to enrich opportunities for children's freedom to play.

PRIORITIES FOR THE FUTURE

Play is a central force in children's development and learning, and must be recognised and championed as such. As the world reels from turmoil brought on by the COVID-19 pandemic, environmental effects and war, play is even more crucial in providing children with a space to grow, understand their world, make sense of their experiences, develop a sense of self and feel well and happy.

The priorities are:

- providing children with essential opportunities to take charge of their own play throughout their childhood
- ensuring rich play opportunities, including outdoors, for all children and overcoming obstacles that limit opportunity for play, including resisting pressure to suppress young children's experiences of play in educational settings
- developing a culture of respect for children's agency in play, including children's purposes being given prime place along the play continuum
- resisting a drive for early attainment (questionable given the very early school starting age of children across the UK) which emphasises adult-determined objectives and can subvert 'playful' activities in ways which interfere with children's own motivations and thinking
- providing CPD for educators, to support growth in the complex pedagogy of play.

Skilled adults who expertly decide when, and know how, to stand back, observe and enjoy children's own learning in play, are essential in educational settings. Knowing when and how to sensitively join play to support a child's own purposes, and when and how to offer opportunities toward adult-identified objectives while maintaining children's agency, takes skill. The quality of pedagogy for play should be a prime focus for educators now and for the future.

QUESTIONS

- What do you remember of play outdoors when you were a young child? What changes do you see for young children today?
- What are the challenges in providing for *free play* in your setting?
- What kinds of CPD do you think you need in your setting to extend children's opportunities for play and adults' skills in a pedagogy of play?

FURTHER READING AND RESOURCES

Early Level Play Pedagogy Toolkit. https://education.gov.scot/improvement/learning-resources/early-level-play-pedagogy-toolkit
An online resource designed to support practitioners working with young children to use play pedagogy to support learning and development.

Learning through Play in the Early Years. https://ccea.org.uk/downloads/docs/ccea-asset/Curriculum/Learning%20through%20Play%20in%20Pre-School%20and%20Foundation%20Stage_0.pdf
A resource to support learning through play with a range of materials.

PEDAL Hub: Resource Library. www.pedalhub.org.uk/play-pieces
An online resource which features research on play.

2

EARLY YEARS CURRICULUM: PAST, PRESENT AND FUTURE TRAJECTORIES

VERITY CAMPBELL-BARR AND SASHA TREGENZA

CHAPTER OBJECTIVES

- To trace philosophical and policy influences in the ECEC curriculum
- To examine the influences of ECEC pioneers in developing high-quality pedagogy
- To consider the concept of child-centredness
- To offer recommendations for a future sustainable, child-centred, early years curriculum.

CHAPTER OVERVIEW

In this chapter, we explore and analyse developments in the early childhood education and care (ECEC) curriculum, tracing philosophical concepts and policy influences, to identify what has shaped current understandings of an ECEC curriculum. This journey of evolving ECEC examines the influence of early years pioneers, such as Friedrich Froebel (1826), Maria Montessori (1912), Margaret McMillan (1919), Rachael McMillan, and Susan Isaacs (1929), identifying how the roles of adults, children and environments within ECEC have developed over time to promote high-quality pedagogy. We critically consider the interplay of policy initiatives in the evolution of the ECEC curriculum in England, highlighting where policy has both drawn on and contradicted the philosophical origins of ECEC. International research illustrates different philosophical conceptions of child-centredness within ECEC and how children can be made 'present' and actively central within early learning (Campbell-Barr and Georgeson, 2021). We conclude with insights and recommendations for a future early years curriculum centred around the child.

INTRODUCTION

The social welfare function of ECEC is now internationally recognised as a social good in supporting parental employment, which relates to an economic good of having more parents in work, while human capital perspectives monetise the role of ECEC in supporting children's holistic development and providing the foundations for their lifelong learning (Campbell-Barr and Nygård, 2014). However, despite the multiple social and economic functions of ECEC, its curriculum is under-theorised (Wood and Hedges, 2016). Historically, there have been different approaches to the ECEC curriculum, largely shaped by developmental theories. Examining the influence of five early years pioneers – Froebel (1826), the McMillan sisters (1919, 1930), Isaacs (1929) and Montessori (1965) – illustrates how the curriculum is historical, social and cultural, holding assumptions about the roles of the adult, child, learning environment and the nature of learning. Here we see how ideas about curriculum have developed over time, and how they have become entangled in policy ideals about what ECEC is for.

Questions of education and learning transcend time, but here we pick up a history of ECEC by observing how, during the Romantic Period (1785–1832), philosophies around the purpose of education, the rights of the child, the role of the adult and the environment within ECEC came to the fore. Growing interest in, and evidence on, child development (Parker-Rees, 2015) increased attention on how ECEC could foster children's holistic development. The 'what' of child development, such as health or education, has a bearing on the nature of curriculum, but developmental milestones and 'norms' have come to guide the ECEC curriculum, despite ECEC pedagogy remaining open to interpretation and learning being a unique and complex process for each child (Wood, 2020). This chapter explores aspects of curriculum, drawing on examples from practice, to critically consider the contemporary ideologies and approaches to ECEC. Finally, we speculate on what a future ECEC curriculum might look like.

THE ROLE OF THE ENVIRONMENT IN ECEC
THE NATURAL WORLD

Froebel (1826) perceived early childhood to be a special and unique stage of life (Jarvis et al., 2017), and he established the 'kindergarten' to support children in developing their innate pureness as they holistically explored their thoughts and ideas. Froebel presented the need for children to understand the world around them, connecting with and caring for the 'garden', encouraging hands-on experiences, self-directed activity, problem-solving and real-world learning. The McMillans further promoted the important role of nature in supporting children's learning and development, establishing an 'open air nursery', where the garden provided many educational activities, enabling children to move freely, enhancing their physical development and mental well being (McMillan, 1919). Similarly, Isaacs' Malting House School (1924–1929) offered provision that embodied the essential role of the garden in education, while Montessori (1965) acknowledged the value of open-air space in supporting children's innate disposition to explore and learn. This reoccurring significance of the garden and nature in ECEC remains evident today, with emphases on outdoor, experiential learning and the benefits of connecting with the natural world (Boyd, 2018) (see Chapters 1, 4 and 5).

Often, the outdoors is seen as a resource which presents learning opportunities for children, as the next example from Ireland shows.

PRACTICE EXAMPLE

Building a snowman

In an urban pre-school in Ireland (where snowfall is rare) the children (aged 3–5) wanted to go and play in the snow. The children worked together to build a snowman, with the educator supporting. One girl talked about needing to find a head for the snowman, so the educator asked how and the child replied 'with a ball'. The educator followed the children's lead, asking questions to help problem solve but with the resource of the snow itself providing the solution.

Connection to nature illustrates the Romantic origins of ECEC, whereby positioning children close to nature was viewed as protecting them from the harsh realities of the adult world (Gabriel, 2017). However, as will be discussed, the natural world is not only a romantic play and learning resource for children, but also a subject of learning (see Chapters 3, 4 and 5).

OPEN-ENDED RESOURCES

Early pioneers also considered the need to add additional resources into the outdoors. Froebel (1826) presented the idea of learning through play, providing 'gifts' and 'occupations' within the learning environment. 'Gifts' consisted of open-ended objects such as balls on a string, creating curiosity and interest, to explore abstract thoughts and stimulate discovery. 'Occupations' were for practising daily skills such as sewing or wood carving to foster invention. 'Gifts' and 'occupations' were presented sequentially, enabling children to start with the simplest resources, building to the most complex, extending thoughts and knowledge over time throughout their exploration (Eugene and Provenzo, 2009). Similarly, the Montessori Method (1912) promoted a carefully prepared and structured environment, within which children had freedom of choice and movement, while interacting with a range of open-ended and natural materials to inspire them, supporting intellectual and social development. This concept of providing open-ended resources is evident in the educational philosophy of McMillan (1919), who suggests that because high-quality development requires opportunities to experiment and discover the properties of natural materials, children should have freedom in their play and learning. Further, Isaacs (1929) emphasised the use of natural materials, imagination, arts, crafts and scientific discovery, believing that – to understand the importance of responsibility – children should be trusted to direct their own play, take risks and explore their ideas in an open-ended context.

The influences of these pioneers are evident in ECEC today. For example, an enabling environment remains a key principle of the English EYFS (Department for Education, 2021a), echoing the need for stimulating resources and spaces; rich, play-based learning opportunities; and support for children to take risks. Its 'Characteristics of Effective Teaching and Learning' mirror the need for open-ended play and learning opportunities through active learning, creating, thinking critically, playing and exploring. These empower children to use their imagination, become a decision-maker, explore their ideas and make sense of the world around them within their learning environment (DfE, 2021a). However, international research shows how the resources provided to children offer signals as to how a space is to be used, which in turn provides messages that might limit a sense of 'free' choice (Campbell-Barr et al., 2018). The adult has a role in pacing and sequencing activities (Bernstein, 2000) – for example, setting up a home corner influences the kinds of role play children might engage with. Similarly, a construction area with construction toys influences what children are expected to do in that space. There is no linear relationship from a curriculum document – like the EYFS – to pedagogic practice, but the resources provided illuminate how the social order will interplay with and regulate pedagogical interactions. English policy identifies ECEC as providing the foundations for children's lifelong learning, thereby shifting the idea of resources from being 'gifts' and open-ended natural materials for children's self-chosen exploration, to being tools for achieving adult-prescribed learning objectives and outcomes. Free choice is reduced as children are steered in prescribed directions to demonstrate the achievement of particular skills.

HOME-FROM-HOME ENVIRONMENT

Froebel (1826) believed in creating a nurturing environment for children to grow and develop alongside nature, and emphasised the importance of parents, particularly mothers, being children's first educators – a concept now acknowledged (see Chapter 6). Froebel's *kindergarten* became an extension of the home, thus requiring educators to hold nurturing qualities. Montessori (1912) and Isaacs (1929) further developed the significance of the home, with child-friendly furniture enabling children to access the environment independently and comfortably. Similarly, McMillan (1930) emphasised how the nursery school should become part of home life, supporting the nurturing of childhood (Liebovich, 2019). The McMillans highlighted that the early years is a time to respect and care for childhood itself, and is about more than the education of a future adult workforce.

Parental partnerships remain a fundamental principle within international models of ECEC, indicating how relationships between educators, children and families, are key to promoting children's outcomes (see Chapters 6 and 11). However, the interplay of 'homely' and 'educator', signals the blurring of the role of ECEC as both 'care', in supporting working parents; and 'education', in supporting children's holistic learning and development. This dynamic varies in different international contexts (Moss, 2006) but indicates how an ECEC curriculum signals what is valued for children, their learning and development, and highlights the expectations of the ECEC workforce.

THE ROLE OF THE ADULT IN ECEC

Early years practitioners have varied roles and responsibilities (see Chapters 12 and 13), but here we discuss two roles traceable across this history of ECEC: observer of free play and facilitator of learning.

OBSERVER AND REFLECTOR

Froebel (1826) believed that documenting important observations of children's development effectively supported learning. Observation, in Froebel's approach, is combined with reflection, where educators reflect on what children can do and their current thinking, then extend and deepen the child's knowledge and skills accordingly. For Montessori (1912), observation enabled educators to understand how children learn, by following the child, identifying individual needs and interests, then changing and enhancing the environment accordingly, to promote children's freedom within a structured and well-prepared environment (Giardiello, 2014). McMillan (1930) used observation to view children holistically, emphasising the importance of providing education and care to best strengthen learning and development. Similarly, Isaacs (1929) considered the role of the educator to be that of an observer, to inform an understanding of children's learning and development, and to shape planning. While all these pioneers promoted observation, their purposes varied slightly. Froebel (1826), for example, supported the *educator's reflections* upon what children could do and how to extend this further, while Montessori (1912) considered observation to be a tool for understanding how children learn and the uniqueness of each child.

Common to these pioneers is the notion that observation facilitates a focus on the child and their abilities – *what they can do* and *how they learn* (see Chapter 3); however, well-intentioned use of observation to plan for future learning risks shifting the focus from the child *in the present*, towards a view of what the child *should* become. This future-orientated vision is embroiled in policy debates about the purpose of ECEC; a child development focus positions ECEC as preparation for the next stages of education, rather than ECEC being of value in itself (Roberts-Holmes, 2021). Yet, without a future-orientated vision of a child's development, there is a risk that a child's development may languish rather than progress. There is also a question around what children are to be prepared *for*. A developmental focus on children, combined with aspects of nurturing, and a recognition that children are at the centre of their world, mean that ECEC can support both their present and future learning.

FACILITATOR OF LEARNING

The facilitation of learning involves many different elements. For Froebel (1826), this meant *guiding*, rather than instructing. For Froebel, *freedom of guidance* meant supporting children to express themselves and explore their interests. This freedom is supported by an educator who plans and provides sensitive guidance, enabling children to develop knowledge and practise skills through real-life experiences. From a Froebelian perspective, the educator's responsibility is to facilitate a rich learning environment and to guide children to think for themselves, challenge themselves and develop self-discipline.

Montessori considered educators as facilitators of learning through creating well-prepared environments, which provide signals to children as to what they might do. The Montessori Method (1912) includes *auto-education*, whereby the multi-sensory environment is prepared to such an extent that, independently, children may discover and learn. The educator then facilitates learning and observes sensitive periods (see Association Montessori Internationale in Further Reading and Resources), stepping in to support and further develop knowledge and skills, when the child shows signs that they are ready for guidance.

According to Isaacs (1929), educators were responsible for creating high-quality learning environments, supporting children's freely chosen activity, without limiting natural curiosity. The roles of the environment and of the educators were equally important, with self-chosen, closely observed play being crucial. McMillan (1930) believed that children need to be nurtured to achieve, with educators responsible for facilitating children's good health, happiness and well-being, regardless of individual differences. McMillan's educators were facilitators of learning, providing both education and care to young children.

European research has illustrated how educators nurture while supporting learning through observing *in the moment* (see Chapters 3 and 4) and adjusting their facilitator role to respond to each child's needs (Campbell-Barr et al., 2018). Observations demonstrate how educators carefully adjust their interactions with children from directly leading or facilitating activities, to observing carefully – intervening only as needed. Educators often engage in several interactions simultaneously, playing directly with children, observing others, soothing a distressed child – at once fulfilling the roles of educator, carer, facilitator and observer. Educator–child interaction may not be overtly physical, and can include facial expressions and careful body positioning to indicate attention, with or without direct intervention (Hayashi and Tobin, 2015). As case study 2.1 illustrates, educators have subtle ways of signalling that they are there to support children's needs, ways that echo responsiveness, sensitive guidance and moments.

CASE STUDY 2.1: BUILDING THE GARAGE

Sasha Tregenza

Two 3-year-old children are building a garage for their toy cars. The educator observes and asks open-ended questions to extend their thinking. Tom's garage design consists of one high side of Duplo, making the structure wobble.

Tom: 'This keeps wobbling, it's too wobbly.'
Zack: 'It needs reinforcing, that's what my Daddy says.'
Tom: 'What's that mean?'
Zack: 'Like this.' [placing a brick beside the wobbly tower]

The educator explains how reinforcing helps to strengthen and support a structure, encouraging Tom to experiment with ways to strengthen his design, suggesting 'I wonder what would happen if we placed the bigger Duplo brick on the bottom instead of the top?' Tom uses his problem-solving skills to experiment with reinforcing his model, with the educator nearby. He becomes frustrated as the Duplo bricks continue to wobble and fall. The educator observes this frustration, offering a hand to steady the structure, while Tom repositions his bricks, smiles and continues to construct his garage, until he has completed this to his satisfaction. Tom places his car inside the structure, commenting 'It's done!', while the educator praises his effort and asks him to explain the process of building his garage.

THE ROLE OF THE CHILD IN ECEC

Our ECEC pioneers saw several roles for children, which chiefly involved them in learning through self-directed play and activity, acquiring daily skills, and caring for and respecting living things.

LEARNING THROUGH PLAY AND SELF-DIRECTED ACTIVITY

The influence of our pioneers has positioned ECEC away from directed teaching and instruction, towards valuing and respecting children's abilities to direct their own playful learning (see Chapter 1). This concept emerged in Froebel's (1826) philosophy of child-centredness with playful activities, outdoor play, music, poetry and nature, supporting both spiritual and educational development. Child-appropriate playful learning experiences – enabling self-activity, construction of knowledge and exploration – were at the core of children's early learning. These required play provision to be carefully planned for, to promote curiosity and interest and meet specific learning objectives (Eugene and Provenzo, 2009). The Montessori Method (1912) similarly acknowledged play as being the *work* of the child; accordingly, children were offered open-ended natural resources, providing greater scope for freedom of imagination and playful experiences (see Chapters 1 and 5). From the Froebelian and Montessorian perspectives, play exists within a structured environment prepared for them, which might limit children's self-directed activity and their active learning.

McMillan and Roberts (1917) further promoted the role of children as free players, providing space to run, dig, explore, and the freedom to choose playful experiences, to take responsibility and make choices within their learning environment, often outdoors. Similarly, Isaacs (1937) valued child-initiated play as a vehicle for expression and development, emphasising that play has the greatest value in learning and development, when children have the freedom to evolve, choose, explore and follow their own course of play.

CASE STUDY 2.2: THE DRIVE-THROUGH RESTAURANT

Sasha Tregenza

Three 4-year-old children are in the home corner. Anthony comments that the window with curtains is like a 'drive-through to get food'. The children use their existing knowledge, imagination and negotiation skills to redesign the 'home corner' to mirror their understanding of ordering food at a drive-through. Anthony collects a note pad and pen to record orders and stands behind the window. Max selects a large cardboard box from the junk modelling corner and discusses with Janet how they can use it as a car to travel through the drive-through. The children use their problem-solving skills to make a pathway for the car to travel alongside the window. The educator observes the interaction and interest between the children and hints: 'I wonder if there is anything else you might need to do before you take the food you have ordered?' Janet suggests: 'Money, we need to pay!' Anthony replies: 'No, we just beep this card against here ... BEEP, see!' (Holding a square piece of cardboard he had found, against the cash register he had also found). The children continue to play, taking in turns the different roles and responsibilities.

The United Nations (1989) Convention on the Rights of the Child enshrines the right of children to play, yet play and self-directed activity are dependent on the educator who observes, facilitates and creates the play space, potentially limiting *free* play. The 'right to play', combined with responsiveness and recognition of the children as being central to their ECEC experiences, must maintain a child-centred philosophy (Chung and Walsh, 2000).

DEVELOPING DAILY LIFE SKILLS

Children learning daily living skills in ECEC was supported by all pioneers featured here, who recognised daily skills as part of being in and nurturing the world, while promoting children's self-care and as preparation for adult life (Eugene and Provenzo, 2009).

DEVELOPING CARE AND RESPECT FOR LIVING THINGS

Our pioneers all championed children's relationships with the natural world, and the ensuing benefits in enhancing physical development, in promoting well-being and in nurturing the environment itself. The settings created by these pioneers embraced the use of the garden and open-air spaces where children learned and practised the skills of caring and respect for living things: growing flowers and food and caring for animals and the wider setting community. Though the concept of respecting and caring for the environment has existed for centuries, the fast-developing technological environment threatens children's engagement with nature, necessitating a re-emphasis of the importance of the natural outdoors for children (Louv, 2013).

Our environment is a dominant focus in ECEC, with an emphasis on education for sustainability (see Chapter 4) ensuring that our youngest generation develops climate and conservation awareness, thus caring for themselves and others (Hirst, 2020). As case study 2.3 shows, the extent to which sustainability is embedded in the curriculum varies, and depends on the individual setting and practitioner priorities (see Chapter 3).

CASE STUDY 2.3: RESPONSIBILITY FOR RECYCLING

In her ECEC setting, it is Estha's (age 3) turn to be responsible for recycling. The practitioner who is cooking lunch calls Estha to the gate at the kitchen entrance, saying 'Estha, I've some recycling for you.' She hands her a cloth bag with the words 'reuse, recycle – save the planet' printed on it. It contains a cardboard egg box, a plastic milk bottle, and a small glass jar with a metal lid. Estha takes the bag outside where there are several labelled recycling boxes. She places each object in the correct box.

(Continued)

The practitioner who introduced the children's recycling responsibilities to the setting is in the garden and says: 'Hi Estha, I see you are responsible for the recycling today.' Esther smiles and, as she skips indoors to return the recycling bag, she replies 'Saving the planet!'

We know the increasingly detrimental impact humans have wrought on the natural world, with global climate change (see, for example, COP26 in Further Reading and Resources) requiring a re-establishment – in education – of a focus on sustainability, stressing a symbiotic relationship between the development, health, well-being and economics of individuals and the planet (see Chapters 4 and 5).

KEY ISSUES FOR THE FUTURE

We need new visions for the future. Policy has perpetuated a narrow and restricted view of education, with the present-day ECEC curriculum becoming synonymous with control, and focused on limited understandings of developmental approaches (Wood and Hedges, 2016). Historical views of ECEC can appear ideological when divorced from socio-cultural and historical contexts, yet modern interpretations of the pioneers' ideals have important messages for curriculum today. A broadening of child development to consider children as part of the world offers opportunities to reimagine the ECEC curriculum.

'Birth to 5 Matters', which was developed by the Early Years Coalition (2021: 6), demonstrates how settings can marry EYFS policy requirements with priorities for children. It reaffirms 'core principles which recognise':

- the child at the centre of practice
- the child's connections within family, communities, cultures and the natural world
- the need to consider the whole child: physical, social and emotional well-being, health and learning
- children's rights under the UNCRC (UN, 1989)
- the sector's responsibilities under the United Nations Sustainability Goals and UNESCO Education for Sustainable Development
- the statutory requirements of the SEND Code of Practice.

With a focus on the unique child, positive relationships, enabling environments and learning and development, curricula legacies of the past are clearly present in twenty-first-century ECEC curricula, where the connection between the child and nature remains evident.

The pioneers' legacies can be seen as ideological calls to allow children to play freely outdoors (Wood and Hedges, 2016). However, recognition of the outdoors is about an engagement with the world, a deeper learning about our world and the life skills needed to survive in it. The EYC has drawn attention to: children's funds of knowledge, equity, sustainability; children's rights; twenty-first-century skills; and professional judgement, within which traditional subject areas combine and meaningfully emerge, as children co-create their learning in partnership with informed, skilful, sensitive practitioners.

Curricula must be future orientated, enabling children, when adults, to care for themselves and live in synergy with – and protect – the planet. The underpinning philosophy towards a curriculum might therefore be focused on the child as being central in their world, which holds much to learn about.

QUESTIONS

- How would you describe the curriculum priorities in your setting?
- How would you explain your approach to supporting children's learning to a prospective parent?
- Can you trace the approaches of the pioneers in your practice?

FURTHER READING AND RESOURCES

Association Montessori Internationale (2022) montessori-ami.org (accessed 11 April 2022).

26th UN Climate Change Conference of the Parties (COP26) in Glasgow on 31 October – 13 November 2021. https://ukcop26.org

EYC Birth to 5 Matters 'Spring Festival' themes. https://birthto5matters.org.uk/spring-festival (accessed 14 June 2022).

Giardiello, P. (2014) *Pioneers in Early Childhood Education*. London: Routledge.
This book traces the influences of ECEC from Rousseau to the present day.

Nutbrown, C. and Clough, P. (2014) *Early Childhood Education: History, Philosophy and Experience*, 2nd edition. London: Sage.
This book, on the work of ECE pioneers, includes fictional conversations with many of them, to highlight their contributions.

Wood, E. (2020) Learning, development, and the early childhood curriculum: A critical discourse analysis of the Early Years Foundation Stage. *Journal of Early Childhood Research, 18*(3), 321–336. https://doi.org/10.1177/1476718X20927726
This article questions the selective use of child development theories as the underpinning knowledge base for EYFS practice.

3

UNDERSTANDING YOUNG CHILDREN'S LEARNING THROUGH OBSERVATION AND ASSESSMENT: HOMING IN ON FASCINATIONS

SUE ALLINGHAM AND NICOLA BRINNING

CHAPTER OBJECTIVES

- To offer a language for early assessment and observation of learning, with ways of defining current terms
- To encourage reflection on practice and provision across the sector
- To discuss and develop thinking about observation and assessment through case study examples.

CHAPTER OVERVIEW

This chapter is built around the policy contexts of Wales and England. This immediately requires a definition of terms, which we seek to do through practice examples throughout the chapter. With an emphasis on observation in the moment and practitioner reflection, we consider how observation-informed assessment should be prioritised over prescribed assessments which can obscure the fascinations of individual children as they learn holistically. Case study material highlights the effectiveness of assessing though naturalistic observation, and the important role of parents in their children's assessments.

INTRODUCTION

We are in a time of change. Since 2020, the COVID-19 pandemic has made a big impact, prompting reflection across all walks of life. Coincidentally, change is running through the way that early childhood education is being reviewed in England and Wales. So, drawing on our experiences of working in England and Wales, we take a fresh look at how young children's learning is understood and assessed. We first consider how various terms are defined, then we briefly compare the relevant policy in Wales and England. This is followed by a consideration of how we understand children and their learning, with a practice case study from a nursery school in Wales. From this, we think about the concept of 'fascination' and the role of adults in observing and scaffolding children's learning. Two further case studies identify the importance of observation-derived assessment, and the role of parents in the assessment of their children's learning. Finally, we suggest some key issues, around observation and assessment, for the future.

A PROFESSIONAL LANGUAGE

Policy and practice use several core terms and phrases, which we refer to throughout this chapter, including: teacher, parent, setting, provision, curriculum, teaching, learning, play, observation, assessment, planning, pedagogy, and sustained shared thinking. It is important that we own and understand our professional language, and remain aware of how it is used in various media, and of our own meanings and usage of such terms. We may not all hold the same understanding of these terms, and so we may understand other people differently. We will return to this later.

EARLY YEARS EDUCATION POLICY IN WALES AND ENGLAND: A COMPARATIVE OVERVIEW

First, we present a brief overview of how, in recent years, the governments of England and Wales have adopted different approaches to reviewing and developing early years policy.

EYE POLICY IN WALES

Chapter 1 introduced the Welsh perspective on play, and here we consider curriculum more broadly. The Welsh Government has recognised the need for a curriculum to reflect the learning styles and stages of child development, through which children organically evolve. This approach, championed by Professor Graham Donaldson, resulted in the development of *The Curriculum for Wales* (Donaldson, 2015). Donaldson recognised that children learn on a continuum, progressing at their own pace, and acknowledged that every child has their very own learning journey.

Observation is necessary to gauge a deeper understanding of where children's learning currently lies and to identify *appropriate* provision for their further development. The Curriculum for Wales for 3–16 year olds is underpinned by 12 Pedagogical Principles and encompassed within six Areas of Learning and Experience (AOLE): Expressive arts; Health and well-being; Humanities; Languages, literacy and communication; Mathematics and numeracy; Science and technology. Wales's holistic curriculum allows children the autonomy and independence they need over their own *learning journey*. It is: evidence-led; based on subsidiarity; ambitious and inclusive; manageable, with pace, passion and professionalism; and unified.

Adults scaffold learning and provide stimulus and provision to meet the needs of all learners. This is the first time Wales has seen a curriculum that is underpinned by *experiences* – this is imperative – and *repetition* to ensure children's skills, knowledge and understanding are acknowledged. There is now no place for paying lip service to teaching topics to tick a box. The Welsh curriculum provides ample opportunity for learners to have ownership of their learning experiences, with enquiry-led learning and opportunities to learn and grow together. Children are growing in an ever-evolving world and need to live and learn through authentic learning opportunities, equipping them for life in a unified society. The Principles and Areas of Learning Experience are supported by cross-curricular responsibilities, and embedded within this curriculum reform are Four Broad Purposes whereby all children and young people will be: Ambitious, capable learners; Enterprising, creative contributors; Ethical, informed citizens; Healthy, confident individuals.

Assessment is acknowledged as a learning continuum throughout the new curriculum which will now support individuals' learning as a journey, working through any progression step at any time. Children are not expected to meet targets at a certain stage, regardless of developmental appropriateness. There are 27 statements which form the basis of learners' progression through five age-related Progression Steps:

1. Age 3–5
2. Age 5–8
3. Age 8–11
4. Age 11–14
5. Age 14–16

These Progression Steps are part of a learning continuum which can be attained at the appropriate point for each learner. Descriptors of learning; Areas of Learning and Experience (AOLE); pedagogical principles, and cross-curricular skills are outlined, with schools having control of designing their own curriculum and pedagogy – bespoke to, and reflective of, each school's ethos and core values.

ECEC POLICY IN ENGLAND

As in Wales, ECE in England has undergone review and change, stimulated – not by an examination of child development – but from a review of primary school assessment. This resulted in the introduction of a statutory baseline assessment to be completed on entry to Reception classes, and changes to the EYFS statutory framework and non-statutory guidance.

Assessment can support good teaching, but this depends on the form of assessment. Revision of the Statutory Framework (DfE, 2021a) and EYFSP (DfE, 2022a) to meet the needs of a government accountability agenda was problematic. This resulted in a feeling that assessment must be based on statements in policy documents designed to *prove* that children take the *correct* steps to achieve the early learning goals (ELGs).

The Statutory Framework sets a context for settings to develop their curricula for children in England from birth to 5 years. A culture had grown up of tick-box assessment, perhaps because of a lack of pedagogical background and professional experience among some practitioners. While the reforms aimed to discourage such practices, this requires extensive culture change and an increase in professional knowledge and confidence.

HOW SHOULD WE UNDERSTAND CHILDREN AND THEIR LEARNING?

Curricular policies in England and Wales have different starting points, yet practitioners' interpretations of policy and their views of 'the child' remain at the core. For Wales, observation has frequent mention in policy, such as:

> The key principles essential for holistic and meaningful learning for all children start with skilful, observant and interested adults, who provide authentic and engaging experiences in effective, exciting environments. Our role is to use our observations to plan experiences and environments that are meaningful and relevant to children's interests. (Welsh Government, 2022: 7)

In English policy, observation receives less prominence, yet it is a vital pedagogical tool of assessment. Practitioners responsible for children's holistic learning know the importance of observing children and taking time to understand their fascinations. Quick tick lists have routinely been used by many, but practitioners can find themselves trying to teach what is tightly prescribed by policy, rather than developed from children's interests (see Chapter 1).

The role of the adult is crucial in understanding children's learning – through observation and assessment practices – which home in on their fascinations. Assessment is acknowledged as an important part of work in early childhood education, in all four countries of the UK, but how this is interpreted varies.

Throughout this book, we see examples of children being naturally drawn to, and fascinated with, natural environments and the natural curiosity this provokes. Effective pedagogues do not rely on 'off the shelf' curricula or assessment programmes and approaches. Rather, they skilfully define, refine and adapt policy and practices to facilitate individual children's learning. Case study 3.1, from a Maintained Nursery School in Wales, demonstrates such practice. With children's fascinations guided by elemental play (Woods, 2016), the nursery's approach is also underpinned by Bronfenbrenner's (1977) theory of 'Ecological Development', which suggested that a child's environment should be a nested arrangement of structures – each contained within the next – organised according to how much impact they might have on a child. Bronfenbrenner suggested that children's development is significantly influenced – directly and indirectly – by the social and cultural forces in their immediate and wider environments.

CASE STUDY 3.1: IN THE ALLOTMENT AND THE POTTING SHED

Yvette O'Reilly, Senior Teaching Assistant and Justin Mills, Teacher

Grangetown Nursery School, Grangetown, Cardiff, Wales

The children have been designing, exploring and preparing our compost and community allotment.

In the afternoon, Fion, Mike, John and Nadia, aged between 3 and 4 years old, all helped dig and transport soil to various parts of the garden, so that we could begin planting. John knew the grass would be good for the 'little creatures'. We came across several worms and talked about how they mix up all the soil when moving around and that this is good for the plants.

The children and Yvette looked at the seeds inside a pepper; with support, they chopped the peppers, gathered the seeds and placed them onto paper towels with water. We considered how we should grow them and how best to ensure they grew; deciding that we should do some collaborative research and follow visuals for the best steps. Our nursery uses Wilson's (1984) concept of Biophilia – so research here is supported by lots of displays, pictures and planning.

The enquiry around planting seeds from food that we eat continued the next day. Fion wanted to see if her seed had grown at all, so she independently went to the potting shed to report back on the progress of her seed.

Zion and a few others moved soil from the digging patch to the potting shed, where they each planted apple seeds, much as they did the day before. They labelled their sticks to keep track of the seeds. When discussing how living things grow, the conversation led to the life cycle of a plant. The children talked about the basic needs of plants and flowers and the essential things they needed to be responsible for, for their seeds to

(Continued)

flourish. Anna, the practitioner, and four children dug out the beds and added the gravel, using tools to dig, fill buckets, and add gravel to the base of beds. The children talked about how plants like water but not too much, and how stones help with drainage so that plants don't have too much water and then won't grow. The children had ownership over the type of plants to place in the beds, deciding they wanted climbing plants, fruit bushes and flowers.

The children were fascinated by the 'snakes' and 'snails' (worms) that they found in the soil. In emptying one of the planters, they came across more worms which fascinated John and Anna who spoke about the length and colour of the worms and which were the 'mummy' and 'daddy' worms. The children also worked together to move the green house to the compost area and the leaf compost to Forest School, to ensure that there was plenty of room in and around the flower beds to grow everything in one space.

A group of 22 children used their senses to investigate three types of fruit: watermelon, pineapple and mango, looking at the patterns on the skin of the watermelon and testing themselves to see how strong they were, by holding and feeling the weight of the watermelon. They made predications about whether these fruits would have seeds inside. Dale, Fion and Tammy lifted one above their heads. Fion said, 'it would be red inside and taste juicy and delicious'. Zion said that he had pineapple at home, and Anna guessed a fruit beginning with 'M' and which was red and green on the outside and yellow/orange inside – describing the mango. Each child took a turn to use a large knife to cut off the pineapple top, bottom and sides, while chanting the 'chopperty chop' rhyme. Most of the children ate the watermelon, and most also enjoyed the mango and pineapple.

Six children talked about their snack and where it came from (many suggesting Asda) and they also talked about how fruit grows. Talking about what living things need to grow, most children recalled sunlight and water and remembered that the soil was very important. The children were surprised to find seeds in their cucumbers, holding cucumber slices up to the sun to see through them and whether they had a seed. Finding many seeds, the children collected them in a bowl to plant the next day. Zion squeezed his orange to see if it also had seeds inside. John said, 'I know oranges have seeds in; when I eat them at home, I find them in my orange and I eat them'. Once all the children had finished their snack, they took their fruit peelings out to the compost area, and Zion said, 'this will help to make sure our soil is very healthy'.

Most children thought the seeds wouldn't grow and that we couldn't grow our own in the nursery. John decided to use the iPad to look up how to do it. The children remembered that the seeds need water to grow and discussed how they must remember to do this. Eddie used a watering bottle to water the seeds planted in the soil, showing that he understood the process of watering a plant, by aiming consistently at the soil and pulling the trigger to water different pots on the stand. He was also fascinated by the cause-and-effect action of this process. Dale, Eddie and Tammy investigated the seeds we harvested from the watermelon, mango and pineapple crown, watching a video of how to grow them. We talked about how the seed grows up through shoots and down through roots. We looked for a sunny spot in the nursery to help the seeds germinate and checked on progress daily.

Tammy, Yunus and Anna were really interested in a pile of sticks in the compost area, and explored them for a sustained period. They talked about where they came from.

Anna pondered: 'They have come from the trees'. 'Why are they different colours?'

We noticed that some were brittle, and some were bendy.

Tammy said: 'I'm making a magic wand and turning you into a frog!' [chuckling as she cast a spell]

Tammy and Anna were able to manipulate the sticks and create loops and circles that they then tied off. Yunus noticed and tried several times, becoming frustrated when he couldn't tie the sticks off. With support, he made a wand and cast spells on the practitioner too, very pleased with this achievement.

On another day, Fion was again keen to check on the apple seed she had planted in the potting shed. Some of the seeds the children had planted had sprouted a green shoot. Fion, Zion and Mike carefully sprayed water onto their plants and some others. They then agreed to water them again the next day, when Fion said: 'I want to go see my seed in the shed.' , and referring to the seeds everyone had planted she observed: 'They are green now'.

It is possible to identify many elements of learning which are relevant to practice in all parts of the UK. We do not intend here to analyse children's learning in terms of subjects, but many Areas of Experience and Learning and Early Learning Goals, are present in the rich case study included in this chapter. The outdoor and indoor environments in this nursery school, together with sensitive, informed and immersed practitioners, and clear theoretical underpinnings and professional knowledge, facilitated many aspects of early years curricula as children learn while engaging in real tasks (see Chapter 4).

WHAT IS A FASCINATION?

Being in awe of something encourages children to become fully immersed; awakening this euphoria results in their intrinsic motivation which influences their learning as individuals and in co-operation with others. This awe and fascination have an effect on our brains as we release endorphins, making the experience memorable and meaningful (Given, 2002).

We suggest that, as practitioners, we should talk about what it means to 'be in your element'; this takes different forms for different people. What sparks that 'state of flow' and allows sustained, high levels of engagement will depend on the individual. This demonstrates that observation should be at the core of all quality early years provision.

Further, we suggest that practitioners need to 'think outside the box' and confront assumptions to stimulate and engage to a deep level. Sometimes, it is the adult's reservations or feelings around a learning experience that hold young learners back, so we need to be self-reflective and assess our own reservations. Ultimately, children will take the risks and provide the provocations that go far beyond those reflections of an adult. Learning and exploring together, in a collaborative way, is key, as children are confronted with elements of challenge and desirable difficulties through their learning experiences.

When adults identify moments of achievement, newly mastered skills, steps in literacy and so on – this is sensitive observation which can be recorded as a form of ongoing, individual assessment. We have not included mention of children identified with special educational needs or disabilities (SEND) (see Chapter 8) because we suggest that the practices discussed in this chapter are inclusive and similarly apply to all children, whatever their abilities, learning, developmental or support needs. To achieve this inclusivity, continuous and enhanced provision are needed. Curriculum and pedagogy are intrinsically intertwined with meaningful observation and formative assessment. *Continuous provision* makes the learning experiences familiar, reassuring and always accessible – independently and with adult support, while *enhanced provision* is where a learning experience has been scaffolded by an adult or provides a challenge above any intended outcome. For example, a builder's yard was set up with all the relevant resources which children could access independently, thus providing a challenge to the children to stretch their critical thinking by posing a 'desirable difficulty'. This might present itself in the adults piercing holes in the bottom of buckets and then challenging the learners to make their own cement with sand and water. By creating holes in the buckets, this will pose a practical problem that the learners will have to work collaboratively on, to achieve their aim. These styles of learning experiences are carefully constructed by the practitioners and allow multiple avenues of learning to solve a problem. Learners will be engaged in sustained shared thinking and display deep levels of learning when experiences are presented in this way. It's vital to stretch learners to the edge of their capabilities and to challenge their creative thinking, while homing in on their interests and schemas (Athey, 2007).

The role of the adult here is to observe, and scaffold children, looking out for those who might need help to deal with frustration, and noting what each child has achieved across different aspects of learning. The extended observations and practitioner notes from Grangetown Nursery School in Wales show how deep engagement of practitioners with children – and the subsequent documentation of activity, conversations and learning – can provide useful information for recording children's ongoing achievements and identifying learning needs or next steps in whatever policy format is required. This is the focus of case study 3.2.

CASE STUDY 3.2: FROM 'IN THE MOMENT' OBSERVATION TO INDIVIDUAL ASSESSMENT

Anya has a real fascination with literacy and is far beyond her age of development. She shows enthusiasm and an intrinsic need for learning more and more about the concept of words and their linguistic connotations. Anya will get lost in story books and read with awe and wonder about the magic of the print on the page. She understands that the written words have sound and meaning, and will independently sound out new words that she adds to her ever-growing word bank.

Anya always seeks opportunity to read new texts and find print within her environment. Anya took on the task of writing signs and labels in our setting. She created a welcome sign in both English and Welsh. She listened intently to the adult and understood the task at hand. Independently, Anya sounded out the words, correlating the right letter to the sounds she heard when speaking aloud. With very little adult support, Anya created beautiful print which we proudly showcased in our setting.

Tuning in to learners' interests and providing opportunities that are rich and authentic ensures that learners have ownership over their learning. These things also demonstrate to learners that the adults within the setting see, hear and respect them, solidifying the meaningful, genuine relationships between practitioner and learner. Anya has a strong sense of belonging and is comfortable in expressing and challenging herself. This results in authentic learning which allows for organic development and progression.

We suggest that all settings, regardless of their location or policy prescription, can hold the child as the centre of the curriculum (see Chapter 2), with clear policies and practices on holistic observation and assessment. And this also means involving children's parents in their assessment and learning records. Chapter 6 focuses on how parents are involved in their children's learning at home in their capacity as first educators, while case study 3.3 briefly illustrates how parents can be invited to contribute to the ongoing assessment of children's learning and development.

CASE STUDY 3.3: INCLUDING PARENTS' KNOWLEDGE IN ONGOING INDIVIDUAL ASSESSMENT OF CHILDREN'S LEARNING AND DEVELOPMENT

To get a full picture of our learners, we hold a parent/teacher consultation during our admission process. We use the format shown to direct conversations to ascertain the child's likes, dislikes, family dynamics, what's important to them and more. This provides us with a baseline that has come direct from the parents. This enables us to start their learning story and provide provision that will meet the learner's needs and engage them from the very beginning. We conduct these during our 'home visits'. These visits allow the families to feel more at ease as it's their own environment and it provides the practitioners with an invaluable opportunity to observe the learners in their safe place. Being able to facilitate these visits and construct these dialogues ensures that we have all the information we

(Continued)

need. It also allows us to experience something that the learners remember and cherish, guaranteeing that we develop meaningful, authentic relationships with the child and their whole family.

It is important to acknowledge that our learners with Additional Learning Needs also have Person Centred Planning (PCP) meetings, where, every term, the parents meet with all professionals involved with their child, and discuss progress, what's working well and what's important for the future. These meetings are facilitated by the school and are all recorded in the learner's Individual Development Plan (IDP).

KEY ISSUES FOR THE FUTURE

The interpretation of any national assessment policy depends on many things, such as: the background knowledge of the practitioner and how widely read and how well informed they are; whether information comes from a primary source or is mediated by another source – such as the local authority (LA), social media, other practitioners; practitioners' life experience; practitioners' professional experience; how professional language is interpreted and defined; and the specific setting ethos and philosophy.

If the adult is the sole decision maker in terms of what counts as learning, they decide what is worth observing and adding to a child's learning profile, within their policy context. We suggest that it is a matter of respect that adults take responsibility to ensure the involvement of all; including the children who have agency and their own thoughts, opinions and ideas, and their parents who are their primary educators. Children's fascinations are theirs alone to explore and indulge. We need to ensure that policies, in every country of the UK, preserve the unique child and their fascinations, and emphasise the skill of observation and formative assessment as being key.

Assessment of young children's learning in the future should:

- highlight and celebrate the learning approaches and qualities of each child
- identify the unique fascinations of each child
- prioritise accounts of children's deep learning in free play – alone, in small groups, and with/without practitioner support
- derive from observations by practitioners and contributions from parents
- be shared with parents
- record child-led learning and adult-identified lines of development.

As the case studies in this chapter show, these priorities are achievable and, in some settings, are already part of established practice where observation and assessment are integral to planning. As 'Birth to 5 Matters' (EYC, 2021: 39) states:

Each child's own unique pathway of development and learning involves many ele
ments woven together in a holistic form. Observation, assessment and planning (OAP)
makes this holistic development visible, so children's thinking and understanding can
be shared with parents and carers, other professionals, and with children themselves.

QUESTIONS

- Look back over case study 3.1, from Grangetown Nursery School in Wales. What
  instances and practices of observation, assessment and understanding of children's learning can you identify? What was being observed? How is it being
  assessed? What is the impact of this on children's learning?
- It is vital that all those working with young children are secure in their professional
  knowledge and understanding, including their professional vocabulary. Consider
  how you use the terminology around learning, particularly how the terms *observation* and *assessment* are used in policy and practice.
- Think about your own practice and your own pedagogic approaches: to what extent
  do you recognise and explore the fascinations of the children you work with?

FURTHER READING AND RESOURCES

Birth to 5 Matters (2021) *Learning and Development: Observation, assessment and planning
as quality improvement.* https://birthto5matters.org.uk/wp-content/uploads/2021/03/
PDF-19-OAP-as-Quality-improvement.pdf
Overview of integrated observation and assessment practices and tools to identify children's achievements and aid planning.

Chesworth, L. (n.d.) *Observing, Recognising and Responding to Children's Funds of Knowledge
and Interests.* https://birthto5matters.org.uk/wp-content/uploads/2021/03/Observing-
recognising-and-responding-to-Childrens-funds-of-knowledge-and-intrests.pdf
Summarises *Funds of Knowledge in the Observe-Assess-Plan cycle.*

Pen Green Centre, Charnwood Nursery School and Rowland Hill Nursery School
(2018)*A Celebratory Approach to SEND Assessment in the Early Years.* www.pengreen.org/
wp-content/uploads/2018/05/A-Celebratory-Approach-to-SEND-Assessment-in-Early-
Years-1.pdf
Focuses on children as unique individuals and their achievements. It emphasises an inclusive approach, useful for observation and assessment.

DEVELOPING A CULTURE OF SUSTAINABILITY IN EARLY CHILDHOOD EDUCATION

ALISON FEATHERBE, LOUISE LLOYD-EVANS AND HELEN MOYLETT

CHAPTER OBJECTIVES

- To outline and exemplify a 'slow pedagogy' of education for sustainable development
- To demonstrate how sustainability in ECEC can be guided by the Three Pillars of Sustainability
- To suggest some actions for the future of sustainable practices in ECEC.

CHAPTER OVERVIEW

In the early years, where our habits of mind and learning dispositions are formed, we can help to cultivate young children's social imagination; supporting them to think creatively, critically and optimistically about the state of their world and their own actions. Here we draw on practical examples from *Young Friends Kindergarten* in Hove, East Sussex where the staff have been working on developing their hopeful 'slow pedagogy' and provision in this way for several years.

INTRODUCTION

PRACTICE EXAMPLE

Stop wasting water

Three-year-old Kit is pouring water into a water butt with an adult. Water is splashing out.

Kit stops, observes the adult, and says, 'You are wasting water, we need to stop wasting water.'

Adult: 'What do you think we should do about that?'

Kit gets a funnel and says, 'Let's pour it in this.'

Kit saw the problem and suggested that the practitioner should do things differently. This kind of short, everyday interaction is an example of a child using social imagination:

> the capacity to invent visions of what should be and what might be in our deficit society, in the streets where we live and our schools. Social imagination not only suggests but also requires that one take action to repair or renew. (Greene, 1995: 5)

The thinking and practice we share in this chapter are inspired by hope and social imagination, as well as by the huge learning power of young children and the adults who live and work with them. Early years education has a vital role to play in creating a more environmentally sustainable and socially just world at a time when we face the need to save our planet and its many life forms from the devastation inflicted by our own species. Issues such as climate change, deforestation, loss of biodiversity and extreme weather are affecting everyone; nevertheless, governments and multi-national companies act slowly to take the global action required and this can be depressing. However, we have also seen that people power can influence national governments and make a local difference. Much of this creative change has been inspired by young people such as Greta Thunberg and others, who have inspired global school-based action (see case study 4.1).

CASE STUDY 4.1: YOUNG FRIENDS KINDERGARTEN - TRAVELLING HOPEFULLY

Louise was embedding sustainability principles at home with her children when she recognised that her strong personal principles around sustainability for herself, her family and her home could, and should, be brought into her work with children and their parents in her childcare business. So began the journey for Young Friends Kindergarten. Alison, an independont oonsullaril, has followed the progress of the nursery closely for some years and, for the last two years, has been employed there on a part-time basis to assist in its development. Helen lives nearby and admires their thoughtful child-centred pedagogy for sustainability.

Young Friends is a flourishing nursery with an exciting curriculum and an ever-developing sustainable environment – a learning community where children and staff are totally engrossed in their play and explorations, as well as being aware of their place in the wider world. Young Friends reaches out locally through the parents and other community members. The nursery belongs to a wider national and international community of educators. It has developed practice through undertaking accreditations such as SchemaPlay, OMEP ESC Bronze Award and the Green Flag Eco-Schools award, as well as winning Nursery World awards. The kindergarten is a member of Eco Wheel, links to the GECCO website and hosts visits and meetings for other settings from across the UK to share the lessons learned along the way.

The nursery uses recycling, composting and upcycling to allow the children to develop skills across all Early Years Foundation Stage areas of learning. Rather than focus on these practical ideas here, we concentrate on what makes planet-friendly actions successful: the underpinning pedagogy, the ongoing professional development and the lessons learned along the way, which may support thinking and practice in other settings.

At the heart of everything that happens are the children. Louise, Alison and the team continue to learn from, and reflect on, how the everyday lived experience of the children and the care and teaching provided by the staff can equip all the Young Friends community to be powerful learners and caring eco-aware citizens.

THE THREE PILLARS OF SUSTAINABLE DEVELOPMENT

The UN Earth Summit in Rio (in 1992) referred to three 'interdependent and mutually reinforcing pillars' of sustainable development. These have since become known as the Environmental, Social and Economic pillars. The challenge for early years educators is to develop pedagogic practices that promote sustainable actions with respect to each of these pillars (see Siraj-Blatchford et al., 2010; Boyd, 2017; Bergan et al., 2021).

One way of meeting this challenge is adopting an early years curriculum that focuses on children as active agents of their own learning (see Chapter 2). Sen (1999: 6) urges the adoption of a 'capability'-centred approach to sustainable development which aims to: 'integrate the idea of sustainability with the perspective of freedom, so that we see human beings not merely as creatures who have needs but primarily as people whose freedoms really matter.'

Young Friends practice is a respectful approach to children as free active agents as well as a clear focus on the environmental, social pillars and economic pillars.

The economic pillar is not just about buying and selling in the obvious way that can be seen in the broken keyboard example below. Today's throw-away culture tells young people that it doesn't matter if we break things – after all, new toys are just an easy computer-click away. At Young Friends, children 'fix' things when they break, which teaches them both to be careful with what they use and to consider how to fix things if they break. Some things, they decide, are not fixable, but many are.

ENGAGING AND INVOLVING PARENTS

One of the lessons Young Friends has learned is that the community has to be parent-centred as well as child-centred. Staff are passionate and committed to making the nursery as sustainable as possible and sometimes their enthusiasm for making the necessary changes has run away with them. Early on, for example, when they 'banned' disposable nappies, Louise remembers having 'to slow down, realise our haste and address concerns from parents. We may have known these things were "right", but it's easy to forget about the planning stage when we got used to the idea, and just spring it on parents. We have learnt our lesson about that.'

More recently, the children broke a computer keyboard. The team decided that they would use this as a valuable lesson to address the economic pillar of sustainability and talked to the children about making things to sell to in order to raise money to buy a new keyboard. The children loved the idea and also enjoyed counting the money as it increased and comparing it to what they needed. Louise explains: 'they gave me the money and I bought them a keyboard and the lessons learnt were incalculable. However, we hadn't educated our parents on the value of this activity and some understandably felt we were asking them by proxy to buy nursery resources! Backtrack again! We did it too soon, so we took time to really explain The Three Pillars. Lesson learnt.'

A SLOW PEDAGOGY

The passion and enthusiasm of Young Friends staff may have sometimes needed slowing down, but it has also achieved amazing results. As the references to the Three Pillars and the wider community of sustainability indicate, Louise, Alison and the team are clear about their philosophy and see it as part of a bigger picture of national and international climate and sustainability initiatives.

Louise and Alison explain how environment and pedagogy work together:

> Young Friends is not built to be pretty (even though it naturally is) – it is the type of place you dreamed of as a child, numerous opportunities to explore loose parts, cardboard boxes to climb in and out of and tape to stick them all together. Children get

into 'flow' quickly as they become absorbed in their play, often carrying on where they left off the day before. It's not always easy to see a child's intentions, and this is where subtle open-ended conversations come in – or not – maybe the children are just getting stuck in and want to be left alone – knowing this is the skill of a great practitioner who is always observing. Not writing or ticking boxes but simply observing and reflecting.

In this description of 'slow pedagogy', children are not rushed too far, or too fast, but rather met where they are, as staff enjoy with them the power of their curiosity and the thrill of finding out what they can do – valuing them as interesting people in their own right – as human beings, not just human 'becomings' who need to be got 'school-ready'! Consequently, there is no rigid 'routine of the day' and, as our bee example shows, the practitioners are as curious and observant as the children.

PRACTICE EXAMPLE

The bee

Angharad (practitioner): Oh, look I found a bee; who wants to come and look?

Drew:	It's lying on the ground; is it poorly?
Angharad:	I think it's a bit sleepy but what should we do?
Harper:	Help it. Pick it up and make it safe.
Angharad:	Good idea! I'll get a bit of paper so I can pick it up without hurting it.
Drew:	Yeah!!! [Jumps up and down with excitement]
Angharad:	What do you think we should do now?
Jesse:	Let's take it to the sugar water. [the children and adults had made a bowl of rocks and sugar water for the bees and put it in a sheltered place in the garden a couple of weeks before]
Angharad:	What a wonderful idea. Let's take it there now.

The children watch happily, while Angharad puts the bee gently by the side of the sugar water bowl.

At the beginning of this chapter, Kit was conscious of the wasted water: both Kit and the children engaged in helping the bee, and are encouraged to talk and think in partnership with adults. Adults do not issue directions or stick to a timetable – rather, they facilitate conversation and support problem solving.

FIXING, RECYCLING, REUSING

At the back of the urban woodland garden is the Nature Workshop. Here, children fix, create and learn about real-life safety. They wear safety goggles and gloves as they saw and drill and learn real DIY skills to fix and make things to play with. Sometimes they will decide they want a toy, like a car, and make decisions about how to make one. Or, perhaps, they will use their real sander to sand down some rough edges of the wood so they don't get splinters. It is a joy to watch any child making their own toy which they then play with for hours, days and often weeks because it has the features they planned and wanted – and *they* made it! The workshop is also stocked with things like masking tape, glue and other materials for when they need to fix something like a book. Seeing a problem and attempting to fix it oneself is part of the package of lifelong learning skills that give children the freedom and capability which Sen (1999) advocates.

While they are fixing, recycling and exploring their environment, children are practising social skills and care for each other, as well as being encouraged to use all the characteristics of effective learning. In case study 4.2, we can see playing and exploring, active learning and creative and critical thinking in action.

CASE STUDY 4.2: THE RIVER

Alex, aged 3, started to gouge a long line in the mud down the bank of a hill at a local woodland. 'This is my river!' she exclaimed proudly. Some of her sticks snapped, so she started to experiment with different types to find the right size and strength for her needs. She passed one to her key person and invited her to join in with her. She told her their task was to 'make the river long enough to reach the water at the bottom of the hill'.

The next day, she was joined by her friends, and they made a larger 'river'. They found worms which one of the children decided were river worms and needed to go back into the riverbed to keep them alive. On day three, Alex added rocks in a line which she said were 'stepping-stones, bridges and cliffs'. Her friends were happy to help her realise her vision.

Back at the kindergarten, the key person showed the group a video about water cycles to explain how their river would work. They then extended it further by conducting a water cycle experiment with boiling water and a mirror, and they watched the water evaporate, condense and precipitate. Over the course of the week, the team inspired the children further by projecting backdrops of different rivers from around the world and reading books that featured rivers.

Alex is free to take risks and develop her ideas with her friends. By tuning in and allowing the time, space and freedom to engage with the environment and her peers, the adult is fostering Alex's ability to focus and concentrate deeply while she is thinking creatively and critically. She is making meaning as she notices patterns, tries out ideas and builds working theories (Chesworth, 2019).

The examples we have shared so far are interactions between adults and children using verbal communication. Babies also confidently interact with peers, older children and nature (see Chapter 5). In the urban woodland garden, staff assist where needed, but otherwise engage by watching, while they function as those secure bases from which the very youngest explore the kindergarten world through their senses, building physical aptitude as they crawl, pull themselves up and toddle around the uneven and varied terrains. They look up to feel the rain, turn to the sound of a bird or buzzing bee overhead, and deepen their learning through schemas, 'familiar and repeated patterns of behaviour' (Athey, 2007: 57), like putting bark in and out of empty vessels, stirring leaves and rainwater, negotiating a bumpy landscape, or watching the tadpoles wriggling in the frogspawn. The animals – eight guinea pigs and the Labrador, Landa – are also a source of fascination and delight, and the children can become absorbed and in a state of flow when observing them. This notion of children being in 'flow' is often discussed at Young Friends. Csíkszentmihályi (2000) talked about flow as an optimal psychological state that people experience when engaged in an absorbing activity – the sort of involvement leading to deep-level learning and high levels of personal well-being (Laevers, 2000).

The educators at Young Friends also experience deep involvement when they are open to children concentrating and becoming oblivious to other stimuli. In their practice, we can see what Van Manen has called 'pedagogical tact', defined as 'the active alertness, ethical sensitivity and practical flexibility that educators demonstrate … in everyday educational situations' (Van Manen, 2015: 190). He has unpacked this idea in many ways but of particular relevance here is the importance of *hope*; arguing that pedagogical hope 'animates the way a parent or teacher lives with a child: it gives meaning to the way an adult stands in the world, represents the world to the child' (2015: 192). He argues that when we are hopeful, we are open, and that we are only truly open to a child's way of being when we are open to ourselves. This can sometimes be very challenging and Young Friends recognises how fundamental staff well-being and professional development are to a truly child-centred approach.

THE JOYS AND CHALLENGES OF WORKING SUSTAINABLY

Over the years, Louise has gathered a strong staff team, but recruiting and retaining the right people who are open to working within the Young Friends approach is an ongoing challenge. Any potential staff member should get just as excited as the children when they find slug eggs and become equally passionate about learning through nature as about understanding 'flow' and 'slow pedagogy'. She says:

> It's important to hire open-minded and environmentally aware people and then we keep up the momentum with regular room observations and relevant supervision targets. Consistency is key to ensuring depth and authenticity. Everyone is encouraged to reflect and take pride in developing their own skills in line with our ethos and alongside the children.

Our days are flexible and flowing without the constraints of 20-minute sessions. What does it matter if children haven't covered all areas if they have been in flow, learning and having a wonderful time at the back of the garden all day? It is clear that this patience and flexibility benefit children's development far more and what does coverage mean anyway? It's just an invitation to tick boxes rather than be a partner in learning.

All of this is impossible without inspiring room leaders and managers who are happy to spend time in the rooms both to help and to role model, and showing it's not about 'paperwork' and 'getting things done' but about genuinely enjoying the children.

Our resources are all-natural and open-ended – no structured shop-bought toys, except for staples like wooden blocks. Rooms are stocked with reused and repurposed items and sustainable loose parts. Parents and new staff do find this extraordinary and often daunting at first. Open-ended everything? What will children play with? How will I work with this? What will they do with these 'things'? However, we ask new staff to be patient – stop and watch their role models and not to worry if they feel lost because, in the end, the rewards are priceless. Over time, they usually (not always – this is not for everyone) find our Young Friends obligatory resourcefulness unlocks creativity and skills for child and adult exploration. Children relish the opportunity to think differently about their play and staff relish the freedom to be authentic, relaxed and creative in their work.

The role of the adult within children's play is a common topic with the team (see Chapter 1). It's so important to get this right, and so we teach our team to OWL (observe, wait and listen) sensitively and attentively. Interacting to a high level is not about always being in the centre, quite the opposite, it is about knowing when to sit back and watch as much as when to get stuck in! Our children are confident and resourceful because they learn their views and interests are valued, but there is consistent encouragement of their independent and critical thinking expertise.

We keep up the momentum with 'flowing' routines that allow children to weave and flow inside and out, while adults scaffold their learning, often without the children realising. Children develop their sense of self and learn about risk and safety and to respect and think of others; for example, serving each other at mealtimes, keeping their environments clean and tidy, looking after plants, recycling and composting (see Chapter 2). Children are never told to finish an activity if they are 'in flow' – made possible by intuitive adults who can see where they need to be in order to facilitate this. All of this encourages a way of thinking and being that helps children to question and have high levels of wellbeing and involvement.

We encourage a daily reflective time for the room teams, to build on our knowledge of each child and share 'teachable moments' (Hyun and Marshall, 2003). Our staff are trained and practised in the Characteristics of Effective Learning (DfE, 2021a, para. 1.5), tuning into each child and seeding environments around challenging and interesting continuous provision. Our team's main objective is to facilitate and encourage the children to be in *flow*.

As the 'bashing together' example shows, the adults model team working for the children, and this helps create a sense of community that we see rolled out in children's play.

PRACTICE EXAMPLE

Bashing together

A group of 3-and 4-year-old children is bashing chalk and charcoal and other things they can find on the wooden table outside – passing things to each other to try and experiment together. They are in conversation:

Taylor:	Try this stone, it's really hard and good at smashing.
Kim:	Shall I show you how to do it?
Addison:	Thank you. [watches closely] Can I have a go?
Kim:	Yes, you try.
Addison:	We need a bit more, don't we?
Taylor:	Yes.

SPACE FOR EXPERIMENTATION, CHALLENGES AND LEARNING FROM MISTAKES

The Young Friends philosophy expects educators to think for themselves and bring creativity to the activities and experiences they provide. The sustainable curriculum has evolved organically and is 'owned' by all the staff.

PRACTICE EXAMPLE

Experiments with painting sustainably

Recently, one of our leaders highlighted that we didn't have enough opportunities to mark-make sustainably, so they went about making paint with powdered spices and other natural ingredients. There was lots of trial and error that the children were involved with (we had a lot of rotting beetroot in tubs for a while!). Because we are doing many things for the first time as we try to be more sustainable, we see these instances as perfect demonstrations to the children that we are learning together and that adults don't always have the answers and are still researching and learning too. In fact, it's often the children who come up with solutions. The search for natural paints that can be cheaply made continues!

The staff create experiences that challenge children and encourage them to work together to solve problems. For example, the plants need to be watered, but how are we going to get the water from the water butt to the plants? Frogs have moved into one of our water butts – how will we make sure it's safe, the water stays clean, and they can get in and out? The children enjoy problem solving and often come up with very practical and sensible solutions. So, we can see that these children are capable thinkers who are developing the life skills they need to live sustainably and compassionately now and in the future.

KEY ISSUES FOR THE FUTURE
THE POLICY PICTURE

The 17 United Nations Sustainable Development Goals (SDGs) are targets that all UN member states have agreed to work towards achieving by the year 2030. They set out a vision of a world free from poverty, hunger and disease. The SDGs aim to be relevant to all countries to promote prosperity while protecting the environment and tackling climate change. They have a strong focus on improving equity to meet the needs of women, children and disadvantaged populations. It would therefore be reasonable to expect that recent policy documents in the UK would reflect those goals. However, it is hard to find any policies on sustainable education which are broader than re-cycling or 'top tips' for teaching.

For instance, the Department for Education (2021b) purportedly responded to the Paris Climate Agreement, with legislation to meet net zero by 2050, and to UNESCO's 'ESD for 2030' with the keys roles of education in achieving the SDGs. We cannot rely on government policy, because it is largely focused on national curriculum subjects, with scant reference to early years as being crucial to a sustainable future. The trauma and disruption of COVID-19 saw governments talk of 'catch up' and 'accelerated learning', as if children were in a race – inevitably with winners and losers. We must trust and support the creativity and infinite capacity of young children to imagine and create different ways of being in the world (see Chapter 2).

THE PEDAGOGICAL PICTURE

Unusual narratives feature in children's play, and they are familiar with not having answers. All kinds of things are possible, for example:

> Macy: I've lost my watch and my umbrella at home.
> Adult: Oh. What do you think might have happened to them?
> Macy: A mystery took it in my house.

We serve children and ourselves best when we embrace imagination and creativity and reject the narrow foci of 'learning outcomes'. So, for the sake of all of us and our planet, let's develop hopeful, relational, slow pedagogies; with time and space for deep-level learning. In a future filled with confident, autonomous learners who think and act collaboratively, people will find ways 'to know what to do when they don't know what to do'!

WE NEED TO

- believe in the capacity of young children to see themselves as custodians of the environment
- reflect and engage in debate so that together we take steps (however small) to live more sustainably
- adopt a slow pedagogy which puts children first, listens to their voices, and values their creativity and problem-solving abilities.

QUESTIONS

- Have you taken time to reflect on your personal values around sustainability and what are you already doing to make changes?
- How might you reach out to parents and others in the community to work together to encourage thrift, conservation and citizenship?
- How do you empower the children through supporting their ways of learning and their thinking skills as they engage with outdoor environments?

FURTHER READING AND RESOURCES

Boyd, D.J., Hirst, N. and Siraj-Blatchford, J. (eds) (2017) *Understanding Sustainability in Early Childhood Education: Case Studies and Approaches from across the UK*. Abingdon: David Fulton/Routledge.
Examines research into education for sustainability within EY education in the UK and discusses how policy and pedagogy support the Sustainable Development Goals.

Eco Wheel: https://ecowheel.org

GECCO: https://gecco.org.uk
A registered charity, established to promote sustainability in early years childcare and education.

The Green Flag Eco-Schools award: https://www.eco-schools.org.uk/about/what-is-eco-schools/

Hadland, C. (2020) *Creating an Eco-Friendly Early Years Setting: A Practical Guide*. London: Routledge.
A comprehensive guide to embedding a sustainable approach in settings.

Huggins, V. and Evans, D. (eds) (2018) *Early Childhood Education and Care for Sustainability*. London: Routledge.
This book combines international examples of best practice and research to support the future of sustainability in ECE.

OMEP ESC Bronze Award: www.omep.org.uk/esc

SchemaPlay: https://schemaplay.com

The UN Earth Summit in Rio (1992): www.un.org/en/conferences/environment/rio1992

United Nations Sustainable Development Goals: 17 Goals to Transform our World – www.un.org/en/exhibits/page/sdgs-17-goals-transform-world

5

A GRASSROOTS APPROACH TO DEVELOPING EARLY YEARS OUTDOOR EXPERIENCES: BUILDING A COMMUNITY OF PRACTICE

ELIZABETH HENDERSON, EMMA GORDON, HELEN MCKINNON, JACQUELINE BREMNER AND MAGGIE MACDONALD

CHAPTER OBJECTIVES

- To share an overview of current outdoor early learning and childcare (ELC) in Scotland
- To exemplify outdoor practices that enhance children's unique development
- To stimulate discussion on helping practitioners find their voice and self-confidence to engage in transformational practices.

CHAPTER OVERVIEW

Taking a Scottish perspective, this chapter shows how, building on the early roots of outdoor learning, recent policy has promoted outdoor learning in the early years. In this chapter, Elizabeth Henderson shares her account of establishing a Community of Practice (CoP) to support practitioners in providing outdoor experiences for young children. Case studies from CoP practitioners, focus on: going to a local green space with children; den building as a provocation; and a child under 2 learning through her senses. The chapter highlights the role of a CoP in nurturing belonging and agency in times of change.

OUTDOOR LEARNING AND PLAY: PAST AND PRESENT

In June 2019, 38 early learning and childcare (ELC) practitioners, from 30 ELC settings, embarked on a collaborative learning journey. With shared values, beliefs and a passion for outdoor ELC, they formed the core of a new Community of Practice (CoP) called *Working in Green Local Spaces* (WIGLS), designed to nurture professional friendships, encourage knowledge sharing and develop a sense of belonging. A commitment to the value of nature and the outdoors in helping nurture young children's healthy, holistic development, connects these practitioners with early pioneers.

In response to the perceived impact of industrialisation and poverty on young children's health and well-being, many pioneers advocated for open-air play spaces, learning about nature, gardening, dance, music, singing and craft. They included Robert Owen (*New Lanark Nursery*, Scotland, in 1816), Friedrich Froebel (Kindergarten, in 1837), Lileen Hardy (*Edinburgh Free Kindergarten*, in 1903), Rachel and Margaret McMillan (*Open Air Nursery and Training Centre*, Deptford, London, in 1914). Today, over 200 years since Robert Owen opened his *New Lanark Nursery*, the same concerns persist.

Today's practitioners, however, face a more complex early years landscape: children spend an estimated 50% less time outdoors, and more time watching screens and using digital devices than the previous generation (Moss, 2012); 5.5% of 2–4-year-olds have identified mental health concerns (NHS Digital, 2018); and a rise in obesity to 14.4% for 4–5-year-olds in England (NHS Digital, 2021) give cause for concern – all further exacerbated by increased poverty. Indeed, Scotland's Chief Medical Officer advised that 'children under five should have 180 minutes of physical activity every day and that should include outdoor play' (Scottish Government, 2020: 56).

Children need to move freely to explore their environment, play, co-construct their world, to connect and to belong; this is their right. However, for some children, outdoor play in general is limited due to: increasingly sedentary lifestyles; fears about children being hurt while playing; a lack of safe outdoor spaces; a suspicion of strangers; and little time for play at the end of an adult's working day. Sandseter et al. (2020: 124) consider parental and practitioner concerns and fears around risk to be 'the main barriers to children's outdoor play'.

Global research, however, affirms the salutogenic, health promoting impact of the natural environment (Lindström and Eriksson, 2005) through valuing the outdoor environment in nurturing healthy, holistic, child development. Sunlight boosts vitamin D intake; exercise increases heart rate, strengthens muscles and promotes bone development; walking among trees boosts our immune system; time spent outdoors prevents myopia (short-sightedness); natural green contexts improve mental health, well-being, concentration and attention; moving outdoors can improve sleep and reduce obesity; and, as children become rooted in their local environment, they develop a sense of belonging (Richardson and McEwan, 2018; Mathias et al., 2020; Lingham et al., 2021).

A 'GREEN LIGHT' FOR GREEN PLAY

In Scotland's ELC, increased use of the outdoors is now encouraged (Scottish Government, 2012, 2017, 2019, 2020; Care Inspectorate, 2016, 2017; Inspiring Scotland, 2018). In 2008, The Secret Garden in Fife was the first outdoor nursery to register. Subsequently, Scottish government policy, encouraging outdoor play and learning (see Chapters 1 and 7), has resulted in over 40 outdoor settings, predominantly from the private and voluntary sector.

Policies signal change, yet practitioners are tasked with implementation, and sustainable change needs support. Kania et al. (2018: 4) identify three levels and six conditions necessary for sustainable systems change:

Structural – policies, practices, resources

Relational – relationships and connections, power dynamics

Transformational – attitudes and beliefs.

Change can be challenging; therefore, barriers need to be identified and overcome.

LEADING OUTDOOR PRACTICES AND CHANGE

Aberdeen City has provided high-quality *professional development* opportunities on outdoor provision, yet local outdoor consultant, Juliet Robertson and I began to question why the anticipated increase in high-quality *outdoor practices* had not materialised. Mirroring research across the western world (Kalpogianni, 2019; Sandseter et al., 2020; Josephidou et al., 2021), many of Kania et al.'s necessary conditions for change challenged practitioners to address:

- inadequate outdoor spaces for children to play and explore nature
- tensions within teams generated by a lack of shared understanding of outdoor play and learning
- limited staffing
- lack of materials and equipment including outdoor clothing
- concerns about health and safety and accountability
- undervaluing of rich learning possibilities in outdoor play by some parents
- practitioners' personal disconnect from nature
- attitudes to weather conditions.

Adopting a solution-focused approach, I asked, where are people 'connected or disconnected from others who must be part of the solution?' (Kania et al., 2018: 18). Isolated practitioners needed to connect with others across the city to share experiences, problem-solve, acknowledge their already rich funds-of-knowledge, and build capacity together. Our CoP quickly expanded to 78 practitioners from 38 settings in the first year, enabling some settings to develop shared perspectives in their outdoor work.

SPIRALS OF SUPPORT

Practitioners are 'empowered learners who build their working knowledge through spirals of engagement over time' (Fleet and Patterson, 2001: 2). One-off sessions 'have limited value in engaging hearts and minds in educational priorities or changing professional practice' (Fleet et al., 2018: 72); therefore, practitioners need access to ongoing support. These factors informed our CoP programme, an ongoing spiral of training and support across Aberdeen, enabling practitioners on their learning journey, to flexibly engage with peers. Our professional development programme, which grew out of a CoP survey, included:

- hospitality visits to settings across Aberdeen to share experiences of developing concrete and tarmac into movement-rich, exploratory outdoor play spaces. The Celtic tradition of welcoming strangers in, providing refreshments and sharing stories resonated with our visits to settings and so they became known as our 'hospitality visits'
- monthly sessions exploring: nature's gifts, learning journeys, stories, poems, songs, games, art, craft
- full-day sessions, exploring the outdoor natural environment as a nurturing context
- supported research in Special Interest Groups (SIG), encouraging practitioners to build, extend and share their 'funds of knowledge' (Amanti et al., 1992)
- a funded ERASMUS+ study programme to enable immersion in outdoor practices at the Saltamontes outdoor nursery in Spain
- peer-to-peer discourse
- fun.

WIGLS provided a safe space in which to explore local solutions to local challenges; every locality has its own unique geography, bio-geography, culture, weather, politics, history, all of which need to be explored.

WORKING TOGETHER AND KNOWLEDGE SHARING

With dialogue flowing across the city via WhatsApp chats, planned meetings and visits, practitioners began to find their voices and the courage to make change, while engaging with Kania et al.'s (2018) six conditions for sustainable systems change. Those who had already initiated change shared their expertise with their peers during visits, illustrating how to develop sensory and movement-rich play spaces with loose parts, and develop areas of green space, enabling children to engage with nature: following snail trails, watching butterflies, spotting birds, discovering spiders, and growing flowers and vegetables.

In the following case studies (5.1–5.3), four practitioners share their experiences, beginning with off-site visits to a green space, which may feel quite daunting for some. The issue of inequitable access to outdoor contexts for families from lower-income households was drawn sharply into focus during the COVID-19 pandemic (Friedman et al., 2022).

CASE STUDY 5.1: ARE THERE BEARS IN THERE?

Maggie MacDonald, Early Years Practitioner, Aberdeen and Jacqueline Bremner, Early Years Excellence and Equity Practitioner, Aberdeen

> 'I'm scared. Are there bears in there?
> I think there might be a tiger or a lion hiding in there.'
> (Lewis (4) on his first local green space visit.)

Our setting is in a noisy, urban main street in an area of deprivation where many children have limited access to green space. Understanding the importance of green spaces for well-being, Maggie enrolled in *Wee Green Spaces* training run by outdoor consultant Juliet Robertson (of https://creativestarlearning.co.uk), which provided the knowledge, skills and strategies to encourage practitioners to go off-site with their children. This helped us to individualise our setting handbook, including risk assessments, and procure vital equipment such as tarpaulins and a portable potty.

Finding a green location

We were introduced to the curator of Aberdeen University's Botanical Gardens to discuss its potential use, and complete the required administration. The gardens and arboretum, where we spent our sessions, met our need for natural beauty, a peaceful atmosphere, wildlife, security and a safe space for use in inclement weather.

Materials and equipment

To support full inclusion and year-round outdoor access, the school leadership team secured funding for waterproofs and a 'day sack' for each child. The children quickly took responsibility and ownership of their kit – packing their own bag and dressing themselves appropriately for the weather, developing independence and self-esteem.

Involving parents

Many parents attended Q&A sessions, with several volunteering to join a rota to support sessions for six children with four adults. Parents saw their children taking ownership of their *Wee Green Space*, building friendships, supporting each other and modelling learning for each other. We discussed the importance of well-being with parents during sessions, helping to build trust as we supported parents while their children's engagement unfolded.

Children engaging with the outdoors, nature, each other and people they met

We have a high number of children with speech and language challenges, so our emphasis was on using nature outdoors to encourage talk. We started small, with children we thought would benefit most. We changed group membership gradually, introducing new

(Continued)

children and withdrawing others. This enabled children, experienced in the group, to be role-models, helping us build on what had been established. We often encountered interesting people: beekeepers, a wildlife photographer, gardeners, engineers, all eager to share knowledge and extend the children's learning experiences.

Being in our green space enabled our children to use their imagination more freely and to look out and up. While lying on the forest floor, the children looked up and one said, 'This is the *best* place to see clouds up in the sky.' They identified cloud formations as a swan, a horse, a unicorn and a parrot, and, on successive visits, this became a favourite activity, raising awareness of the weather, extending imagination and vocabulary, and simply 'being' and breathing with nature.

Reflection

Our regular visits to our quiet natural space provided positive outcomes that surpassed our expectations. Over time, we noted changes in children's attention, listening, speech, language and communication. Quiet children spoke more confidently, children with EAL spoke more English and some children developed more clarity in their speech. We believe that the impact is due to small groups, relationships and the peacefulness of the setting, enabling children to engage and learn in an unhurried way.

CREATING THE TIME AND SPACE TO LISTEN TO CHILDREN

The concept of 'affordances' is frequently presented as a normative model, without recognition that an affordance is 'both relational and a resource' (Rietveld and Kiverstein, 2014: 327). Children act on affordances that are relevant to their needs and imagination, as and when they are ready. Case study 5.2 shows what is possible when children have the space to move and play freely outdoors, with loose parts resources, and practitioners engage in intentional listening and reflective practices after a provocation.

CASE STUDY 5.2: BUILDING OUTDOOR DENS

Helen McKinnon, Senior Early Years Practitioner, Aberdeen

In December 2020, I undertook a small-scale research project entitled 'What happened when we decided to build dens outside?'. In talking with the children aged 3–5, a theme emerged of dens built from materials such as wood, being enclosed spaces for play. Some children drew dens as enclosed spaces. I began by setting up a simple den as a provocation, selecting loose parts (crates, poles, tyre stands, long sticks, monster pegs, tarpaulin, organza material) which the children would be able to use independently. In the days that followed, I built unfinished dens, hoping to motivate children's involvement in the building process. I then observed and listened to the children and several themes emerged.

The builder

John (aged 4) replicated my original provocation, focusing solely on the construction and, once he had successfully achieved his goal, he left. I discussed John's den building with him and he said, 'I needed to lift wood. Get crates to put some sticks in to make them stand up. I popped on a cover, needed a grabber for that. I thought it would be fun.' John illustrates the cognitive and physical learning involved in den building.

Building to connect

Amelia (aged 4) is quite shy in nursery, so she watched others building a den then began to help. The next day, she built her own den, furnishing it with crates draped in material. She 'cooked' for the children who had gathered around her, following her lead. The social aspect of the den seemed most important to Amelia, who invited others into her den.

Finding my place

After the initial provocation, Layla (aged 4) was the first to enter the den, saying: 'It's amazing!'. Thereafter, she played in the den with friends but didn't get involved in the building process. Six days later, she accepted my invitation to build a den, taking control of the space and creating a place where she felt safe. In March 2021, when the second lockdown in Scotland ended, den building provided Layla with a purpose to attend to and engage with others, creating a place for herself and engaging others without overt invitation.

Hide-aways

Some children used their den as a quiet space, to just be and look out on the world. For others, the den provided a space for them to relax, rest and manage their emotions.

Reflection

Having developed a movement-rich outdoor play space with access to loose parts, I was intrigued to research the impact of den building, as a provocation, on our children. They engaged deeply over several days, extending their learning, problem solving and team building. They created dens throughout the pandemic, confirming that initiating den building with accessible resources enabled them to take ownership of their play. Did this mean more to the children during the pandemic?

These observations highlight the influence I have as a practitioner over a child's environment and how my decisions impact the potential for children's learning. Providing carefully considered open-ended resources empowered the children to take ownership of the den-building process, and to drive their own learning, in a way that met their individual needs.

BABIES OUTDOORS

Nature is essential to human growth and well-being from birth. Before walking, babies' neck and back muscles develop the strength to support their spine and head, freeing their hands for exploration. Babies can then build their understanding of the world by reaching out and exploring it with their senses. 'We learn that learning itself is movement', yet 'sensing bodies do not yet know what it will mean to sense' (Pacini-Ketchabaw et al., 2017: 24, 53). Coming to know the world involves an element of curiosity, wonder and courage, while being porous to the surrounding environment. Case study 5.3 explores the unhurried and courageous encounter between one toddler and a puddle.

CASE STUDY 5.3: THE COURAGE TO LEARN IN AN UNHURRIED WAY

Emma Gordon, Nursery Manager, Aberdeen

I aimed to better understand how children under 2 years old in my setting take risks to learn about the world and themselves outdoors.

Very young children generally have few words, therefore observations of their actions and interactions help to identify their learning. Ruby's story shows how she used her hands to engage with her world.

Ruby (1:2)

On a rainy day in the nursery garden, a practitioner places Ruby (who is not yet walking) on the ground next to a puddle. Ruby sits for a moment looking around her as other children move about the garden. The practitioner splashes Ruby's hand in the puddle. Ruby watches intently then places her own hand in the puddle while remaining balanced on one knee with the other leg propped up on her foot. Ruby moves her hand in and out of the puddle, touching the water, watching the movement of the water rippling away from her hand. Ruby repeats this motion several times before lifting her hand up and, turning it over, looking intently at her wet palm. Ruby touches her palm with her other hand then returns her hand to the puddle, splashing a few more times before lifting her hand again, turning it palm up. She moves her hand to her mouth, sticks out her tongue and licks the palm of her hand, tasting the water, then returns her hand to the ground and the puddle.

What are Ruby's thoughts as she interacts with nature? Is she making connections? What new learning is evolving? Could Ruby be making a connection between the water on the ground and the water she drinks from a cup?

Ruby used her hands to explore the world around her, demonstrating care and dexterity in her coordinated movements, while utilising her existing skills of balance and muscle memory to remain upright. Using her senses engendered a holistic experience of her environment.

Children engage in courageous adventures every moment of their day to explore and to consolidate, develop and extend their learning. Ellis et al. (2021) note that children use their bodies to engage with the affordances of their environment, and self, peer and adult interaction. Multi-layered observations help overcome our reliance on language in understanding children's learning, and avoid marginalising those yet to speak, who express themselves differently.

DEVELOPING AND SUSTAINING PLAY AND LEARNING IN THE OUTDOORS

Our communities need to be enriched and revitalised by learners who have a strong sense of place and who are committed to the common good. (Scottish Government, 2012: 12)

This statement holds true for all, everywhere, in the UK and beyond. However, before we can ask children to protect their environment, they must come to love it first. They need time to connect and develop a sense of place (Kudryavtsev et al., 2012; Cumming and Nash, 2015), to become 'a "grounded" or "rooted" learner stand(ing) within the world' (Sobel, 2013: 17); and practitioners, too, need time to know nature (Button and Wilde, 2019).

To support this, we need:

- policy-makers, informed by practitioners' voices and research, integrating and aligning initial training programmes, regulatory guidelines and professional development
- planners whose work is underpinned by child-led outdoor practices, and an understanding of natural affordances
- practitioners who are given time to explore nature and outdoor contexts within a collaborative community, to strengthen their professional voice
- outdoor spaces which are well-resourced, accessible throughout the year, and valued as a rich, resourceful context for all learning possibilities.

LOOKING TO THE FUTURE: WE ARE NATURE

Our relationship with nature and place is visceral and emotional; a process of embodiment that should be unhurried, helping to nurture an attachment to place which, ultimately, engenders belonging (Kudryavtsev et al., 2012). Yet, coming to know and understand that we and nature are interdependent is something that cannot be forced.

'A journey of a thousand miles begins with a single step'… even in the smallest of welly boots (quote attributed to Lao Tzu).

QUESTIONS

- What is your relationship to the outdoor environment? Do you notice changes in your mood, feelings, breathing, thoughts after a walk in the park, by the shore?
- Identify the strengths of your outdoor context and consider how you might build on these to extend children's opportunities for movement, sensory and nature explorations. Can you involve the children in adapting their outdoor space?
- Where can you learn more about nature and the cycle of the year, and how might you draw on this in your work?

FURTHER READING AND RESOURCES

Cree, J. and Robb, M. (2021) *The Essential Guide to Forest School and Nature Pedagogy.* London: Routledge.
There are diverse approaches to being outdoors with children and this book helpfully covers several aspects, though it is not early years specific.

White, J. (2015) *Every Child a Mover: A Practical Guide to Providing Young Children with the Physical Opportunities They Need.* London: Early Education.
Providing a wealth of knowledge and practical examples, this book highlights why children need to move outdoors.

https:// www.childrenandnature.org
www.earlychildhoodoutdoors.org
Two resourceful and interesting websites for practitioners.

Outdoor ELC for practitioners: https://youtu.be/nte7WYO60Jc
This film shares practitioner experiences in outdoor ELC.

ACKNOWLEDGEMENT

The case studies in this chapter are based on a project booklet for practitioners in our CoP, reproduced here with permission.

6

WORKING WITH FAMILIES TO SUPPORT YOUNG CHILDREN'S LEARNING

CATHY NUTBROWN AND BECKY COOK

CHAPTER OBJECTIVES

- To provide an overview of research on families' roles in young children's learning
- To consider national and local policies to support family learning
- To show how settings can work with parents to help them to support their young children's learning.

CHAPTER OVERVIEW

Early childhood education settings are, increasingly, developing work with parents to help them support their young children's learning at home. With examples from a Maintained Nursery School and a Trust Pre-School in Yorkshire, this chapter considers how parents can help their children's early learning and development, and how ECE settings can support them. We summarise some key research findings, consider the importance of family learning, demonstrate current practice and anticipate the future.

PARENTS SUPPORTING THEIR YOUNG CHILDREN'S LEARNING: RESEARCH LESSONS

Parents are key to their young children's development and learning, having long been described as their children's first teachers. Indeed, some 30 years ago, the Rumbold Report (DES, 1990) was unequivocal about parents' central role and what this means for practitioners:

> What is needed is for educators to be able, and willing, to explain to parents how the experiences offered to children contribute to their learning, and to describe how their children are progressing. They need to be prepared to share responsibility with parents. This places considerable demands upon the educators: they need to be ready to spend time on it, and to exercise sensitivity; they also need to have enough confidence to invite parents to share in their children's education. They must ensure that they have the necessary skills to work effectively with parents. (DES, 1990: 13, para. 100)

Many settings work with parents to enhance young children's learning, and in the last 40 years families increasingly are recognised as important sites for young children's learning. That parents have a role in their children's learning is not a new phenomenon, and many settings now have embedded policies and well-established, effective practices to support parents as educators. Indeed, Nutbrown et al. (2022: 5) assert that 'Focussed family learning can change things, making learning more enjoyable and parents more confident.' Since 2020, the COVID-19 pandemic has shone a spotlight on parents as educators, in the UK (Murray, 2020; Nutbrown et al., 2022) and internationally (Dayal and Tiko, 2020; Kim, 2020; Duran and Ömeroğlu, 2022; Pasifikus et al., 2022).

Strong support at home can predict children's later educational achievement (Taggart et al., 2015), so what family members offer children can make a real difference to children's progress, especially their language (Hillman and Williams, 2015) and early literacy (Hannon et al., 2020). How parents support their young children's early learning can enhance their holistic development in the early years and beyond (NLT and DfE, 2018). So, when early years practitioners share their knowledge, skills and understanding with parents, they are helping to extend the learning support parents give their children.

Family economics and parents' own educational achievements can impact on children's outcomes; children of better-off parents generally do better in school than their peers who live more disadvantaged lives (Hayes et al., 2018). Poverty exacerbates the educational achievement gap and threatens life chances (NLT and DfE, 2018). However, early years settings can support *all* parents in ways which help them to enhance what they do to support their children's play and learning. Hannon et al. (2020) showed that the Raising Early Achievement in Literacy (REAL) programme was particularly effective for children whose mothers had no formal educational qualifications, thus helping to address the cycle of underachievement that inhibits the success of children at risk of educational underachievement. REAL Approaches are based on parents providing four things:

- *Opportunities* for their children to learn (toys, books, experiences, space, time)
- *Recognition* of their children's learning (pointing out and celebrating small steps in effort and achievement)
- *Interaction* around learning activities (spending time in shared activities, talking, taking turns, talking about what they are doing together)
- *Models* of learners (making a point of letting children see them doing real-life activities and jobs such as reading, writing, household repairs or gardening).

REAL Approaches to family literacy have been particularly successful in involving fathers who, though sometimes unseen in settings, play an important part in their children's learning, and it is important that settings find meaningful ways to involve fathers (Morgan et al., 2009) and are sensitive to and respectful of the diversity of families and shared parenting.

After four decades of research, particularly in family literacy, there is strong evidence that supporting parents as their children's educators is a worthwhile investment (Hannon et al., 2020; Lynch and Prins, 2022; Nutbrown et al., 2022). As case study 6.1 illustrates, ECEC settings have worked with parents to help them better value and facilitate their children's play (Singer et al., 2006; Veitch et al., 2006) and to understand the pleasure and importance of reading with children every day (Demir-Lira et al., 2019).

CASE STUDY 6.1: STAY AND PLAY – SUPPORTING PARENTS IN READING WITH THEIR CHILDREN

The setting holds regular Stay and Play sessions focusing on reading with children. Parents and grandparents are invited to stay when a librarian from the local library visits, reads animatedly to the children and talks about the books she has brought. She talks with parents about the importance of frequently sharing books with children and explains dialogic book sharing: a process of talking with children about the book, while reading, asking questions to help children explore the book more deeply, explaining new words, and thinking together about parts of the story.

The librarian encourages the children to choose a story to share with their parents and encourages families to visit the library soon to borrow from the wider selection of books. Adults and children enjoy sharing stories together, and children borrow a book from our family library.

We visit the library with children and parents, where the librarian reads a story before children enjoy art and craft activities linked to the book, which are then displayed. The children were delighted to see what they had made when they next visited the library with their family. As a setting, we regularly share regular anecdotes, reminders and ideas about reading and sharing books and stories with families through their social media.

In Australia, Hayes et al. (2018: 1405) found that 'Higher levels of parental involvement at 2 years were associated with better learning outcomes at 6 years'. Further, poorer families and boys were linked with less parental engagement when children were 2 years old. Thus, tackling inequity in opportunities at home, long before children begin school, is essential.

Parents using and building on everyday activities at home make a difference to their children's all-round development, and talk, especially, is a crucial aspect of toddlers' development (Hutchings et al., 2017). Settings and services need further investment to establish and extend opportunities for parents to learn more about supporting their young children's learning (see Chapter 11). However, many interventions seem designed to make home learning more like school learning, whereas Nutbrown et al. (2005) make clear that home learning is often less formal, more spontaneous and closely related to children's lived experience and interests than some more abstract activities encouraged in schools and early years settings, as case study 6.2 illustrates. See also The Sheffield REAL project. (https://sheffield-real-project.sites.sheffield.ac.uk)

CASE STUDY 6.2: COOKING AT HOME – FUNDS OF KNOWLEDGE

Pearl, mother of 3-year-old Naomi, enjoyed the Adult Learning class organised by Naomi's nursery. The group of six mothers had tried and shared several easy recipes that they could make at home. The aim had been to help families cook nutritious meals on a limited budget. The women chose ingredients from the Fare Share (https://fareshare.org.uk) delivery to take home to try out more recipes. Talking with Naomi's key worker, Pearl said that she remembered cooking with her mum as a child in Jamaica, but that she found it hard cooking with Naomi around. Key worker Stella explained how Pearl might involve Naomi in the cooking process – in simple chopping, weighing ingredients, counting, talking about the colours, smells and tastes of the food, and so on; she suggested that taking time over the process was really beneficial, and if Pearl had time, there was no need to rush. Pearl said she didn't think Naomi would be interested, but said she'd give it a go that weekend.

When Naomi next attended nursery, she talked excitedly about 'making supper' and went immediately to the home corner kitchen and started filling pans with various objects to represent the food. Chatting to two other children, she explained how to chop – naming some foods, counting ingredients herself – '1, 2, 5, 6, 90, 100', demonstrating her 'funds of knowledge' (Chesworth, 2019) around food which had been enhanced through cooking with her mum. The opportunity to cook, and participate in preparing a family meal, had extended Naomi's personal cultural capital around food and sharing a meal, which she brought to her play.

When Pearl collected Naomi, she made a point of seeking out Stella to tell her how she had found cooking with Naomi. Pearl said she had been overwhelmed at how capable and interested Naomi was, how she listened about how to chop vegetables safely, got involved in preparing the meal, and now she stayed in the kitchen without getting fed up or bored, really concentrating on what they were doing together. Pearl said that she hadn't realised quite how much Naomi could do and was amazed by her chatter. Pearl added that she now felt more confident in helping Naomi with simple counting, talking when doing real household jobs, and letting things 'just flow'.

Pearl told Stella that she'd never thought she could do 'the kind of learning with her that you do here', but Stella's encouragement made her realise that – as Pearl put it – what she could offer Naomi was different, 'more natural, and everyday things where learning just happens'. Stella promised to organise some more workshops for parents who wanted to find out more about young children's learning, to help develop parents' confidence in supporting their children's learning through everyday tasks.

When parents are attuned to the possibilities of the everyday, they can take advantage of spontaneous occurrences to extend their children's talk, play and learning – building on the cultural capital of their family and community. Once a parent realises that activities such as counting while shopping, weighing while baking, singing rhymes in the car, spotting letters from the bus all support learning, they can make use of unplanned opportunities. The challenge is how to help parents maximise and extend what they already do, in the everyday – digging in the garden, woodwork, cleaning, shopping, washing the car. Practitioners sharing knowledge of what matters in early learning, and how parents might best support their children, can increase parents' confidence to notice what their children have achieved already, build from what they know their children can do, and recognise new achievements.

PRACTICE EXAMPLE

#50things to do before you're five

Our pre-school settings in the Yorkshire and Humber region are champions of *#50things to do before you're five* which originated in Bradford and 'helps parents develop their home learning environment, suggesting a wide range of low-cost and no-cost local activities. The *#50things* approach improves early language and literacy, motor skills and resilience'.

Ideas of activities in the local area which parents can share with children are on a free-of-charge digital app. Settings support parents who use the app, by identifying *#50things* activities that link with planned activities each week, so that if parents do not follow up the *#50things* at home, children still have opportunities to try them.

The setting makes a point of facilitating some of the suggested *#50things*; for example, all children took home a paper bag to collect leaves, seeds and other things they might find on an autumn walk; and then they brought their collections into the setting to talk about. Parents were given suggestions of what to look out for, questions to ask and things to wonder about with their children. Families say they enjoy the activities, finding them

(Continued)

> fun and easy to do together, and many use our online interactive tracking tool to share pictures or comments about their child's engagement. For families, following the *#50things* suggestions is primarily about spending time together, talking and exploring the locality in a relaxed and confident way.

POLICY SUPPORT FOR FAMILY LEARNING

The policy position on supporting *all* parents as educators of their children is unclear; there is a considerable amount of 'guidance' on supporting home learning in the early years, but national policy is less concrete. While government endorses (and in some cases funds) guidance and reports (NLT and DfE, 2018; EEF, 2022), there remains a lack of national investment and policy.

The Education Endowment Foundation (2022) identified that a high level of parental engagement in children's learning is consistently associated with better academic outcomes, yet not all parents find this role easy. The *quality* of what parents do makes a difference, and success here need not be defined by parents' own levels of education or income. The EEF (2022: 6–7) suggests that settings should:

- review how they work with parents
- offer parents practical strategies to support learning at home
- shape modes of communication with parents to encourage positive dialogue about learning
- offer more sustained and intensive support when families need it.

These four suggestions imply considerable responsibilities for parents, so in the case studies which follow we examine how settings might practically approach them. Case study 6.3 shows how a setting can offer parents practical ideas to support their children's learning, sometimes in the most difficult circumstances, and demonstrates the commitment and creativity settings can dedicate to offering meaningful support.

CASE STUDY 6.3: SHARING WAYS OF SUPPORTING HOME LEARNING DURING THE PANDEMIC

A major part of our practice during the lockdown periods of the COVID-19 pandemic in 2020 and 2021 when many children were at home, was to utilise and build on our positive relationships with parents to support them to sustain learning at home. We knew many families' difficulties in everyday life throughout the pandemic: financial problems due to job losses, limited time due to working from home, needing to support older children with schoolwork, social isolation and the subsequent effects on mental health and well-being.

At a time of unprecedented difficulty, we wanted to offer materials and ideas that families could use as when they needed or had time. We created a Busy Bag for each child, containing bubbles, chalks, pencils, paper, a ball, a tub of playdough, a small soap, a copy of our handwashing song, a book and a leaflet of ideas about including children in everyday activities that would support their learning. We added straightforward ideas to our website and included some printable resources for those who could access them. We uploaded, and provided links to, audio stories and suggestions of related activities – with links to suitable websites that children could use.

Knowing that most parents used social media, we used this daily to share material for families, including storytelling, singing, nursery rhymes, cooking demonstrations, playing with playdough, talking about favourite toys, suggesting an activity or sharing an action song or a dance. Parents said their children looked forward to these each day, which generated lots of comments and shared exchanges between staff and parents.

We held weekly 10–15-minute Zoom meetings with small groups of children and their parents; these took the form of 'show and tell'-style discussions, sometimes with a treasure hunt, with children finding things around their homes, or a chat about the week. For many children, these were the highlight of their week and parents gladly made time to join them whenever they could. When children returned to the setting, we noticed that those who had engaged with us while at home settled back quickly into the nursery.

Practical support, in the form of ideas, materials and opportunities to talk with staff, is important for families. While welcomed during pandemic lockdowns, we know that these are also important in terms of supporting home learning outside of such restrictions (Nutbrown et al., 2022). In case study 6.4, we see how settings can tailor how they communicate with parents to facilitate constructive conversations about their children's learning.

CASE STUDY 6.4: MEANINGFUL COMMUNICATION FOR POSITIVE SETTING-HOME CONVERSATIONS ABOUT CHILDREN'S LEARNING

Following the pandemic lockdowns of 2020 and 2021, as restrictions eased, we have continued with the forms of communication that worked for our families during periods of COVID-imposed social isolation. Our *social media communication plan* sits alongside our weekly activities plan and we think about what we want to share with families about their children's learning and how they can enhance this at home; we might share a song, rhyme, story, or what's been happening in the setting with 'Ask your child about ...'. This could be a visitor we've welcomed or a great game that we've played – anything to stimulate more conversations at home! We share 'top tips' and advice around health and well-being, including dental care, sleep routines and healthy snack ideas, alongside information about local family-friendly events or places. Many parents comment that our posts help them to

(Continued)

understand our ethos and feel valued as partners. Though this takes time and commitment to sustain, it adds value to our relationship with families and has a positive impact on children's learning, development and experiences.

We continue our *newsletter* with an overview of what the children will be exploring each half-term, making these available in hard copy and digitally. We maintain our *online tracker* for each child so that parents can see what their child has been experiencing in the setting, and upload pictures and comments to share what they have done at home. Returning to in-person contact, we resumed open mornings and face-to-face discussions with individual parents, after two years of online meetings and phone conversations.

Where families use English as an additional language, it is important that their home or heritage languages are valued and that children are encouraged to use all the languages of the family. Family learning and family literacy can happen in all languages and learning is enhanced. This places a responsibility on settings to find effective ways of working with families where their home language is different from the main language or languages spoken in the setting, to address inequalities around home languages and increase accessibility to family learning for *all* families.

In their *Manifesto for Family Learning: Birth to Five*, Nutbrown et al. (2022: 172–173) are unequivocal:

> We believe that family learning must become a priority of policy nationally, locally and in each setting or service. Effective policy needs to be made and evolve over time; too much short-term policy making with little reference to research or recognition of what has gone before is wasteful. Longer-term goals need to be set and sustained through necessary funding and professional development.

Good home learning practices with parents must be supported by policy, which carries with it responsibility and funding. Recently, Ofsted (2020) appears to have prioritised parents' perspectives as service *users* rather than *partners* in their children's learning. Policy for England is less strong than those of many regional local authorities (LAs), some of which have embedded excellent practice in work with families around early learning, into local policy, such as in Sandwell MCB's (2020: 26) plan which states: 'We know that supporting families so their children are ready for the next stage in life is important. Children being ready for school, schools being ready for children and families and communities being able to support that readiness are vital.' To realise such LA ambition, national policies must be coherent so that LAs and individual settings can draw on the financial support which is often aligned to policy.

CASE STUDY 6.5: SUPPORTING FAMILY LEARNING

For some parents, getting more involved in their children's learning in the setting has brought great benefit. Lauren did not work outside the home, but rather stayed at home with her three children, aged 2, 5 and 7; she enjoyed spending time with her youngest and found it difficult when he started nursery, aged 2. She really enjoyed our Stay and Play sessions and volunteered regularly to help in the setting, playing with the children and quickly establishing positive relationships with them. After one Stay and Play session, co-hosted with local adult education colleagues, and funded by Adult Learning, Lauren enrolled at the college to gain a childcare qualification. She studied while her children were in school and worked as a lunchtime supervisor with us until she finished the course. She obtained a position in a local school as a support assistant for a child with additional needs. She loves her work and said it's something she never saw herself doing before she became part of our nursery family.

This is no isolated incident – several mums and a grandma – following our Stay and Play sessions exploring, for example, play, healthy eating, communication, reading and behaviour – have enrolled on and successfully completed adult education courses on supporting learning in schools or working with young children. The setting was funded for hosting Adult Learning for parents which supported their confidence and enabled them to gain a qualification and the chance of employment.

We always welcome parents who'd like to experience work in the early years and volunteer with us as part of their training, and those parents really understand the need to interact with their children and spend time with them, completing activities as part of their own learning; hopefully this will continue throughout their children's educational career.

KEY ISSUES FOR THE FUTURE

Three areas need attention if settings are to maximise parents' confidence and support for children's learning:

- **There is an urgent need for policy support for family learning**, at national, local and setting levels. Policy should endorse and support work to help parents learn more about their central role as educators, especially in how to make the most of those spontaneous, everyday opportunities for learning.
- **Funding family learning work is essential** for material and human resources for home visiting, and for working with small groups of parents to share professional knowledge about child development, early literacy, making the most of outdoor spaces and opportunities for children to play.

- **Early years practitioners need initial training and subsequent CPD which includes theoretical and practice knowledge, to develop high-quality family learning** if they are to successfully involve and support parents as their children's first teachers. CPD opportunities can enhance educators' confidence in sharing their professional knowledge with parents, and in listening to parents to learn from them about their children (see Chapter 12).

Policy commitment to family learning must lead to action, build on the wealth of experience which already exists, and regard practitioners' work with parents as a key part of working with children. The work ECEC settings do with young children is enhanced when parents recognise and build on their central role in their children's learning, and is an important element in addressing disadvantage (see Chapters 11 and 14). The Education White Paper (DfE, 2022b: 3) pledged to reform English education so that every child should 'get a great education and the right support', including 'high-quality early years provision' (p. 16); and, though it included many mentions of parents as *receivers of information* about their children's progress, there was no mention of the need to work with parents as their *children's first educators*; the omission of this critical symbiotic relationship is a huge oversight.

QUESTIONS

- What recollections do you have of learning at home with family members when you were young?
- What are the challenges of establishing work with parents to promote young children's learning?
- What makes for the successful involvement of *all* families in supporting young children's learning?

FURTHER READING AND RESOURCES

Lynch, J. and Prins, E. (2022) *Teaching and Learning about Family Literacy and Family Literacy Programmes*. New York: Routledge.
An international review of family literacy research, identifying examples of successful programmes.

Nutbrown, C., Clough, P., Davies., K. and Hannon, P. (2022) *Home Learning Environments for Young children*. London: Sage.
Research and case studies of effective partnerships with *all* families, using REAL Approaches.

#50things to do before you're five. https://50thingstodo.org
Created by St Edmund's Nursery School, Bradford, and launched at the Houses of Parliament in 2018. Adopted by many local authorities nationally.

The Sheffield REAL project website – https://sheffield-real-project.sites.sheffield.ac.uk
Provides resources for organising work with parents in many aspects of curriculum, and for developing home visiting.

Parents' roles in children's literacy development: https://drive.google.com/file/ d/1WI3jubsF9I5ZiKJxgI6W3SK_A4Anz9LD/view

7

TRANSITIONS IN EARLY CHILDHOOD EDUCATION AND CARE, ACROSS TIME AND DAY TO DAY: A SCOTTISH PERSPECTIVE

ALINE-WENDY DUNLOP, LISA BARNES AND MYRA MCROBBIE

CHAPTER OBJECTIVES

- To provide an overview of research on transitions
- To present a critical explanation of transitions policy in Scotland
- To demonstrate the realities of transitions through case studies of practice
- To set out key issues around the future of transitions in Scotland and beyond.

CHAPTER OVERVIEW

In this chapter, we have chosen a transitions lens on an ecological model to address contemporary issues around well-being, play, curriculum and leadership in the evolving Scottish early childhood world: a world which itself has made significant transitions and where change has been a constant factor. As authors, we come together from three different contexts within ECEC in Scotland, representative of research, policy and practice in Scotland.

INTRODUCTION

At the heart of our early years practice lies a shared belief in the creativity, competence and contribution of young children in all that affects them, as also enshrined in the United Nations (1989) *Convention on the Rights of the Child*. This core belief in children's strengths, leads us to a set of shared values which respect:

- the central importance of relationships
- the cultural context of learning, especially home culture
- how theory informs our actions
- the importance of adults embracing their own continuing learning to inform their practices
- children's intrinsic curiosity and motivation, which drives their explorations and learning
- capturing the interests of all children and celebrating their discoveries.

Key to these values is trusting children through the very important skill of following childrens' lead, looking 'beyond the act' (McNair and Cerdan, 2022: 22) and 'following ahead' of children (Dunlop, 2018a) through child-focused 'know-how' (as many chapters in this book also demonstrate).

By attending to what is already understood about childhood transitions, we relate research and policy to day-to-day values on the ground, using six case studies of work with children aged 2–6 years. We conclude by reflecting on what careful attention to transitions and their capacity as arenas for change might bring to reconceptualising transitions.

A TRANSITIONS LENS

Early childhood transitions have been a focus of research for over 50 years and research interest grows; perhaps because as human beings in an ever-changing world, we are always in transition, and this is most obvious for our youngest. Research and practice offer various ways of defining transitions. At its simplest, change is a constant as human development takes place, so we must ask 'what is the difference between change and transition'? For us, transitions are more than circumstantial change; they are phases and points in time when, with agency, we can create new developmental, emotional, social and cognitive shifts.

Transitions research uses informative work from different disciplines, for example Sameroff's (2009) transactional approaches, Bruner (1996) and Trevarthen et al.'s (2018) strong evidence that children create culture together, Bourdieu's (1990) thinking about 'rites of institution', van Gennep's (1909) 'rites of passage' and Bronfenbrenner's mature bio-ecological systems (Bronfenbrenner and Evans, 2000), which consider the mutual impact of children, environment, home, contextual factors and children's self-generated cultures. (A reading list is available at https://early-education.org.uk/centenary-book.)

Recent themes in transitions studies (Dunlop, 2018b) focus on ethical encounters in transitions research; children's perspectives, agency, advocacy and voice; family engagement; diversity in transition to school; professional responses; children as learners; school readiness; changes in identity as a home, nursery and school child; peer play and peer relations; continuity and discontinuity; and social justice and equity in the links between research, policy and practice. These multiple perspectives are expanded by new thinking on parental, infant, early childhood and professional transitions (Dunlop et al., 2022) and their impact on practice.

These themes lead to reflection on children's spaces, attunement and relational approaches – both day-to-day and longer term – and what this means for leadership. This type of 'know-how' supports transitions for each child to develop a sense of belonging within settings, which children and families may have never entered before or may have been excluded from in COVID-19 times. Meeting daily transitions in this way has the potential to build everyone's capacity to meet future transitions positively by:

- creating *transitions networks*
- supporting children to feel *ready for transitions*
- developing *transitions ease*, and thereby
- building child and family *transitions capital* – social, emotional, cultural, educational. (Dunlop et al., 2023)

This means taking a careful look at how systems work best.

CONTEMPORARY ISSUES

Scottish early childhood education provision began with Robert Owen's infant and nursery school in New Lanark, over 200 years ago, and is a history of change and transition. (A brief history of the past century of ECE change in Scotland can be found at https://early-education.org.uk/centenary-book.) In today's Scotland, much of what happens for young children, in what is now referred to as early learning and childcare (ELC), is driven by government policy and interpreted in different ways by each of our 32 local councils. Guidance for pre-birth to age 3, and later curriculum experiences and outcomes for 3–6-year-olds, drive what practitioners do. A dual approach to quality of provision encourages self-evaluation of practice through 'How good is our early learning and childcare?' (Education Scotland, 2016) and 'How good is our school?' (Education Scotland, 2015), with quality now being measured through inspection bodies. This combination of self-evaluation and ELC inspection criteria could, we suggest, be used through to the first phase of primary school.

The evolution of the politics of early childhood education and care in Scotland has seen:

- the advent of a written curriculum framework for early childhood
- the aspiration to close the poverty-related attainment gap
- the move to offer every 3- and 4-year-old child and some 2-year-olds 30 hours a week (term time) of funded early learning and childcare.

This inevitably leads to serious questions about the commodification of childhood, the language of 'services', 'provision' and regulation, rather than contemporary practice which prefers to focus on children's spaces, relational approaches and giving children time. The latter offers the renewal of a focus on children's capacity to lead the way and adults who anticipate but do not over-direct through their understanding of what we describe as 'following ahead' (see Chapters 1 and 4). Aspirations for children in Scotland are ambitious at both policy and practice levels.

CONTEMPORARY POLICY LANDSCAPE

Policy in Scotland emphasises the importance of practitioners working with parents to ensure that the transition from home to ELC setting and from ELC setting to Primary 1 is positive. In four separate policy documents (Standard for Childhood Practice; Realising the Ambition: Being me; Getting It Right for Every Child; and Scottish Early Childhood, Children and Families Transitions Position Statement), children are at the centre of thinking about well-being in context. Seeing transition spaces as opportunities to promote the well-being and learning of young children, while recognising the complexity of daily transitions and their connection with resilience in transition over time, is paramount. A common feature across practice advice and support is the importance of communication between ELC settings and children's parents and carers, and with a range of professionals with a shared commitment to the professional values of social justice, trust, respect and integrity (GTCS, 2021).

Taking an ecological view, this acknowledgement of the significance of personal transitions across place, relationships and curriculum in both national standards and practice guidance aims to approach each child with dignity, respect and compassion, so that children feel included by responsive and supportive staff. The five principles of the Health and Social Care Standards (Scottish Government, 2017) can be understood as being inclusive of the principles in the Scottish Early Childhood, Children and Families Transitions Position Statement (of 2019). The 'my world triangle' ('Getting It Right for Every Child'; Scottish Government, 2017) takes an ecological view of the child, giving equal credit to the importance of these same principles having a focus on children having opportunities to develop confidence in who they are. The focus on child-centred positive transitions – founded on consistency, communication, culture and collaboration, documented in the practice guidance – upholds the thread of continuity across policy documents, and the clear values in 'Realising the Ambition: Being me' (Scottish Government, 2020) set sound priorities for working with young children. Policy in the end is only as effective as the people implementing it – it relies on leadership in practice and on informed practitioners to focus on children's attributes, well-being, opportunities for play and access to curriculum as they journey through the transitions of early childhood. This includes work that supports children in daily transitions as they develop strategies for coping with change and transition over time, and a sense that they will manage and are competent.

TRANSITIONS IN ACTION

The six brief case studies which follow illustrate approaches to ensuring positive child and family experiences in transition, in the context of policy. Each case study emphasises that, at its best, policy must be enabling, research can be informative, and transitions handled well in early childhood not only enhance present experience but also promote well-being, confidence and resilience in future transitions.

CASE STUDY 7.1: RECOGNISING AND BUILDING MEANINGFULLY ON CHILDREN'S INTERESTS AT ELC START

Myra's 2-year-old grandson has a real interest in agricultural machinery, as his family have a strong agricultural background which he has been exposed to from an early age. He can talk about five different types of tractor, recognising them in pictures, on the road or in a field. Most of his play involves loading bales onto trailers, 'scooping up' items with loaders and placing them in dumper trucks. Sand play, too, involves scooping up sand, filling containers and transporting them to another area. He also wheels his wheelbarrow behind his grandfather, collecting general garden waste and depositing it in the bin. A typical transporting schema is visible (Athey, 2007).

It is important that parents are aware that sharing what they know about their children's learning can aid transition from home to setting, so that practitioners can provide for children to do the things they are familiar with as they join a new setting, making them feel valued and safe in an environment which is prepared and ready for them.

CASE STUDY 7.2: TRANSITIONS FROM A CHILDMINDER'S PERSPECTIVE

Childminder, Zoe Sadler has been inspected by the Care Inspectorate as part of their new inspection approach, which noted: 'Time had been taken to discuss and plan for transitions so that the care offered at these times supported children's confidence and wellbeing.'

One new family started with her during the COVID-19 lockdown and so she had to review and change her usual transition process. She held garden meetings with the family and put together a selection of photographs and videos for the family to view the environment. Ben had started at the local playgroup during lockdown and Zoe worked closely with the staff to support his transition to the new setting. Parents' working pattern meant that it was challenging for playgroup staff to follow their usual practice of home or garden visits for new children. Zoe, Ben's parents and the playgroup staff formed a plan together whereby Zoe was in a better position to support the transition process. She took Ben for short visits, pointed out the new setting while on walks with the children, and talked about the activities they saw the children participating in. This supported rather than replaced the parents' role as work commitments and setting hours were incompatible. Ben, secure in Zoe's care, was eased towards a meaningful and successful transition.

Sustaining positive approaches has never been more challenging than during the COVID-19 pandemic when restrictions became the norm in daily life, consuming enormous personal energy. The childminder and the setting worked within the limitations to create a positive transition for Ben.

CASE STUDY 7.3: THE BENEFITS OF HOME VISITS

Westfield ELC in Aberdeenshire is registered to take children from six weeks old, and home visits prior to the child starting with them has long been established practice. Two members of staff visit the family home, one to talk and complete paperwork with the parent and the other to start building the relationship with the child, in an environment where the child feels safe and secure. This begins a positive relationship between the setting, practitioners and the family.

Westfield ELC caters for vulnerable families and when COVID-19 sent the country into lockdown, the setting moved to operate its own hub, knowing that it was important for parents to maintain regular contact to support their well-being.

As COVID-19 restrictions eased and new families began to be enrolled, Westfield staff developed a new process of welcoming them. Families visited the setting's garden to meet staff and complete paperwork, and videos of all areas of the setting were made and shared with parents so they could view the environment their children would attend. It has been a high priority for Westfield ELC staff to ensure they maintained communication with parents and achieved positive transitions for the children. The setting introduced an app, 'Evidence Me', enabling learning, information and photographs to be sent by the child and keyworker to parents who, in turn, are encouraged to share learning from home. These different ways of working and maintaining contact ensured that parents had support to meet both their own and their children's needs.

Practitioners working in hub settings consistently tried to maintain good contact, communication and relationships with all families: those attending under new rules, and those remaining at home. Digital technology and social media helped family members stay in touch with practitioners without the usual face-to-face contact.

CASE STUDY 7.4: THE IMPACT OF FATHERS' NETWORK SCOTLAND ON AN EY SETTING APPROACH TO TRANSITIONS

Insch Nursery, **in Aberdeenshire**, provides a nurturing experience for children and their families. After attending an Early Education Aberdeen event with Chris Miezitis from Fathers Network Scotland (www.fathersnetwork.org.uk), the staff team began to evaluate our *family nurture* approach.

From March to August 2020, Insch Nursery was closed due to the lockdown. Over this time, we set an optional daily challenge for all our nursery families. The expectation was that families would use our online interactive learning diary to post photos, videos and comments about the daily challenge they did at home. Before the lockdown in March 2020, we had encouraged fathers and mothers to create and access a login for their child and, while the numbers of fathers engaging in this increased, there was still a clear imbalance between mothers and fathers. Lockdown saw the number of fathers engaging with the learning diary triple; they posted photos and videos of their child doing the daily challenge, which they had set up following our advice. It was fantastic to see so many male role models engaging with our service and using our advice to support their children's learning. As well as engagement online, we offered visits to returning and new families during the summer to support the transition back into the setting. Almost all children had both parents come with them for the visit which allowed staff to meet and build a relationship with both parents right from the start. Returning to nursery, fathers' engagement has been sustained online and more fathers now drop off and pick up their children. This could be linked with many men being furloughed from their jobs over lockdown and, on our reopening, many fathers working from home with an increased flexibility for childcare.

(Continued)

Moving forward, our setting encourages both fathers and mothers to attend the settling-in visits offered during the school holidays. This allows practitioners to build a relationship with both parents from the initial meeting, demonstrating that they value the input of both. These positive relationships mean that practitioners confidently talk to whichever parent brings and collects their child, rather than identifying a 'main' caregiver. Positive relationships with all parents help them feel comfortable and relaxed at the setting, creating a positive atmosphere for children, and allowing adults to share information and advice around individual children's development, including strategies to support transition to nursery and to school.

The impact of the pandemic has been huge, with loss of full parental contact and limitations on the range of experiences offered. Arranging a bespoke start in nursery and school, meeting children and families where they were, required practitioners to create good alternatives, while they too may have been struggling with illness and loss. When settings are committed to maintaining relationships, they find ways to do so.

CASE STUDY 7.5: MAYFIELD NURSERY SCHOOL, MIDLOTHIAN

Mayfield Nursery School is at the heart of the Mayfield community in Midlothian. It serves a mixed catchment, with most families living in areas of multiple deprivation. Its vision is *learning through play – freedom to be me*, which reflects the importance staff place on each child being able to develop *who they are*. This vision is underpinned by the interconnected values developed as a holistic school community: respect, positive relationships, nurture, inclusion and equity, learning through play, community, and freedom with guidance. The curriculum and our pedagogy have been specifically constructed to meet the children *where they are* culturally and developmentally, with a specific focus on emotional well-being and self-regulation, social development and skills, nurturing competent, enquiring children through self-directed play in all areas of language development – receptive and expressive language, social communication and attention, and listening.

In 2018, the school doubled in size as part of the expansion of ELC in Scotland. From an experienced and highly skilled team, the school now has 26 staff who, as across Scotland, are at different points in their professional learning.

Mayfield's work to support transitions is ongoing and focuses on the opportunities that transition offers children and their families, specifically opportunities for agency. Huge importance is placed on the development of warm, nurturing relationships for parents and their children as they transition to nursery, from the first contact with the nursery, both verbal and written. With attachment theory firmly at the heart of our work and the knowledge that good practice is relational, the nursery has examined the vital role of the key person for parents and children. For most children, Mayfield is the first setting that they have attended. Parents are often concerned about what this will be like for them and their child. Staff recognise that several approaches are needed to ensure that all families and children receive the kind of relational support they need, and, during the COVID-19 pandemic, personal approaches have proved even more essential. Transitions are supported in many ways, including: verbal and written communication; home visits; visits to the nursery; informal sessions for parents and carers about what coming to nursery looks like; and Parents as Early Education Partners (PEEP) groups with time to play in nursery afterwards.

This range of support for transitions aims to give parents opportunities to engage with the nursery in ways that suit them and make them feel valued. Conversations are focused on parents' knowledge of their children and what, as parents they want to know more about. Parents report feeling welcome, heard and valued, happy to leave their children in the nursery and at ease in asking questions and seeking feedback about their child's settling: this is a shared endeavour.

Offering multiple forms of support for transition maximises the success of a smooth and pleasurable transition, forming the start of positive home–school relationships foundational to learning and well-being.

CASE STUDY 7.6: A PLAY JOURNEY – PRIMARY 1 AND BEYOND

Leanne Sweaton

In recent years, my Primary 1 (P1) practice with 5-year-olds has been challenged in a way that I have never experienced before. Understanding why play is so important for children and their development at this stage has forced me to re-think my teaching, learning and assessment more than any other approach in my career. I still question why it hasn't always been like this, and I could never contemplate returning to the more traditional methods I once used. As a classroom practitioner for over 20 years, I have taught across all stages; my favourite stage by far is and always will be Primary 1. It is a privilege to be the first teacher that children begin their school journey with, and I never take that for granted.

At the beginning of my play journey, I provided a more playful classroom to aid the transition from nursery into P1, but it quickly became more than *just* a transition approach. As I engaged with professional reading on play, listened and followed anyone on social media who was an advocate for play, I quickly realised that, for children, play really was the best way to learn. I was hooked. Play excited me, challenged me, empowered me and left me with a sense of wanting to find out more, do more and try more, and this is where

(Continued)

my journey began. Now my teaching day revolves only around play pedagogy; I live and breathe it and I will always embrace the chance to talk about it with others and inspire them to try it for themselves

The approach works best when you achieve the correct balance between teacher-directed, child-directed and child-initiated learning (see Chapters 1 and 2). The children play for large parts of the day, and I have become skilled in observing, assessing, extending and challenging their play so that it meets both their needs and the requirements of the curriculum. I observe, record and act on what I see as quickly as I can so that the opportunity for child-led learning is not lost. The children can all read and write but you won't find a jotter or workbook in my setting. Their skills in literacy and numeracy have been developed through play and this never ceases to amaze me.

What empowers me is how motivated, engaged and purposeful the children are in their environment and their learning through play. In leading the learning, they too have become empowered and, as a result, the children have become natural problem-solvers, curious, creative and fiercely independent (see Chapters 3 and 4). Play does exactly what it says on the tin, and I dare anyone to try it and not fall in love with it. Play is natural, enjoyable, all-consuming and the best way children learn. So, logically, a play approach in school complements the skills and 'know-how' that children bring with them.

This testimony demonstrates that taking play pedagogy into the school system can promote learning when teachers are committed, and this also requires visionary pedagogical leadership (see Chapter 13).

Having considered relevant research, Scottish policy and practice in some of Scotland's early years settings, we close this chapter with our summary of what is needed in the future.

KEY ISSUES FOR THE FUTURE

Big questions remain, not least how we are moving from the impact of the pandemic on young lives. From a Scottish perspective, we offer some key issues which may also prove useful to practitioners elsewhere.

How does government funding and entitlement to designated hours of early years provision assist positive transitions? Can the combination of strong policy, appropriate curriculum guidance, play pedagogy, the new Froebel movement in Scotland, the moves not to rush children, and practitioner development, guarantee attuned leadership in local, regional and national arenas to enable a system (itself in transition) to provide well for all of Scotland's children? **Could similar circumstances bring similar benefits to transitions elsewhere in different policy contexts and settings?**

Persistent issues and repeated efforts to create change recur over time. Reflecting on our early childhood tradition in Scotland and the many local and national initiatives, we suggest that a transitions lens helps to consider how perpetual issues, about children's well-being and learning, and nurturing families, might be tackled differently and more successfully. **Can we see transitions themselves as tools for change?**

The association of poverty, working women and childcare is not new: both Owen and the Scottish early childhood pioneers were highly political. Present-day political motivation in Scotland to invest in young children must be met with vision and imagination. New beginnings are needed: the knowledge exists to do this well and to renew our Scottish model. This requires building on the strength of our rich heritage – to step off from it in contemporary ways, including forward-looking CPD (for example, https://early-education.org.uk). System transitions mean that skilled and experienced nursery Headteachers are being redeployed; it is to be hoped that their expertise is not lost to the ELC sector at such a crucial time of change. In Scotland, we need immediately to support the many new practitioners to develop their knowledge and skills (Dunlop et al., 2020). **How can early years practitioners in all policy contexts and types of settings be supported to enable effective, holistic transition experiences?**

It is people that will make the difference. Lileen Hardy (1913) talked of the 'quiet spells when an adult has an opportunity of playing the important parts of observer and learner'. These moments could ensure that working in many different early childhood spaces values in action will reconceptualise transitions as a modern interpretation of the early years pioneer's legacy is alive and relevant in our settings.

QUESTIONS

- Reflecting on transitions approaches in your setting, could you help build transitions networks for children and families as they start in early years and when they move on to school?
- What could you do to support children and families to feel ready to make these transitions with ease?
- By enhancing communication and relationships between settings, could you foster play approaches to transitions?

FURTHER READING AND RESOURCES

White, E.J., Marwick, H., Amorim, K., Rutanen, N. and Herold, L. (eds) (2022) *First Transitions to Early Childhood Education and Care*. Dordrecht: Springer.
Focuses on the first transitions infants make into early childhood settings.

International Journal of Educational and Life Transitions (https://ijelt.dundee.ac.uk). Publishes articles and multimedia outputs on educational and life transitions across the world.

SERA Early Years Network Special Issue (2020) www.sera.ac.uk/wp-content/uploads/sites/13/2021/01/SERA-REB-Special-Issue-Early-Years-Network-2v2.pdf
Focuses on early childhood research in Scotland, including on leadership, play pedagogy and love-led practice.

Getting It Right for Every Child (Scottish Government, 2017)

Realising the Ambition: Being me (Scottish Government, 2020: Section 8, 88–97)

Standard for Childhood Practice (SSSC, 2015: 8, 14–15)

Parents as Early Education Partners (PEEP): www.midlothian.gov.uk/info/851/early_learning_nurseries_and_childcare/334/peep_-_learning_together_programme (accessed 18 September 2022).

Scottish Early Childhood, Children and Families Transitions Position Statement (2019, updated 2022) https://education.gov.scot/improvement/self-evaluation/scottish-early-childhood-and-families-transitions-statement/#:~:text=%E2%80%8BThe%20Scottish%20Children%20and,local%20policy%20and%20transitions%20practice (accessed 18 September 2022).

ACKNOWLEDGEMENTS

We warmly acknowledge all who contributed case studies for this chapter.

8

INCLUSIVE EDUCATION FOR YOUNG CHILDREN WITH SPECIAL EDUCATIONAL NEEDS AND DISABILITIES (SEND): MULTIPLE PERSPECTIVES

JAN GEORGESON, HELEN ADAMS, EMMA SHORT AND KATE ULLMAN

CHAPTER OBJECTIVES

- To briefly set out legal and policy contests for young children with identified SEN/D
- To describe practice for young children with SEN/D in three different settings
- To identify key issues for the future.

CHAPTER OVERVIEW

This chapter traces a brief history of provision for very young children with identified special educational needs and/or disabilities (SEN/D). It considers the promise of the UN Convention on the Rights of the Child (1989), with – as yet – an unfulfilled focus on legal rights to provision. The remainder of the chapter demonstrates, through the experience of early years leaders, how policy plays out in practice.

INTRODUCTION

Looking back at the history of provision for very young children with special educational needs, we see how this has been shaped by society's understanding about differences between individuals, what causes these differences and what we should be doing about them. Over time, collective responsibility for more vulnerable members of society has been influenced by moral codes and pragmatics. Disability, in England, might historically be attributed to the presence of demons or the misdeeds of parents, but individuals with impairments were also assimilated in the community; religious orders provided care for those who were abandoned or found it difficult to live within prevailing conditions and, from the mid-1700s onwards, charitable foundations offered care and (sometimes) education for children with sensory, intellectual or physical impairments. Gradually, responsibility has devolved to the state, although, even when it became law in 1870 that all children should be educated, some children were still classed as ineducable and a lottery of care or incarceration continued until the 1970 Education (Handicapped Children) Act (www.legislation.gov.uk/ukpga/1970/52/enacted) made education universal.

Though today we might seem a long way from the unenlightened practices of the past, tensions remain between the needs of those requiring support and the systems of support available. The UNCRC (United Nations, 1989) offered the prospect of change; no longer should provision for young children with disabilities depend on how others felt about their situation (either out of kindness, prejudice or pragmatics); instead, the focus should be on their legal rights to equality of opportunity, dignity and having a voice in decisions about their lives. UK legislation enshrines some UNCRC rights, however international monitors have noted the slowness of progress towards full incorporation in England. Despite this, the influence of the UNCRC is apparent in many aspects of legislation affecting children, viewing things from the child's perspective and managing the dilemma of difference. So, how can we provide support to enable children to have the same opportunities without drawing unwanted attention to the way in which they are different?

While the legal status of children's rights has been changing, our understanding of child development has increased. Decisions about who should receive extra support rely on those around the child – child, family, neighbours and those providing services – noticing that they are different and moreover that their difference suggests the need for support. This 'noticing' goes beyond spotting physical differences to detecting delays in doing things already achieved by their peers. Much research has resulted in identifying developmental milestones which can be used to recognise children whose development seems delayed or compromised. Interventions might then be offered to enable a child to 'catch up' so that they might have the same access to educational opportunities as their peers once they start school. Indeed, the 'Levelling Up' agenda for England identified support for children with SEN/D as a 'challenge', and stated:

We must also do more to ensure children with SEND and children with a social worker have the same opportunities for success as their peers. Whether improving the early identification of need and the quality of mainstream support, or providing effective and timely specialist support, we have a moral duty to do better by these children. (DfE, 2022b: 36, para. 89)

We must await the outcomes ensuing from the SEND review (DfE, 2022c), to see what resources are committed to turn any stated intentions into realities.

If we map the story of advances in understanding child development against the history of early provision, we notice shifts in the purpose of educational provision for young children away from time and space to support them to grow and learn at their own pace. Alongside legislative changes that foreground the role of public institutions in keeping children safe, and policy shifts towards provision of ECEC to enable parents to work (earning money to move families out of poverty and reduce social exclusion), the emphasis on identification and remediation contributes to an ethos of surveillance and preparation for future schooling. The experience of supporting a child with SEN/D in an early years setting is now shaped by many more factors than benevolent concerns to care and nurture individuals whose developmental trajectories are different from those of other children around them; parents and practitioners can feel that their intentions are frustrated by systems that do not respond with flexibility and sensitivity to individual children's needs.

In three case studies, Helen, Emma and Kate share their experiences of leading support for children with SEN/D in different early years settings.

Helen considers how supporting children with SEN/D can vary between mainstream settings. All settings need to find ways to manage challenges to appropriate provision, including adequate funding, the functionality and accessibility of early years buildings and staff's skill and competence, alongside the 'postcode lottery' that influences the range of provision available in an area. Provision is also shaped by the principles and expectations of policy makers and those in practice, including school leaders, governors and government.

CASE STUDY 8.1: WHERE DO SPECIAL EDUCATIONAL NEEDS FIT IN THE EARLY YEARS FOUNDATION STAGE?

Helen Adams, Headteacher, Truro Nursery School, Cornwall

In our Maintained Nursery School, we go out of our way to be inclusive and do what is right for the child and family – my background in SEN/D is therefore a driver in our vision and practice. Other settings might have other priorities, particularly if they are concerned

(Continued)

about upcoming inspections. The Ofsted Inspection Handbook (Ofsted, 2021) makes frequent reference to meeting the needs of children with SEN/D alongside references to knowledge and skills acquisition and curriculum, yet these two expectations may work in opposition. Practitioners can sometimes assume that a child is ready to learn, or perhaps they *should* be ready to learn. However, the acquisition of knowledge and skills can only be achieved if a child is in a state receptive to learning, and so much has to come first. Children need to be able to self-regulate, to manage their emotions, thoughts and behaviour; they need sufficient auditory/visual or spatial perception, and they need to be warm and free from hunger. Faced with monitoring and inspection, practitioners need to have the confidence to pay close attention to each child's basic needs, and perhaps give them something to eat, allow them a rest, or provide them with some sensory feedback. This can be difficult for practitioners to bear in mind if their focus is primarily on getting the child to comply so that those inspecting or monitoring view the outcomes of the activity as successful.

All too often, this can lead to an approach of just 'dealing with' children with SEN/D in mainstream settings and schools, providing a bit of extra support so that they can achieve within the periphery of the mainstream curriculum. Such children might be allowed extra 'play' time because they are unable to take part effectively in whole-class sessions. Where funds allow, children with SEN/D might be offered individual support when their peers are involved in whole-class sessions, making it difficult to achieve an outcome for the child which is both meaningfully inclusive and enjoyable. If practitioners understand that what a child needs is developmentally appropriate provision, they are more likely to help them to be successful. The EYFS (DfE, 2021a) provides for differentiation, and skilled staff can enable this. For example, a group of children are exploring clay: some may be demonstrating symbolic representation of something they know with creative likeness to the real object; they may be able to use sophisticated language to describe their creations. Others may enjoy the process of making and re-making while describing their sensory experiences, and others may feel the same sense of joy by being supported to touch the clay and feel its properties against their skin. All outcomes are valid and developmentally appropriate for each individual. The EYFS allows for variation within broad parameters; however, as the curriculum narrows, so might opportunities for children with SEN/D to succeed alongside their peers.

The EYFS maintains a focus on the individual child within a supportive relationship between a child and their key person – an essential factor in meeting the needs of all pupils. Emotional warmth and attunement ensure that children feel they are genuinely cared for and safe; both fundamental prerequisites for children to be able to learn. The key person relationship remains important in Reception classes but less favourable child-to-adult ratios can make this more challenging to develop in the same way; a key person needs time to get to know the child really well so that they might better meet their needs. They also need a strong understanding of child development as an individual iterative process rather than as a sequence of milestones.

In our Maintained Nursery School, we endeavour to allow children a degree of choice over who their key person is; we watch for a few weeks and see which adults the children seem to turn to for help and support, which adults they seem to develop a connection with and, whenever possible, this helps to determine the key person. Other relationships are also important; we recognise that we have everything to gain from learning about a child and their family. Our approach is to find out as much as we possibly can about a child before they begin nursery. We engage in multiple ways to equip ourselves with as much knowledge as we can so that we feel confident to fully support a child. *Instead of expecting the child to fit in with us, we want to adapt to fit in with the child's lived experience*, as the following example illustrates:

> A place was requested for Sam, a child with a complex medical syndrome, significant physical needs and developmental delay coupled with various medical complications and the requirement for ongoing medical treatment. Had Sam not been offered a place in our Maintained Nursery School, it would have been difficult to consider where else their needs could be met; there are very limited places in our special schools for children who are not yet of statutory school age and someone like Sam requires a high level of support from highly qualified and experienced staff. Maintained Nursery Schools have long been considered as leaders in meeting the needs of young children with SEN/D and children who are disadvantaged.
>
> Home visits were undertaken to understand what Sam could access at home and how the family supports sensory, physical and emotional needs at home. Families know the nuances in a child's behaviours and how these translate into needs. We evaluated our own learning environment and any adaptations we felt would benefit Sam; this was always from a positive view of what Sam could do, rather than a deficit model.
>
> We take care at every stage to ensure our environment is as inclusive as possible so that it is easy to adapt to different children's needs rather than expect them to fit in with the existing provision. We quickly attuned to Sam and, as a result, we were able to offer interventions rapidly to help them to self-regulate, before any other expectation of accessing provision or the curriculum.
>
> ***
>
> In contrast, Jordan came to us with seemingly no additional needs and nothing had been highlighted by parents or other professionals. Jordan's behaviours soon led us to question aspects of their development. Jordan spent a significant part of sessions pushing others, lying on other children and being over-physical with others. We had to manage this situation to protect the other children's wellbeing but we were also determined to discover why Jordan was behaving in such a way. It might have been easy to jump to conclusions about their social skills, previous social experiences or parenting; however, by observing closely

(Continued)

we recognised that they seemed to be seeking physical feedback rather than responding to others' behaviour. A strong sensory programme was put in place to allow Jordan to gain the feedback they desired from sensory play, so that they became less reliant upon gaining it from pushing others.

The EYFS provides practitioners with an opportunity for great inclusivity, allowing children to develop at their own pace, given their own lived experiences, and understanding that for some children their developmental trajectory will be different from their peers. However, the same cannot always be said of most mainstream provision as children get older. Comparisons, catching up and closing the gap appear to be the focus and somewhere what is right for an individual child appears to be lost.

Working in early years settings offers a particular kind of professionalism, informed by early years traditions and an understanding of child development, as case study 8.2 shows.

CASE STUDY 8.2: LEARNING HOW TO MEET SPECIAL EDUCATIONAL NEEDS

Emma Short, Headteacher, Cambourne Nursery School, Cornwall

In the early years, our teaching and learning follow children's interests. We teach key skills through play, extending children's knowledge through a rich curriculum and following their lead to support their next steps. We love what we do as every day is different and the children take us on their learning journeys. We observe children at play and watch out for schemas, interests and milestones. We come together as a team and talk through each child's learning so that we can all recognise how to support their next steps.

In the past, this approach might have changed if a child was identified – perhaps by parents, Portage or a health visitor during a home visit – as needing additional support. Children were then supported by an Education Health and Care Plan (EHCP) with individual one-to-one support from a designated teaching assistant (TA), who would stick to the child during the session, completing individual targets and ensuring the safety both of the child and other children.

This worked well for parents, who had a designated key person to speak to at the beginning and end of the session, and for the Special Educational Needs Coordinator, who had only one person to liaise with. However, it did not work well for:

- the TA, who became isolated from day-to-day practice
- the child, who became dependent upon one adult
- the rest of the team, who panicked whenever the TA was absent
- the class teacher, who became detached from working alongside that child

- other staff members, who did not experience the richness of working with all the children in the class
- the children in the class, who often saw that TA as the 'friend' of that child alone, and so didn't play with them.

In recent years, the staff team has developed a new system of supporting children with complex needs in our mainstream Maintained Nursery School in an area of high deprivation, with a history of supporting children with SEN/D. The move towards a new way of working followed considerable staff training and development, two years of disruption from COVID-19, many mistakes and precious moments of success. The school has built a culture of inclusion that celebrates *all children's possibilities*. All staff have recognised that they have the skills to support all children and at any time. Staff are comfortable to ask for help and to share concerns. The children have access to all areas of the nursery and are supported to take part in the rich curriculum.

The process of transforming our practice began with whole-school staff development which included emotion coaching, use of total communication, sensory development, speech and language training, movement play and autism awareness. Staff have worked alongside educational psychologists, specialist speech and language therapists, autism and communication workers, Portage workers, occupational therapists and senior Area Special Educational Needs Coordinators, as well as specialist teachers from the local Child Development Centre.

Staff work with parents too. We have listened closely to parents and built up honest and open relationships. Sometimes this has been difficult for everyone, especially during the pandemic when services were limited and support for parents was restricted to virtual contact. We support all children to achieve their full potential and we have worked hard to include all children.

Children who have an EHCP are now supported by everyone in the session. Careful planning is carried out with regular meetings to ensure that all staff have a clear picture of the expectations for each child. Staff use intervention plans throughout the day, including sensory, language and social targets – now carried out by all staff members and including several children. Some members of staff have described it as 'tag teaming' – being there for children throughout the session. The key is knowing what a child's next steps are as well as their individual needs. This requires helping all staff to build confidence in their own capacity to support any child, and understanding that behaviour is a means of communication.

By enabling children with an EHCP the opportunity to be supported by all staff in the nursery, our new way of working means that they have access to a variety of strengths. However, children still have a dedicated key person who can observe, assess progress and support relationships with parents. The key person system ensures individual support is carried out every day; therapies and focused work are recorded and monitored by the key person and the class teacher.

Paula, a highly trained and experienced TA who has worked at the nursery for over 12 years, reflected on the new way of working. Having worked one to one with three children

(Continued)

and more recently in a class with four children with EHCPs who were supported by the whole team, she felt that the new system of not working solely with one child for the whole session or sometimes the whole day, meant that a child who needed additional support was now seen differently by their peers. For Paula, one of the biggest changes was for the children in the class, who interacted spontaneously with the child, whereas, before, the adult offering one-to-one support could act as a barrier between a child and their peers. She felt the whole class benefitted from being more inclusive, with the staff team noticing how children were learning that we are all different. Explaining to children that the loud noises some children make are not to scare others but could be a sign they are happy, builds warm relationships instead of isolation. They learn to respond to difference with understanding.

The pandemic has led staff to prioritise well-being and focus even more on supporting emotional resilience and ensuring children have opportunities to enjoy the nursery at their own pace. This might mean offering children opportunities to explore the sunlight through the trees or watch the sand pour through their fingers. It has also been important to learn about giving space and having the confidence to step back sometimes from a child with high levels of need. This has been the biggest challenge for our team; allowing independence whenever possible by scaffolding support when needed has been our biggest breakthrough.

The importance of play in laying down the foundations of future learning – enabling children to develop in all aspects of their lives – is at the heart of EYFS pedagogy (see Chapters 1, 2 and 4). This is no different when providing a learning environment and curriculum for children who have special educational needs. Some children are offered places in specialist provision, although access to these settings and children's early years experiences can vary due to many factors. A special early years setting can adapt practice to the needs of individual children, usually grouped in small classes with a high staff–pupil ratio. Pupils have contrasting and complementing needs which need to be balanced. The setting will need to support the development of communication skills – often referred to as a 'total communication' environment. For many other children and families, the journey is not so straightforward. Complex and severe learning difficulties, particularly where autistic spectrum disorder (ASD) is concerned, may not be identified until a child enters early years provision – or even when they enter their Reception class. The process of writing an EHCP can take time to initiate and then time to write and may also delay a decision on an appropriate placement. Consequently, children who might benefit from specialist provision in the long term are often placed in mainstream classes because a specialist placement is unavailable or until a final decision has been reached. Special schools can receive children from a variety of backgrounds, some having had no experience within an early years setting. Often, children may have had access to educational provision only for an hour or two a day because their needs are such that they require constant one-to-one support and funding is unavailable.

In case study 8.3, Kate shares her experience of teaching in special schools where very young children are in classes who fit the age range for the EYFS and who have complex needs that were identified at or soon after birth. These children and their families may have had support from home-visiting services such as Portage, which provide expertise before the child enters a nursery or school setting – whether mainstream or special.

CASE STUDY 8.3: SPECIALIST PROVISION FOR SPECIAL EDUCATIONAL NEEDS/DISABILITY

Kate Ullman, Early Years Teacher, Mill Ford School, Devon

When children have a very complex or severe learning difficulty, it is often the case that children are interacting with the world around them at a significantly younger development stage than their chronological age. It is vital that these children have an opportunity to learn in a play-based learning environment and there is great value in allowing children to access this type of environment during Key Stage 1. The priorities for their development will be highlighted in an EHCP and will typically be around communication and interaction, as well as cognition. Without a focus on working with the children and parents to develop the early foundations of good communication, a child cannot successfully take part in more structured learning when they are older.

The EYFS offers an ethos that recognises the fundamental importance of the prime areas of learning (Personal, Social and Emotional Development, Communication and Language, Physical Development) which underpin all learning, and helps children to develop the essential skills they will need to be able to begin to make sense of the world around them. Children with complex and severe learning needs will be working within the ranges described in 'Development Matters' or 'Birth to 5 Matters' and are unlikely to attain the 'Early Learning Goals'. Extending the time for developmentally appropriate provision with a focus on playful learning until the end of Key Stage 1 is a valuable approach for schools to adopt to support their youngest children.

This is the time to look at how the child learns – using the 'Characteristics of Effective Learning' to underpin observations and help to shine a light on their individual ways of learning. Indeed, as children progress through a special school setting, staff will be thinking about what kind of learner they are and which pathway they will take. Following on from the Rochford Review (Rochford, 2016), special schools are implementing the Engagement Model (Standards and Testing Agency, 2020) and considering whether children are pre-formal (or informal) learners, semi-formal learners or formal learners. Informal learners will follow the Engagement Model (2020), rather than subject-specific approaches. The seven areas of the Engagement Model – responsiveness, curiosity, discovery, anticipation,

(Continued)

persistence, initiation and investigation – will seem very familiar to early years practitioners used to working with the Characteristics of Effective Learning; working within the EYFS therefore suits informal learners well.

The importance of a play-based curriculum extends to early learners with ASD. Rita Jordan (2001) discusses the challenges that children with autism and severe learning difficulties can face in developing those skills, but says it is a mistake to not pursue play as an important part of their development. The staff are the most valuable 'resource'; they need to be able to model and scaffold play, to spot when a child is interested and captivated to begin to join in or try things for themselves. The adults around the children need to support them to develop a sense of their own individual identity and their own self-determination by valuing, encouraging and building their confidence.

Cognitive skills and development need to be planned for in creative ways, ensuring children are excited to try new experiences. Flexibility needs to be built into the curriculum so that practitioners can quickly adjust the focus, based on what the children respond to well, while being certain that they are providing a broad and balanced programme which allows for progression. This means that there is a place for objective-led, structured teaching activities, developed after observations of emerging skills, which the adults around individual children plan to support. Special school practitioners develop a toolkit of strategies to draw upon from very child-focused and more gentle approaches, such as Intensive Interaction (Nind and Hewitt, 2005) or making use of sensory methods, such as stories or TacPac (a sensory communication resource using touch and music), to more structured approaches such as TEACCH and PECS. When contemplating the more behavioural approaches, the long-term benefit to each child should be considered.

KEY ISSUES FOR THE FUTURE
INCLUSIVE PROVISION FOR CHILDREN WITH SPECIAL EDUCATIONAL NEEDS AND DISABILITY

Meeting the needs of children with SEN/D can be challenging, time-intensive and financially demanding, it requires a great deal of effort, but it is, equally, fulfilling, exciting and a journey of professional learning and love.

Taking a principled approach to inclusion in the education will directly affect our success in meeting the needs of all children, including those with SEN/D. When we think more deeply about those needs, however, we find ourselves questioning how important and relevant it is to focus on narrowing the gap between children with SEN/D and their peers. Following the UNCRC, we take the view that children with SEN/D have a right to have their needs met in the most appropriate way for them and their future development, rather than the view that they should be supported towards particular goals so that they can 'fit' into mainstream settings. It is our moral duty to put the needs of children first, rather than the needs of the school and an education focused on a narrow range of attainment.

It is vital that we have high expectations for all children and also to recognise that some children require very different provision in order to make progress, and that the steps they take might seem small and repetitive in comparison with others. We should also remember that, for some children with life-limiting conditions, the concept of 'progress' might be less valid than the concepts of a life well led and living in the moment. We need to change the narrative whereby children with SEN/D are constantly compared to their peers in order to judge their progress, so that we do not inadvertently orchestrate a situation where children with SEN/D are always viewed as failing and their considerable individual achievements are not duly recognised.

QUESTIONS

- What does inclusive practice in your setting look like – are all children equally included?
- How do your national curriculum and inspection policies support inclusive practices?
- How can we move to a situation where all children are regarded for who they are and their individual achievements celebrated as personal successes?

FURTHER READING AND RESOURCES

Bomber, L. (2007) *Inside I'm Hurting: Practical Strategies for Supporting Children with Attachment Difficulties in Schools*. London: Worth Publishing.
Explores the importance of attachment and practical strategies for promoting inclusion in mainstream settings.

Conn, C. and Murphy, A. (eds) (2022) *Inclusive Pedagogies for Early Childhood Education: Respecting and Responding to Differences in Learning*. London: Routledge.
Theoretical, research and practice perspectives on a children's rights approach to inclusive ECE pedagogies.

Jordan, R. (2001) *Autism with Severe Learning Difficulties*. London: Souvenir Press.
A guide to working with children who have dual diagnoses of ASD and severe learning difficulties, which includes consideration of the importance of play.

9

RACE, ANTI-DISCRIMINATION AND WORK TO COMBAT THE EFFECTS OF DISCRIMINATION ON PRACTITIONERS AND CHILDREN

STELLA LOUIS, SALLY CAVE AND NAZMA MEAH

CHAPTER OBJECTIVES

- To define the terms used in discussion of race and discrimination
- To provide examples of practice to bring about change and tackle bias
- To offer ways of combatting the effects of discrimination in early years settings.

CHAPTER OVERVIEW

This chapter outlines what anti-discriminatory practice is and the steps needed to promote and implement it in schools and settings. It has been written for all educators who may want to examine their own feelings and attitudes about race and discrimination. In this chapter, Stella Louis sets out the key issues and practices necessary to combat the effects of discrimination and draws on case studies by two experienced leaders, Sally Cave and Nazma Meah, to highlight some challenges and dilemmas in practice. It also reflects on the importance of training and policy development.

RACE AND ANTI-DISCRIMINATION: DEFINING OUR TERMS

Anti-discriminatory practice is defined as a professional method of continually challenging racism, sexism, stereotypes, bias and inequalities. Discrimination may manifest itself in many different ways, including someone's attitude, behaviour, the curriculum and resources they provide, or their values, beliefs and ideologies.

Britain is a rich and diverse country, made up of people from a range of cultures and different parts of the world. There are seven protected characteristics under the law – which include race, gender, disability and religion – but Britain is not an equal society. It is one in which many children from diverse communities find that educators are often unfamiliar with their background, resulting in their achievements and interests not being understood or valued in the assessment of their learning outcomes (Louis and Betteridge, 2020). Without learning about the values of other cultures, and questioning their own assumptions, educators cannot know what children from diverse communities bring with them in terms of knowledge and understanding.

The time is long overdue for every educator to talk more openly and honestly about race and discrimination and how it affects children's development and learning. Research has found that children's initial awareness of their own and other people's race begins at about six months old. Kelly et al. (2005) found evidence that, from three months old, babies look more at faces which match the race of their caregiver. This shows us that babies are more familiar with, and have a preference for familiarity with, people who look like their caregiver – not necessarily differences associated with race. Similarly, between eight and nine months old, babies begin to display a fear of strangers. This is when babies have a physical and emotional reaction to people who are unfamiliar, which demonstrates a responsiveness to people who look like them.

Hirschfeld (2008) provides evidence of children as young as 2 years old using race to reason about other people's behaviour – for example, a child saying, 'the Black boy took the cake', when the cake goes missing and there is no Black boy in sight. This shows that from the age of 2, children not only categorise others by race, but they also begin to internalise racial biases that they come across from interactions with parents, family, picture books, movies and television. Children will gather information from all of these sources about cultural and social norms. Disturbingly, Hirschfeld also found that 5-year-old 'children of colour' were consciously aware of the stereotypes attributed to them and their racial group. This is very similar to the conclusions of Aboud (2008), who found that 'children of colour' were more aware than their 5-year-old White counterparts of prejudice and stereotypes about their racial identities and social group, and how they were affected by them.

THE ROLE OF EDUCATORS IN TACKLING RACISM

Our role as educators is to be positive about children's many attributes. In contrast, Aboud (2008: 62) found evidence that 'White children rarely exhibit anything other than a pro-White bias'. This is reinforced by Kinzler (2016), who found that, by the age of 5, White children had learned to associate some groups with higher status than others. This suggests that children learn messages from everyday encounters that White is superior and Black is inferior. This is because whiteness in society is seen as the default and everything else is seen as othering. Young children have limited life experience, which makes them much more open to seeing the world through the stereotypes they are presented with in books, television, magazines, and so on.

TALKING WITH CHILDREN ABOUT RACE AND DISCRIMINATION

Why should we talk about race and discrimination with children? Children are not colour blind. They need to learn about equality, equity, respect and acceptance of others. Educators need to think carefully about how they can begin to teach children about difference and diversity, from the age of six months. According to Katz (2003), when educators engage in safe, candid, regular and developmentally appropriate discussions about race and discrimination, less bias is seen in children's behaviours and attitudes. Talking to children about diversity matters, even if educators are working in an all-White or monocultural rural school or setting. Young children should be exposed to diversity and difference and have stereotypes and assumptions challenged, particularly if the images and materials being used represent White people only or portray a negative image of people from diverse communities. Early years education is an effective forum where toys and resources can reflect the diversity of society, and practices can support values of equality. It is also an important starting point for talking about and tackling racial discrimination in society and building inclusive educational practice.

FOUR ELEMENTS OF ANTI-DISCRIMINATORY PRACTICE: ATTITUDE, BEHAVIOUR, PRACTICE, REFLECTION

In anti-discriminatory practice, the role of the educator is about four interconnected things: *attitude, behaviour, practice* and *reflection*. As a first step, it is necessary for all educators, whatever their race, to examine their own attitudes, feelings, assumptions and preconceptions about children and their families. This will help you to acknowledge your own tendency to stereotype and to recognise your privileges and your unconscious bias.

BE AWARE OF CONSCIOUS AND UNCONSCIOUS MESSAGING

As a starting point, educators need to consider what messages they themselves have consciously or unconsciously received about the way that different racial groups behave. How does this affect the way that you think about and behave towards them in practice – whether positive or negative? Do you have feelings of authority or superiority which prevent you from recognising children's achievements?

ENGAGE IN CRITICAL REFLECTION

Secondly, just doing what you have always done without reflection avoids thinking about your behaviour and ultimately addressing it. Discrimination in Britain today is not only about skin colour – it affects Black, Asian, Mixed Heritage and Eastern European people too, as shown by Brexit. It can have negative consequences for white Irish, Roma Traveller and Jewish children as well. Taking ownership of the problem of discrimination means reflecting critically on your practice to ensure that you have high aspirations and expectations for all of the children. Do not expect Black and/or Asian colleagues to solve the problem for you – do the necessary work, such as reading and researching, for yourself.

CHANGE BEHAVIOUR

Thirdly, practise is a verb. It requires action. Educators need to think critically about what they do. This may mean reflecting on unfair policies and biased practices based on race, and being confident enough to challenge the stereotypes, procedures and discriminatory attitudes that continue to exist. Babies' and young children's identities are embedded within the family culture in which they live. They learn with others in their family and in cultural and community contexts. This is a rich source of teaching for educators. Educators need to provide children with meaningful opportunities to learn about their own cultural selves and others. This is vital as it will help them to become aware of, and grow to respect, value and recognise difference.

DON'T DISCRIMINATE

Lastly, it is important for all educators to ensure that they do not discriminate against children and their families. Children learn from everyday interactions and experiences with people and the physical environment. Children are keen observers – they absorb information quickly, including discrimination, stereotypes and prejudice. Educators must be active in challenging negative attitudes and practice within the school or setting, including in themselves. Although talking about and reflecting on racial discrimination can at times feel difficult, it is important to educate yourself.

ANTI-DISCRIMINATORY APPROACHES

If educators are to embrace an anti-discriminatory approach, then they need to consider all of the interconnected issues involved *(attitude, behaviour, practice* and *reflection)* and demand change in the systems that lead children from different communities to feel that they are worth less than their White peers. Ultimately, educators will need to do the work necessary to take an anti-discriminatory approach as well as be able to listen to the experiences of children and parents without questioning or denying their validity. Such was the case at Guildford Nursery School and Family Centre, as Headteacher, Sally Cave explains in case study 9.1.

CASE STUDY 9.1: WORK AT GUILDFORD NURSERY SCHOOL AND FAMILY CENTRE (GNSFC) TO COMBAT THE EFFECTS OF DISCRIMINATION ON PRACTITIONERS AND CHILDREN

Sally Cave, Headteacher, GNSFC, Guildford, Surrey

Following the tragic killing of George Floyd in America in May 2020, it was obvious to me that we urgently needed to talk about Race and racism.

GNSFC is a Maintained Nursery School on two sites in Guildford. In addition, the school is the lead provider for the borough's family centre. In total, there are 54 staff, and almost all are White and female. Our children are, however, much more diverse, with 42% multilingual.

Ever since I started at GNSFC as Headteacher in January 2017, senior leaders have written a weekly newsletter for staff. In early June, I wrote about my horror of the killing of George Floyd and my intention that we should, as a whole staff, consider what it means for us. One of the teachers, Rachel, came to see me the following week to ask if she could lead on this work, an offer I accepted. One of the family support workers, Britt, volunteered to support Rachel.

Through June and July, Rachel, Britt and I discussed and debated our own thinking and we also talked to Stella Louis about ways to start discussions with the rest of the staff. We all agreed that it was imperative to begin with ourselves as staff. We each needed to know ourselves before we could think about changes to the environment and curriculum.

In September 2020, Rachel and Britt began a series of small group staff sessions to talk about our understanding, thoughts and feelings related to concepts such as Race,

(Continued)

racism, White privilege, and the *Black Lives Matter* movement. We acknowledged from the start that this would be a journey and that we would probably all begin at different stages. We also included all staff without exception, regardless of whether they worked directly with children and families. Each session began with an agreed code of conduct so that everyone felt safe to be honest.

Staff embraced the opportunity to talk about these issues, and without exception they were open. This was not without its challenges as there were individuals who at times expressed quite opposing views to the facilitators. We held a debrief after one particularly difficult session and discussed our options. After considering asking Stella to facilitate or whether I should be present at each session, Rachel and Britt decided to carry on, however challenging, as it was felt that my presence or that of Stella could result in staff feeling less able to be honest around their feelings. As Britt said: 'Those conversations were definitely difficult, but that's nothing compared to the lived realities and racism experienced by Black people and other ethnic minorities.'

Our Froebelian principles really helped at this time as they reminded me that we believe in starting where the learner is; in giving choice; in learning through reflection. I firmly believe that Froebel's principles should apply to our work with adults as much as with the children. In the next newsletter, I reaffirmed that we were on a journey and everyone had their own starting point, but reiterated that there was an expectation we would become an anti-racist organisation. The journey may be long and different from others' but the destination is defined. The Chair of Governors wrote a statement supporting our work so that all staff knew that engaging in this work was not optional!

From September 2020 onwards, I have included something on which to reflect in most weekly staff newsletters. This might be an infographic, a quote, a photo, some facts or thoughts. In this way, everyone is constantly considering issues to do with Race, equality, equity and discrimination.

We have also asked our Black and Asian colleagues, friends and family members to talk to us about their own lived experiences as people of colour. We do this in order to learn and also to practise being braver about having conversations about Race and discrimination. Much has been done virtually due to the global pandemic but, in some ways, this has made it easier for all. Three housemates of one of our colleagues videoed themselves talking about their experiences as young, female, newly qualified midwives whose parents had all been born in Ghana. While it was reassuring to hear that none had known the overt racism suffered by their parents, I found it very distressing to learn of the more insidious, covert racism that they had all experienced.

Through our work, we became more aware of unconscious bias and the need to do more to reduce its effect. To this end, our HR manager, Jeanette, has completely revised our recruitment procedures. This includes masked shortlisting (names, ethnicity, gender, address and other identifying details are removed from the application form prior to shortlisting); written tasks are assessed without knowing any identifying features of the candidates; and all shortlisting and assessments are carried out by at least two people. Each candidate completes some psychometric assessments and meets with an occupational psychologist who then provides feedback and a report to the panel. One of the psychometric assessments focuses on six components of cultural capability which identify the inclusive behaviours that underpin an individual's capability to work fairly, respectfully, and engage with all types of people, regardless of how similar or how different they are to them. Finally, there is an observed task and a panel interview. Interviewers have all received training on unconscious bias, how to recognise it and how to reduce its impact.

Personally, I am much more aware of my own biases, such as the fact that I have definitely interviewed previously with a 'halo' or 'devil' effect, when one's overall impression of a person is either positive or negative and this impacts on individual evaluations of that person's specific traits. So, I have been in a situation where an interviewee says something I completely agree with and then I find myself agreeing with everything else they say and not truly listening to exactly what they are saying and not effectively assessing them against our desired competencies.

We continue our work and anticipate and embrace the fact that this work will be never-ending.

One of the biggest challenges that the early years sector faces is its commitment to confronting and eradicating racial discrimination. Although no one can force educators to acknowledge and speak out against inequalities, they do need to understand that their silence is loud, powerful and complicit. We cannot continue to turn away and pretend that discrimination does not exist. As educators, we work with children and their families with a promise of equality, which means treating children fairly and equitably, meeting every child's diverse needs, supporting inclusion, and valuing what the child brings from home – their whole self.

NURTURING CHILDREN'S RACIAL IDENTITIES

According to Manning-Morton (2013), a child's racial identity is at the core of their sound psychological development as it is important for children to develop a strong sense of self. This needs to be nurtured by educators as children are developing their identity, working out who they are and where they fit in all at the same time. It is vital that children feel good about themselves and their physical characteristics, such as their hair texture and skin colour. The effects of a lack of understanding about a child's racial or cultural background on their mental health and sense of identity should not be underestimated. Being excluded on the grounds of race, or feeling uncared for and treated negatively, can have an impact on a child's sense of belonging and well-being. In case study 9.2, Nazma Meah shares her approach to leading a setting where racism is not tolerated.

CASE STUDY 9.2: A LEADERSHIP AND MANAGEMENT PERSPECTIVE ON TACKLING RACISM AND ANTI-DISCRIMINATION IN EARLY YEARS SETTINGS

Nazma Meah, Manager of The Village Community Nursery and Owner of Aston Pre-School

This case study looks at how managers and leaders can support staff and children with tackling racism and anti-discrimination in early years as this is more important now than ever in the ever-changing field of racism and discrimination.

As managers and leaders of early years settings, we have a huge responsibility to keep our children and staff safe from racism or anti-discrimination, as well as educating them about it. Children as young as 2 may learn that they are different, and this may not always be in a good way. This is why it is important that, as managers, we support staff and children to ensure that their experiences are positive and inclusive.

First and foremost, it is vital that your setting has robust and effective policies and procedures for inclusion. This must be promoted from the outset, so that staff and parents are aware that no form of racism or discrimination will be tolerated. This gives a good signal to prospective applicants, for jobs and child places, that racism and discrimination are not welcome and will not be tolerated. Statements on job adverts and setting application forms should be clear and concise to this effect.

Supporting staff starts right at the beginning from when they apply for a job, and your interview should stress the importance of staff being inclusive. As a manager, one of the things I tend to do is question applicants on various scenarios to see what their answers are and challenge them on any ambiguities. As an example, we discuss children from same-sex families and whether that would impact on how staff view the child. Historically, there has been some concern with staff that are Muslim, as same-sex parenting goes against their religious beliefs.

So, communication and dialogue are very important when dealing with such issues; such conversations cannot be blocked, and the issues cannot be ignored. They must be addressed head on, via training and awareness-raising. We cannot ignore religious beliefs, values and morals; they form a huge part of our behaviours and attitudes, and this is why, as managers, we must ensure we manage this appropriately and effectively.

Once we have recruited, we must ensure staff have the appropriate ongoing and relevant training. Many staff have just a two-hour awareness session in their induction and then the subject is never touched on in the rest of the time they work in the setting.

What needs to be discussed in training will differ depending on the make-up of the cohort of children in the setting. As an example, a setting with predominantly South Asian and Muslim children but no White or Black children, will need training in diversity and inclusion on how to ensure any White or Black children who join the setting, are not excluded and the well-established Asian children are aware of them. In insulated communities, it is quite easy for children not to see people different to them. For example, a parent once advised me that their 2-year-old was scared of a Black member of staff. I was told that the child had never seen a Black person. On observation, I noticed that it was not the child that had an issue, it was the parent's own direct prejudice that was being played out. The parent withdrew their child.

Over the last few years, there has been an influx of Eastern European families in the areas that I work in, and it has been important that I support staff with this as many staff live in insulated communities and struggle to understand other communities. Some staff had a pre-conceived idea about Travellers and Roma/Gypsy communities, leading to comments such as 'since they have come into the area, crime has gone up'. When small numbers of children from this community joined the setting, staff struggled with their prejudices, commenting on the children as playing 'rough' or not being 'clean'. As a manager, I quickly realised that I need to train my staff on this community and bring awareness about it as the staff were acting on prejudices that have been formed within their own communities.

Making sure that everyone has access to anti-discriminatory professional development must be a priority as this will help to ensure that all educators become more aware of the effect that school and nursery can have on the lives of children. Having such training in schools and settings can create a safe space to make mistakes and learn from others without being judged. Turning away is just not an option – all children deserve to receive an anti-discriminatory education. Reflecting on and challenging negative racial bias or misunderstandings will help educators to recognise discrimination and call it out. Sharing training with whole staff teams will also ensure that everyone comes to an understanding of respecting and valuing difference, sharing the commitment with children and parents, and dealing with discriminatory behaviour. It is crucial to make it clear that discrimination harms children's development and will not be tolerated. All these actions seek to encourage an active interest in learning about anti-discrimination by offering regular statutory training sessions, particularly aimed at assessment processes. This sets the scene for ensuring that all staff have a basic understanding of issues of difference and diversity, so that educators can ensure familiarity with the child's cultural background, develop knowledge about their interests, and work in partnership with parents. Stella Louis ends this chapter with a reminder that tackling racism is the responsibility of every one of us.

TAKING RESPONSIBILITY FOR TACKLING RACISM

The responsibility for tackling discrimination within society lies with everyone, not with one individual. It is a societal problem. Policy makers, stakeholders, educators, families and other agencies, such as higher education, health, housing and justice, must all work together to develop equity and anti-discriminatory practice. This requires the following:

- Governments must provide statutory funding for policies that seek to combat race discrimination, and the development of workshops and courses in response to the needs of local communities.
- All educators must attend statutory training on issues relating to racial discrimination and developing an anti-discriminatory practice – until then, educators have a duty to actively seek out and attend training. Educators, and children, cannot wait until it is a statutory requirement.
- Stakeholders and educators should include children and their families in their discussions around developing anti-discriminatory practice.

A FUTURE WITHOUT RACISM

In 100 years from now, issues of racial identity will be discussed as regularly as literacy and numeracy. The training of all educators will finally prevent any manifestations of racial inequality from taking root in schools or settings. For that to happen, changes are needed in the other aspects of life mentioned earlier in this chapter, to complement and support early education. Regular training will stand educators in good stead to effectively counter all forms of discrimination they face, thus ensuring that babies and young children receive a high quality of early education and preparation for life.

Ultimately, promoting an anti-discriminatory approach is about taking responsibility and action.

This is a call to action for educators.

QUESTIONS

- What do you think of when you hear the term 'racism'?
- Consider how you might begin to address issues of racism and racial discrimination in your setting.
- What changes have you made in your practice to develop anti-discriminatory practices?

FURTHER READING AND RESOURCES

Agarwal, P. (2020) *Wish We Knew What to Say: Talking with Children About Race*. London: Dialogue Books.
A clear and concise book on how to tackle and embed anti-racism.

Louis, S. (2020) Let's talk about race. *Nursery World*, 16–17.
This article looks at how language can be a barrier when talking about race.

Pemberton, L. (2020) Wakanda forever. *Nursery World*, 18–19.
This article shows how educators can use stories to help children build a positive sense of identity.

10

GENDER AND LGBTQ+ INCLUSIVE PRACTICE IN EARLY CHILDHOOD

SHADDAI TEMBO AND FIFI BENHAM

CHAPTER OBJECTIVES

- To explore contemporary research and policy regarding gender and LGBTQ+ inclusive practice in early childhood
- To provide a historical overview of issues surrounding gender and LGBTQ+ inclusion
- To consider how issues of inclusion are presently received in public and scholarly arenas
- To examine strategies for gender and LGBTQ+ inclusive practice for young children
- To propose a future agenda towards wide and embedded gender and LGBTQ+ inclusion.

CHAPTER OVERVIEW

This chapter examines the role of gender and LGBTQ+ inclusive practice to understand how we, as educators, might raise children unlimited by the gendered and heteronormative beliefs which negatively impact their identities. This chapter is written in three parts. Initially, we provide an overview of the field across the past century and consider how gender and LGBTQ+ inclusion is received today within both the public and scholarly arenas. Secondly, we turn to practice and consider strategies for inclusion based on our own experiences with young children. Finally, we look forward to an agenda for the future, considering what kind of change might be needed to maintain, and heighten, a focus on gender and LGBTQ+ inclusion.

INTRODUCTION

At the dawn of the twenty-first century, the question of how we might raise children unlimited by the gendered and heteronormative beliefs that continue to shape the ways in which they develop their identities, remains a central topic of concern. While views are changing in positive ways, opposition persists. Traditional beliefs about who we are and how we should be as individuals still hold a considerable influence over how we understand our own identities and those of other people. Many of these beliefs establish themselves as norms and are internalised through social and moral practices, and in state legal systems. Early childhood, as it pertains to both the profession and the experiences of children themselves, is by no means free from the norms of wider society. Yet, the perception of childhood as an innocent time, untouched by broader issues, remains prevalent. This is a dangerous view, given what is known about how children come to form their identities, in more and less equal ways.

GENDER AND LGBTQ+ INCLUSION TERMINOLOGY

Our use of the term 'gender' refers to a system of social and material practices, norms and expectations within society that constitutes people as being different in socially significant ways (Lorber, 1994; Ridgeway and Smith-Lovin, 1999; Connell and Pearse, 2014). From birth, children are socialised differently based upon their assigned sex. Throughout their childhood, they come to learn what it means to be a 'girl' or a 'boy' or a 'man' or a 'woman'. In receiving these messages, children come to reproduce (as cis-gender) and challenge (as trans, non-binary or gender-diverse) gender norms in their own identities. This is what Judith Butler (1993) foundationally refers to as 'gender performativity', a term that enables an understanding of gender as a constructed performance mediated by broader social practices, norms and expectations. Where we discuss *heteronormativity*, we are referring to practices that socially exclude or marginalise non-heterosexual people and preserve heterosexuality as the norm (Warner, 1993; DePalma and Atkinson, 2009). Finally, we use *LGBTQ+* as an umbrella term to refer to all current and future minoritised sexual orientations and gender identities, with the plus symbol used as a proxy to represent both the wide variety of established genders and orientations beyond the initialism, and those who are part of the community but have a more fluid sense of identity and do not necessarily feel drawn to particular labels. We deliberately use *minoritised*, rather than minority, to draw attention to the active process of certain groups being subordinated according to issues of power, instead of simply their quantifiable number.

RESEARCH AND DEVELOPMENT IN GENDER AND LGBTQ+ INCLUSION

This section provides a brief overview of the field of gender and sexuality, tracing the key themes in scholarship over the past century and considering how such issues are considered within contemporary early childhood contexts.

Over the past several centuries, various models of thought have sought to examine the nature of differences according to gender and sexuality. Of the former, these have ranged from Enlightenment-era 'brain size to body size' calculations, classifications of the shape of 'civilised' and 'uncivilised' skulls, through to early physiological research concerned with finding essential hormonal differences, and then to functionalist perspectives that sought to naturalise the social roles between men and women in society (Murdock, 1949; Schiebinger, 2000; Connell, 2005; Rippon, 2019). Research on sexuality had similarly been concerned with classifications accorded by way of biological and physiological difference (Fausto-Sterling, 2000; Seidman, 2015). Yet, each of these approaches was met with resistance in light of the contributions of feminist and queer scholarship in the second half of the 1900s. In revealing the social constructions of gender and sexuality differences, and challenging universalisms, such efforts have proved insightful and continue to inform understandings in the present day.

The intellectual progress made since the 1950s pushed back against the naturalisation of gender roles, shed light on patriarchal structures and situated the question of gender identity within the political realm (Beauvoir, 1956; Young, 1980). Feminist scholars also identified the need to decentre the hegemonic status of the (White) male subject that was central to the reproduction of sexism and domination against women. Feminist research toward issues on gender intersects with the writings of queer theorists arising from the 1960s' Women's and Gay Liberation movements, as well as the Stonewall Riots, which represented a cultural shift in attitudes toward LGBTQ+ people (Jagose, 1997). Anthropologies of sexuality were beginning to articulate other possibilities for sexuality and to refigure homosexuality as a social issue, away from biological narratives of deviance. In Britain, Mary McIntosh, Jeffery Weeks (2016) and Kenneth Plummer were germinal in establishing LGBTQ+ studies as a field of research (Segal, 1997).

Further intellectual work during this period provided important analyses of patriarchy and the precise nature of women's subordination to men. Adrienne Rich (1980), for instance, addresses how a context of compulsory heterosexuality serves to disempower women. For Rich, the erasure of lesbian existence from history and culture by a range of cultural practices which constrained women into personal subordination to men, contributed to the hegemonic status of heterosexuality. She writes that 'some of the forms by which male power manifests itself are more easily recognizable as enforcing heterosexuality on women than are others' (1980: 20), and argues that many characteristics of male power enforce heterosexuality and produce sexual inequality. As Jackson (1999) summarises, this serves as a double bind where women are kept *in* the boundaries of compulsory heterosexuality and kept *down*, subordinated.

The influence of a child's assigned sex in relation to how they would then be treated by adults also became a central issue around this time (Seavey et al., 1975; Greenberg, 1978). Greenberg's (1978) text on child-rearing practices observes the ways in which parenting practices reflected broader patriarchal norms within society. Advice to parents and carers tended to assume a nuclear family set up entrenched in moralistic notions of how young children should be treated according to their gender. Against this, Greenberg articulates a clear need to challenge gender stereotypes and liberate children from determinate societal expectations. As Osgood and Robinson (2019) write in their review of feminist approaches toward childhood, several scholars during this period were similarly keen to point out how children were already learning about gender and sexuality from family, educators, their peers, and via media narratives about what it meant to be a girl or a boy, a woman or a man. Inevitably, these continued to perpetuate traditional views on how children should be treated differently according to their perceived gender. Scholarship challenging these approaches enabled an understanding of how children come to construct their identities in ways that are mediated by broader social norms, thus problematising historical beliefs in childhood innocence that continued to naturalise gender differences (Stockton, 2009).

It is difficult to gauge, broadly, the extent to which the increase in research and awareness had an effect on children's experiences in the early years in the second half of the twentieth century. The Sex Discrimination Act 1975 sought to address sex discrimination against women by promoting equality of opportunity, but the belief that schooling should have little to do with discriminatory practices remained pervasive (Weiner, 2006). As Browne (1986) notes, any work in the early years profession to combat inequality was given little-to-no attention by the 'gentlemen in Whitehall'. Sexist attitudes meant that 'women's work' was seen as a low priority in the eyes of government. According to one chief education officer in the mid-1970s, 'We are having to jettison everything we can to keep the ship afloat. Unfortunately, nursery programmes are one of the most jettisonable items' (Browne, 1986: 31). Elsewhere, the pervasive influence of developmentalism had been noted as an obstacle (Yelland, 1998; MacNaughton, 2000). As such, inequalities according to gender in the early years persisted into the twenty-first century.

Over a decade since the introduction of the Equality Act 2010 (which repealed the Sex Discrimination Act 1975), one might reflect on what has changed. In our now digital era, the 'Everyday Sexism project' (Bates, 2014) and the '#MeToo' (Jaffe, 2018) movement are pertinent feminist fourth-wave examples of the continual routine and habitual nature of sexism and misogyny in contemporary society (although the latter movement is not without critique; see Phipps, 2021). Additionally, the visibility of transgender people and their experiences within society has increased; this notably being recognised by the Women and

Equalities Select Committee (2016). The report on Transgender Equality makes clear how transgender people were being failed, according to the Equality Act 2010, citing a 'complex and extensive hierarchy of issues that need to be addressed' across society. However, despite an initially positive response, the UK government had enacted only a few of the recommendations five years later and questions remain as to whether such efforts sufficiently challenge increasing levels of discrimination against transgender people.

The broader public awareness may be said to have increased personal, professional and institutional awareness of issues around gender and sexuality within education (Neary, 2018, 2021), and specifically in the early years (Warin and Price, 2019). In England, inclusive practice is recognised within 'Development Matters' (Department for Education, 2020) as being central to high-quality early education, with the need to avoid the gender stereotypes specifically cited, yet, norms according to (hetero)sexual orientation are not noted in the same way. The 'Birth to 5 Matters' (Early Years Coalition, 2021) guidance, another non-statutory document intended to support the EYFS, states that:

> Attitudes toward gender and sexual orientation can limit children and create inequality. During the early years a child's attitudes and dispositions are continually being shaped. Children are influenced by their environments and the adults around them in ways which often affect children's own ideas about themselves. In terms of gender and sexual orientation, young children can develop stereotypical ideas about how they should be and who they should become which can limit their potential. (Early Years Coalition, 2021: 25)

Many other sources pertain to the need to address gender-based discrimination and prejudice (Improving Gender Balance Scotland, 2017; Rae, 2017; Care Inspectorate: Zero Tolerance, 2019; Fawcett Society, 2020), however, apart from the LGBTQIA+ Working Group (2021), there is sparse discussion of how children's sexualities are shaped, and may be shaped, otherwise from heteronormative conceptions. This is in part due to the persistence of 'childhood innocence' that works through a disavowal, or a denial, of the power relations that research shows are already in place in early childhood spaces:

> Discussing sexuality, especially lesbian and gay subjectivities and gender non-conformance, with young children is always constituted as a hazard that frequently ends in controversy ... Risks are constructed regulators; they are the potential consequences of the normalizing judgments, which are inherent in the societal gaze, and which discourage people from stepping outside the boundaries of socially-sanctioned values and practices. (Robinson, 2013: 81)

The perceived risks in enabling children to learn about LGBTQ+ identities must be reconciled with the risks of not doing so; a smoothing over of the ways in which children experience and learn about sexualities leaves them in ignorance surrounding this topic, and in fact perpetuates heteronormativity. Conservative MP Esther McVey's 2019 statement that parents should have the choice to remove their children from lessons about LGBTQ+ relationships in school until they are 16 years old is a concrete example of the logic of childhood innocence (Allegretti, 2019). Heterosexuality is positioned as the default identity formation until a choice is made otherwise and children are seen as more in need of safeties over and above the granting of more liberties. In the next section, we consider how best to support gender and LGBTQ+ inclusion in practice.

GENDER AND LGBTQ+ INCLUSIVE PRACTICE

In this section, we share examples from our experience in practice with young children to support gender and LGBTQ+ inclusion. Opportunities to discuss gender and LGBTQ+ identities are often *already* continuously presented in play, so it is initially important to keep in mind that inclusive practice involves utilising *existing* opportunities, and developing *new* ways to proactively support children.

PRACTICE EXAMPLE

Home corner and family play

Play is crucial to enabling children to develop their sense of self (see Chapter 1), serving a key role in the formation of children's identities. One of the most frequently occurring opportunities for inclusive practice is the home corner, which usually replicates a conventional Western domestic space, replete with pretend food, dining tables and chairs, and general kitchen apparatus. It represents 'family life' and children often adopt the roles of 'mummies and daddies' who look after their babies, cook for each other and 'dress up' according to the materials available. This is not a neutral process – the cultural discourse surrounding 'family' in Western societies is laden with heteronormative and gendered assumptions about *which* children can take up *what* roles. In our experience, discussion, if not conflict, over who adopts which role, is common. It is often assumed that the 'mummy' looks after the baby and dresses up with pretend make-up, while 'daddy' acquiesces to her authority on such domestic issues.

As a practitioner, the home corner offers an ideal way to start conversations about gender and sexuality in terms of different family structures. Conflict over who will play 'mummy' can be an opportunity to either introduce or reiterate that families can come in various forms beyond the traditional nuclear model. We have found that they are usually open and willing to continue the games with two mummies, and this may lead to them queering (looking differently, reframing and challenging) 'what counts' as the family even further: *what about having four mummies?*

The play that children engage in is often stimulated by their own experiences, so introducing them to books with greater diversity, according to gender and LGBTQ+ identities, can broaden their experiences and unsettle habits of thought.

CHILDHOODS, AND DIVERSITY IN BOOKS

Children's books can make space for longer conversations about gender and sexual orientation, although we have found that young children often do not recognise books with LGBTQ+ characters as anything out of the ordinary. As practitioners, we have used *Julián is a Mermaid* (Love, 2018), a picture book that represents the trans experience through the metaphor of mermaids. Julian watches the mermaids and tells his grandma that he wants to be one. She supports him and he uses her things to dress as a mermaid. This visually pleasing book has some pages of wordless illustrations of Julian's transformation. The few words, combined with the stylised, colourful artwork, make this an engaging read for young children and something they can enjoy looking at independently. The use of mermaids as a metaphor means it can be read without discussing gender in any literal sense; because children of all genders can (and do) dress up as mermaids, the message of coming to discover one's gender identity can easily be neglected and could need adult mediation.

When Aidan Became a Brother (Lukoff, 2022) is a book about a trans boy realising his identity and making a social transition. Just before his younger sibling is born, Aidan becomes anxious that his parents might choose the wrong name, room or toys for the new baby as they did for him. He is reassured that if that happens, his sibling will be well supported, because they will have Aidan as their big brother. We have used this book because it offers a clear example of social transition, using the phrase 'transgender children'. This book doesn't utilise metaphor or euphemisms as many others on the subject do, leaving practitioners better prepared to engage in open and direct discussions about gender identity.

Finally, traditional fairy-tale stories tend to reproduce, rather than challenge, norms according to gender and sexuality. There are some excellent books that challenge the norms and actively flip the script to provide a more diverse and inclusive narrative. We have enjoyed reading two versions of *The New Goldilocks and the Three Bears*, one with Daddy and Papa bear, the other with Mummy and Mama Bear, by Beth McMurray (2012). For children already familiar with the story, understanding that there are multiple ways this story can be told has the benefit of presenting different families as having equal value. It also presents an opportunity to side-step the gendered and heteronormative stereotypes often present in the story.

SMALL MOMENTS ...

Outside of particular areas or resources, small moments throughout the nursery day with children can often be insightful and provide an opportunity to discuss their identities. We are first mindful of the language that children hear that can feed into wider issues of sexism, homophobia and transphobia. For instance, telling a girl not to get their dress dirty implicitly teaches them to value appearance over fun, and that self-worth is based on how they are viewed by others. This feeds into broader cultural norms where a woman's value is seen to emanate from their appearance. Similarly, telling a boy not to cry teaches them that emotions cannot be expressed in a vulnerable manner. This can cultivate aggression becoming the main route of emotional release for men, ultimately fuelling issues such as male violence and men feeling unable to ask for support with their mental health. Comments about a boy being a 'ladies' man', referring to children's friends as their girl- or boyfriends, or talking about getting married when grown-ups enforce the assumption of heterosexuality, should be avoided in everyday language.

Throughout the nursery day, there are moments when it is perfectly ordinary for young children to talk about which friend they are going to marry one day, and in our practice we have seen boys saying this about boys and girls saying this about girls. This could, of course, mean very little, but it is important that such moments are not trivialised by staff. Brushing such issues aside risks undermining the child's agency and repressing their views. We have also had conversations wherein a child has expressed in some way that they do not like or identify with their assigned gender. We recall one child who would occasionally declare 'I'm not a boy', another who said that they 'don't want to be a girl', and another who had three different names, depending on the specific shirts they wore, of which one name was typically given to girls and two names typically to boys. We recognise that many practitioners may be uncomfortable in responding to this, yet validation of the child's experience, even with a simple response of 'that's OK', is a good starting point. Practitioners must then be prepared to listen when a child has more to say on how they feel about their identity. In the instance of the child expressing that they did not want to be a girl, Fifi had a longer conversation about what that meant to them. They replied that they hated dresses and having long hair, that boys were just 'better' and had 'cooler stuff'. We did talk about how clothes, hair, toys and so on, do not belong to a certain gender; it would have been inappropriate to dismiss their distress as just bias. What mattered was taking the time to actively listen, ensuring that the child knew that their gender identity should not be limited by any particular constraints about 'who they should be', and reminding them that they should be able to express themselves as they choose.

PARENTS, CARERS AND COLLEAGUES

On occasion, our efforts toward inclusion have been met with resistance by the child's family members who have not wanted their child to be dressed in a particular way or spend too much time with a particular toy for fear it might 'harm' them. While it may be easy to pander to such requests, it would not be appropriate to police any child's agency in their play, nor would it be legal, according to the public duties outlined in the Equality Act 2010 on advancing equality of opportunity.

For parents seeking advice on how to affirmatively support their child's developing identity, we have discussed with them the need to support free choice to enable the child to make decisions on matters that shape their sense of self. The clothing that they wear, their hairstyle, how they wish to be referred, and how they might want their room to look are all decisions related to gender that they can make themselves, rather than having these things imposed on them. Settings should be well prepared to have these conversations, and to signpost to other support services if necessary. External training on gender and LGBTQ+ inclusive practice is a good way of achieving this.

Issues of homophobia and transphobia exist for practitioners, too. As Shaddai has noted elsewhere (Tembo, 2021), there is a need to problematise calls for more men in the early years (MITEY) that implicitly advance essentialist notions of masculinity. Rather, a more inclusive call for more men *of all kinds* in the early years (MMOAKITEY) signals an acknowledgement of the diversity of being a man away from traditional conceptions.

AN AGENDA FOR FUTURE GENDER AND LGBTQ+ INCLUSION

We live in an increasingly divisive political period regarding issues of gender and LGBTQ+ inclusion. Recent attacks have surfaced from right-wing political parties across Europe against gender studies as an academic discipline and legitimate focus of scholarship (Apperly, 2019). The notion that gender may become untenable as a subject area within university seems distant in the UK context, yet it is already the reality in Hungary, where the government has effectively banned university programmes in gender studies, 'citing low enrolment numbers that waste taxpayer money and because it is "an ideology not a science"' (Parke, 2018). Recent UK government (DfE, 2022e) guidance for teachers to promote 'political impartiality' in schools, swiftly criticised as unnecessary by both Amnesty International UK (2022) and the National Education Union (2022), speaks to the broader regulation of issues deemed too 'woke' for children to be taught (Miles, 2022). The accompanying rise in trans-exclusionary radical feminist groups is also noteworthy (Faye, 2021; Phipps, 2021), for their transphobic dog whistles (covert appeals to particular groups), under the guise of 'sex-based rights' which serve to oppressively police claims to who a woman *is* and *can be*. Together, these issues speak to the fractious social context in which we propose this agenda for gender and LGBTQ+ inclusion.

ACKNOWLEDGING PRACTITIONER POWER

We first return to the insights of Paulo Freire, a Brazilian educational philosopher whose writings are foundational to the critical pedagogy movement. Freire's (1972) work has salient implications for those engaged in social justice work today, for his contention was that education is, fundamentally, either for *domestication* or *freedom*, and an initial choice is always required of the educator. Applied here, this maxim compels practitioners to reflect on their own position and power with young children in either enabling or disabling their capacities in terms of gender and sexual orientation. We thus encourage practitioners to reflect on Freire's claim and make this initial choice in relation to their approach toward the purposes of their educational practice.

UNCONDITIONALLY VALUING INDIVIDUAL DIFFERENCE

Freire (1992, 2005) further saw the educator's role as having an ethical and political duty toward children. A distinction here may be drawn between the 'neutral' and the 'political' educator. Of the former, the position might be taken that issues of gender and sexuality are perceived to be irrelevant to young children, or that childhood is in a bubble from the wider social issues discussed within this chapter. A neutral educator may insist on 'treating all children the same'. This is a position which, while appearing progressive on the surface, may ignore individual differences and issues of power. Conversely, the figure of political educator marks a positionality whereby the need to actively challenge systems that continue to perpetuate gender inequality and heteronormativity, is central to their role. Further, wider political issues are understood as directly affecting educational practice, and individual difference is unconditionally valued.

This distinction is a slippery one and masks the fact that a position of neutrality might, in itself, reflect an implicitly political motivation to maintain the status quo. Hence, 'the question before us is to know what type of politics it is, in favor [sic] of what and of whom, and against what and for whom it is realized' (Freire, 1992: 22). Our politics is one of social justice in favour of children who are too often perceived to be transgressive against the normative expectations placed upon them. We affirm and celebrate the existence of transgender children in particular, who challenge and unsettle the deterministic limits of the gender binary, thus signalling other ways of being within the world. We ask that practitioners advance a similar affirmation in their daily pedagogic practice with colleagues, parents and the children themselves. The creation of clear policy guidance, or a manifesto, for existing and new staff and parents might be one approach to ensure this. Against the perception that gender and LGBTQ+ inclusion is risky work, taking action in this way can make a meaningful difference to the children and families that we support.

A COALITION APPROACH TO CHALLENGING INEQUALITIES

More inclusive practice will not occur at an individual level alone; a collective, coalitional approach is equally as important toward challenging inequalities accorded by gender and sexuality in childhood. Working together against these issues and sharing our experience of supporting children in practice can shape resistance on a broader level, beyond individual settings, and challenge the more structural issues present, such as there being a lack of recognition accorded to these issues in curriculum models. **Holding those in positions of power to account and maintaining a critical position against the status quo is an ongoing and necessary task in the face of gendered and heteronormative inequalities**.

Ultimately, our agenda for the future calls on practitioners to recognise their agency in shaping the lives of young children in ways unlimited by broader social norms around gender and sexual orientation. **We ask that practitioners move away from a position of neutrality on such issues, toward an explicit and unconditional acceptance of children who wish to play with the boundaries of conventional identity formation**. In doing so, those working with young children can sustain and extend the rich vein of feminist and queer activism, such that the child's lifeworld may be less foreclosed, less fixed in place, and more open to new ways of being in the world.

QUESTIONS

- Based on our examples in this chapter, how do you now plan to put inclusion into practice?
- Since this issue is coalitional, who do you know that needs to read this chapter that might not usually engage within gender and LGBTQ+ inclusion?
- Issues of gender and sexual orientation can often be exacerbated by other equalities issues such as race or dis/ability. How might this impact your practice?
- How do the issues raised here intersect with what you have read in other chapters?

FURTHER READING AND RESOURCES

www.letterboxlibrary.com – Letterbox Library is an online, not-for-profit social enterprise and a co-operative committed to celebrating equality, diversity and inclusion in children's books.

www.lettoysbetoys.org.uk – Let Toys Be Toys is a campaign to dissuade retailers from categorising toys by gender. It provides good quality resources to support gender equality in practice.

Price, D. (2017) *A Practical Guide to Gender Diversity and Sexuality in Early Years*. London: Jessica Kingsley – case studies and reflection points for staff teams.

11

COMBATTING THE EFFECTS OF POVERTY ON THE OUTCOMES OF YOUNG CHILDREN AND THEIR FAMILIES: THE ROLE OF CHILDREN'S CENTRES

KATHY SYLVA AND LESLEY CURTIS

CHAPTER OBJECTIVES

- To set out the research into the effects of disadvantage on children's life chances and outcomes
- To describe current CC practice in work with disadvantaged families
- To consider research into the benefits of CCs and the impact of closures of such provision.

CHAPTER OVERVIEW

This chapter explores the role of Children's Centres (CCs) in serving the needs of disadvantaged children and families. The chapter first considers research on the way that poverty, minority status and family mental health are powerful influences on the life chances of children, pre-birth to old age (Eisenstadt and Oppenheim, 2019). All four nations within the UK tell a similar story, yet each has pursued different policies to combat the adverse effects of disadvantage. Children's Centres are an exception, however, because all four nations have instituted some form of neighbourhood centres in poor communities to enhance the life chances of those who live in them (see Belsky et al., 2008; Eisenstadt, 2011). Next, the chapter provides a brief description of Children's Centre policy

(Continued)

---

in England, from the early twenty-first century, including a case study detailing the aims, staffing and activities of Everton Children's Centre, Liverpool. The chapter then focuses on the national picture in England, reporting the large-scale national evaluation of the Sure Start Children's Centre programme (Sylva, 2014; Sammons et al., 2015a), which demonstrated the beneficial effects for families. The chapter closes with a discussion of recent research on the decline of Children's Centres in England, and key issues for the future.

THE EFFECTS OF DISADVANTAGE ON THE DEVELOPMENT OF YOUNG CHILDREN

There are marked disparities across the UK in the development of children before they begin school usually around 5 years of age (Social Mobility Commission, 2020a). Differences attributed to social class and or/parent education have been found in school readiness (e.g. language, attention, managing behaviour and emotions, and social relationships; Hughes et al., 2015). Marked social class differences in the quality of home support for children's development have been identified (Melhuish et al., 2008; Sylva, 2014; Sylva et al., 2015; Moore et al., 2019). These differences are apparent at ages 2 (with the developmental check) and 5 years (EYFSP) and widen during primary school before diverging even more sharply in secondary school (Allen, 2011; Centre for Social Justice, 2014). Higher levels of parental education are associated with positive support for learning at home (Hoff, 2006), and Justice et al. (2020) showed that even among low-income families, higher maternal education is related to children's improved language acquisition compared to children of mothers with lower educational achievement. Such an early start usually leads to greater school readiness, giving children whose mothers have a higher level of education a stronger start to a positive life trajectory in education, health and employment (Marmot et al., 2010; Heckman, 2011; Sutton Trust and Social Mobility Commission, 2019).

THE SURE START CHILDREN'S CENTRE PROGRAMME IN ENGLAND

The English Sure Start children's programme was announced in 1998, with Children's Centres becoming its main engine for change from 2002. The (then) Labour Minister Tessa Jowell described the explicit aim of giving disadvantaged children 'the best possible start in life' through neighbourhood-based centres open to all (Eisenstadt, 2011). Sure Start was a comprehensive, inclusive, community-focused initiative designed to combat disadvantage through supporting disadvantaged families. The roll-out of CCs began in 2002 through heavy investment in services, and often new buildings, for families delivered through a 'centre' at the heart of the community. With Jowett's announcement, the original Sure

Start programme was transformed into a 'one-stop shop', providing families with childcare, parental education, advice on home safety, health and social welfare services – ranging from breastfeeding support to advice on weekly budgeting.

Children's Centres were originally required to provide a core 'offer' of specifically defined services, revised in 2013 to a core 'purpose', allowing local authorities (LAs) to decide which services were most needed. The new core purpose was:

> 'to improve outcomes for young children and their families and reduce inequalities between families in greatest need and their peers in:
>
> - child development and school readiness
> - parenting aspirations and parenting skills
> - child and family health and life chances.' (Department for Education, 2013a: 7)

Funding for the Children's Centre programme was highest in 2010–12, with approximately 3,000 Children's Centres, many in deprived neighbourhoods; later, CCs were established in more advantaged communities. At its peak in 2010, Sure Start funding totalled an annual spend of £1.8 billion (Cattan et al., 2021), but budgets had been cut by 60% by 2020 due to austerity policies brought about by the financial crash in 2008 and changing political priorities. Successive Conservative governments had new ideological commitments favouring reductions in public services and encouraging private providers (Smith et al., 2018).

So, what does a Children's Centre do? Case study 10.1 describes what can be achieved when developing an innovative centre with a nursery school and Children's Centre for children up to 5 years of age and their families, in an area within the north-west of England. It highlights the challenges of leadership that are particularly acute in pioneering such innovative and complex services, and provides a rich picture of the services, leadership and organisation of a CC, and its embeddedness within its community.

CASE STUDY 10.1: LEADING AN INTEGRATED EARLY YEARS CENTRE IN A DISADVANTAGED COMMUNITY

Lesley Curtis, Head of Centre, Everton Nursery School and Children's Centre

Undertaking a leadership role to develop an integrated centre combining a state-maintained nursery school (MNS), a number of social services day nurseries and creating a Children's Centre has been a challenge on many levels – not least managing different budgets, and staff on varying terms and conditions of service.

Everton Nursery School and Family Centre grew from an ambitious amalgamation of a traditional nursery school established since 1932, with a range of social services and day nurseries that closed as Everton developed into an integrated centre in 1999/2000.

(Continued)

The original Headteacher role, 23 years ago, was to develop a one-stop shop of services for under-5s for the community of Everton, and, at the time, a flagship for Liverpool. Ironically, 23 years later, my role has seen the dismantling of the nursery school and Children's Centre as funding nationally is progressively reduced. In an area of deprivation, this is so disappointing for local families with young children who require support before starting primary school.

Characteristics of Children's Centre leadership

Leadership is full of 'c' words: challenge, caution, careful, calm and courage. No one can prepare you for the challenge of the role, not even the National Professional Qualification in Headship or Executive Leadership (NPQH/NPQEL), which Headteachers of integrated schools and early years centres have completed over the years. Leadership is like spinning plates at times. I must be able to turn my hand to the many different challenges faced each day and be courageous in responding to them. The need to build strong support structures is important when leading and managing an innovative early years centre. Having a clear vision for early years and a strong belief in learning with and from others, certainly helps when developing this leadership role.

The complexity of teamwork

It is important to recognise that running a large, complex organisation requires a wide range of strategies if one is to meet the huge multiplicity of demands that are faced each day. The complexity brings with it immense challenges, but any small success is an achievement. When I became an early years leader, I believed I would be leading the curriculum (Curtis, 2002), but suddenly realised I had to be an expert in finances, human resources, buildings maintenance, catering and cleaning, and stay calm throughout. The larger the staff team and the larger the site, the more additional areas of expertise are needed. I sometimes spend more time working with adults than children. Being able to understand the contracts, pay and conditions of service for varying staff, meeting unions and developing innovative job roles over the years, has tested my strength and character many times.

Coming from a previous advisory team role to a leadership role was, and still is, lonely at times, and I have, over time, recruited a leadership team around me that covers all areas of Everton's work. Adopting a distributed leadership model (Curtis, 2007a), I developed an innovative leadership team, including a site manager, a business manager, two assistant heads of 2–5s and a Children's Centre co-ordinator. Our distributed leadership model within the school/centre team is supportive and effective, all integrated schools/centres can benefit from this model, and the necessary funding is essential. The role of leader of a nursery school and Children's Centre can be both operational and strategic. The success for me has been in acknowledging the importance of operationally running the school and centre as well as the strategic role Everton plays locally and nationally. This entails 'pushing boundaries' to innovatively develop the school/centre with staff over the years, and reshaping children's services. The Everton Nursery School and Children's Centre has been a trailblazer over the last 23 years (Curtis, 2007b). Our successes lie in our provision being part of the local community of Everton, with links to families, local primary schools and health services; providing a one-stop shop of services for families or signposting them to others. Everton provides nursery education for 3–5-year-olds, and many direct forms of support for parents, including 0–2 years' groups, advice on toilet training and weaning, understanding how young children learn, speech and language sessions, support around domestic violence, managing on a low income and other individual difficulties parents may face from time to time – such as a family with an imprisoned parent, and refugee families. Working alongside parents and hearing their complaints and worries is rewarding as well as demanding. Creating the services families want is complex and physically and mentally draining at times, but worth the time and energy. The role is demanding, involves great challenge and requires stamina.

Sustaining staffing and services

A major challenge over the years has been sustainability and funding. Securing the long-term stability of funding has always been a key part of my role. After 23 years of leading a successful Nursery School and Children's Centre, the challenges remain and increase, as sustainability and finances become increasingly problematic. I have become very entrepreneurial – generating income just to survive and remain open. This is becoming the norm for many Maintained Nursery Schools and Children's Centres across England; despite proven effectiveness in raising children's outcomes, many are withering on the vine. At times, the national policy has been enabling, and supported the development of Everton NSCC. However, more recently, this has become more challenging; we review budgets regularly and have restructured staffing many times over the years to manage within our budget and sustain the services we offer families. Such an immense period of change in a centre like Everton is difficult. A role such as mine can be rewarding and frustrating, with many 'battles' over the years in the pursuit of excellence for young children and their families; it is a privilege but by no means easy.

Continuing professional development

During the last 23 years, staff team members have extended their professional development in all areas of the EYFS, sharing their expertise in local, regional, national and international arenas as the school and centre developed. At times, Everton has been a training institution to support practitioners, leaders and managers through Schools Direct and Teaching Schools initiatives. High-quality learning and teaching are at the heart of everything we do, and have not been compromised when we have expanded our services, or faced budget cuts. Our practice is grounded in the theories and principles of early childhood education with care, and informed by staff action research and research across the early years field.

A political act

Like other early years leaders, I have developed my own philosophical stance on early years leadership, becoming more established in my role, more politically astute and, now, less naïve. Early years leaders must be aware of their political context and aim towards

(Continued)

> an agenda of removing poverty barriers, if they are to be effective (Curtis and Burton, 2009). At Everton, leadership has a political dimension aimed at ameliorating the effects of poverty; we adopt a more innovative, needs-led approach which builds upon education, health and social work to meet the needs of children and families. Inadequate funding, through changing governments and initiatives, threatens our capacity to meet families' needs and to ameliorate poverty and its effects on children's outcomes. Innovative and effective practice cannot be accomplished on a shoe-string budget; quality is compromised when funding diminishes.

The effects of poverty and disadvantage are pernicious, and many ECEC settings across the UK, including Maintained Nursery Schools and Children's Centres, have introduced a practical mitigation measure. In 2019, an Early Education survey found that:

> Many settings were offering practical and financial support to parents to provide food, household equipment, and additional services. Without doubt, increased funding would make a difference to how settings can support families who experience poverty. Settings were clear about what would make the most difference including: how funding was allocated and to whom; the need for improvements in public services (Social Care, NHS, housing, benefits) which had been reduced through government cuts; support for families on child development; building a multidisciplinary team; more funding for children with Special Educational Needs and who are disabled; practical support and resources for families.

As well as offering children more sessions in their settings, provision also gave practical, immediate support to families, far beyond their core purpose of providing education and care for children. These many forms of support for families living in circumstances which disadvantage them, make it possible for young children to benefit most from the high-quality education and care their settings provide. We turn now to an examination of the effectiveness of the Sure Start Children's Centres.

EVALUATION OF CHILDREN'S CENTRES IN ENGLAND (ECCE): HOW EFFECTIVE ARE CHILDREN'S CENTRES AT ACHIEVING THEIR AIMS?

The government evaluated its Children's Centre (CC) programme in 2010–15 through a large-scale, longitudinal, mixed-method design (see Hall et al., 2015; Sammons et al., 2015a; Sammons et al., under review). The ECCE study sought an in-depth understanding of CC services, including their effectiveness for children and families and an assessment of their economic cost and value for money in relation to different types of services (Briggs et al., 2012).

Through a proportionally representative sample, around 300 randomly selected CC managers were interviewed at the start of the study to document the range of services their centre offered to families and to gather basic information about size and organisation. This resulted in the individual centre profiles of staff and services. A further sub-sample of 121 randomly selected centres was made in order to dive more deeply into the: range of activities and services delivered; leadership; evidence-based practices; parenting support services; and partnership working (Sylva et al., 2015). Visits to CCs (in 2011 and 2013) provided detailed information on each CC, including administrative data, observations and interviews (Goff et al., 2013).

An in-depth study of over 2,600 families, drawn from the 121 profiled CCs, was carried out to identify links between families' engagement with services and the subsequent child and family outcomes.

CHARACTERISTICS OF THE 121 CENTRES IN THE 'EVALUATION OF CHILDREN'S CENTRES IN ENGLAND' (ECCE) STUDY (SYLVA ET AL., 2015)

SERVICES AND ACCESS

Some CCs were large, stand-alone buildings, while others were clusters of smaller centres led by a single senior manager or team. In 2011, the 'top five' services (mentioned by over 90% of centres) were 'Stay and Play', evidence-based parenting programmes, early learning and childcare, developing and supporting volunteers, and breastfeeding support. By 2013, CCs appeared to be shifting away from services for *all* families in the neighbourhood towards services for high-need families, sometimes in their own homes. This shift was in line with the new core purpose (DfE, 2013a) of targeting vulnerable families. Services most affected by policy change were those open-access services for everyone such as 'Stay and Play', whose opening hours decreased. Staff reported their conviction that open access was vital for engaging with families across a broad range of user groups, and believed that families' use of CCs stopped if they thought that 'only families whose children are at risk attended them', a sure sign that attendance was stigmatising.

PARENTING PROGRAMMES

A strong focus was on improving parenting behaviours through parenting groups/courses, (many of which were 'evidence based' with demonstrated effectiveness; Evangelou et al., 2017). There was a marked increase between 2011 and 2013 on using proven intervention approaches for targeted families, with 'Incredible Years', Triple P and Peep being the most common (Evangelou et al., 2013).

LEADERSHIP

The Everton case study showed effective leadership to be essential in running a multi-professional centre capable of changing parents' and children's lives. ECCE developed a new 'Centre Leadership and Management Rating Scale' (CLMRS: Sylva et al., 2012) to assess the quality of leadership and management. Its sub-scales were: Vision and Mission, Staff Recruitment and Employment, Staff Training and Qualifications, Service Delivery, and Centre Organisation and Management. The highest leadership scores were found in stand-alone CCs like Everton, compared to a cluster of settings. Higher scores were associated with lower staff absence and typically were found in CCs where managers had 3–5 years of experience in the role. Importantly, CCs with higher CLMRS leadership scores were rated higher on 'overall centre effectiveness' by Ofsted (Sylva et al., 2015).

EFFECTS OF CC USE ON CHILDREN AND FAMILIES

The impact evaluation of CCs (Sammons et al., 2015a) is based on a longitudinal study of 2,600 families registered at 117 of the 121 randomly selected CCs. These all served disadvantaged communities in England, often in the top two deciles of disadvantage. Unlike previous evaluations of Sure Start (Belsky et al., 2008), ECCE collected detailed information on individual families' engagement with services (quantity and intensity) to estimate the effects of using CC services on a large group of families and children.

IDENTIFYING OUTCOMES OF CC USAGE

Analyses of naturally occurring patterns of use by local families revealed associations between CC use and both family and child outcomes. The statistical analyses linked information on service use by individual families and child or family outcomes. Pre-test data were collected when the focal child was around the age of 1 year and post-test data when the child was around the age of 3. Cluster analysis identified several distinct user groups. Multilevel statistical models revealed associations between engagement with CCs and child, mother and family outcomes to answer the questions:

1. Does Children's Centre engagement/use predict better child, mother and family outcomes?
2. Which aspects of Children's Centres (management structure, working practices, services offered, and services used) promote better family, parent and child outcomes?

Six measures of child outcomes were studied: children's internalising behaviours, externalising behaviours, pro-social skills, language, non-verbal reasoning, and health. Two measures of mother outcomes were studied: one focusing specifically on mental health, the other on a more general measure of the mother's health status. For family functioning, five outcomes were measured: household economic status (HES), which identified a household in which no adult had a job; Confusion, Hubbub, and Order within the home Scale (CHAOS); the home learning environment (HLE); parental distress; and parent–child dysfunctional interaction.

FAMILIES' USE OF THEIR LOCAL CC

The CC policy was a complex intervention with no one single pattern of service use. Some families used many services when the child was very young, but then visited just occasionally when the child was a toddler, at one-off events such as a Dad's workshop on a Saturday. Other families were heavy users of a range of services, including Stay and Play or support for mothers' mental health.

The strongest predictors of child, family and mother outcomes were all related to family background, including parental qualifications, family socio-economic status and household income. These findings accord with much previous research (see Melhuish et al., 2008; Marmot et al., 2010; Sammons et al., 2015b; Social Mobility Commission, 2020b) and confirm the strong rationale for investing in Children's Centres: family disadvantage plays a major role in shaping the life trajectories of parents and children, with the most disadvantaged families showing the most adverse trajectories.

STATISTICAL EFFECTS ON FAMILIES AND CHILDREN

We turn now to the statistical effects on families, parents and children of *actual engagement* with services. The ECCE evaluation showed that *use* of CC services and certain *features of centre organisation* were significant predictors of positive family, mother and child outcomes. In general, statistical effects tended to be small, but a clear pattern of consistent and positive effects was found across the majority of outcomes. A greater number of positive effects were found for mother and family outcomes (improved mother's mental health, less chaotic family life, reduced *parent–child dysfunctional interaction*) compared to child outcomes (*improved pro-social behaviour*). This was not surprising as most CCs did not offer childcare places directly but instead 'signposted' families to ECEC settings in the neighbourhood. This limited the possibility of finding strong direct effects of CC use on child development, because, in most cases, the children did not attend childcare in the CC where the family was registered. By contrast, parents' engagement with CCs predicted better scores for the early *home learning environment* at age 3. This is an important finding because the HLE at age 3 predicts better child outcomes at school entry that continue to age 16 (Melhuish et al., 2008; Sylva et al., 2010; Sammons et al., 2015b).

The ECCE evaluation showed the positive impact of attending early education in provision *outside* the family's CC. Few children attended childcare at their local centre, but those who attended formal childcare in a local nursery showed positive effects on both cognitive and social outcomes. ECCE concluded that engagement with the local CCs had more positive benefits for parents and families than for children, whose outcomes were more influenced by attending nearby provision.

THE EFFECTS ON CHILDREN, PARENTS AND FAMILIES OF THEIR USE OF EARLY YEARS SERVICES

The use of a mixed methods design, combining quantitative measures and qualitative interview data, provided robust evidence for drawing conclusions about the effects of family use of ECE services.

MOTHERS' OUTCOMES

- Using CC services in a consistent way was associated with improved *mental health* for mothers.
- Mothers whose families used a CC with expanding services, or stable budgets, showed improved *mental health* compared to mothers at centres experiencing budget cuts and reduced services.

FAMILY/PARENTING OUTCOMES

- Engaging in parenting activities at the CC was associated with improved early HLE for children between 1 and 3 years.
- Families using services early or for longer showed greater gains in early HLE and decreases in CHAOS.

CHILDREN'S OUTCOMES

- Higher levels of childcare (but not at the registered CC where only 8% of children attended) were associated with higher *cognitive attainment*, lower levels of *internalising* behaviours (e.g. anxiety, nervousness) and better *pro-social* skills.
- Families attending CCs offering more programmes for parents known to be effective, had a positive impact on children's externalising behaviour.

- Better *pro social* behaviour in children was found for families registered at particular types of CC: 'stand-alone' (single-centre) units; school-led centres; centres with more named programmes known to be effective; and centres with higher levels of partner-agency resourcing.
- Children whose families had used more CC services showed more positive impact on *externalising* behaviour (e.g. hitting, screaming), by age 3+ years.

A more recent study (Cattan et al., 2021), based on national health data from England, revealed health benefits for children in primary school who had lived, before school entry, in a neighbourhood in which there was a CC. These children were found to have fewer hospital admissions compared to children who had not lived near a CC during the pre-school years, an effect more pronounced in poorer children.

THE DECLINE OF CHILDREN'S CENTRES IN ENGLAND

From 2011 onwards, England experienced wide-ranging cuts to local government budgets, leading to decreased public services over many years. CCs were a flagship policy of governments in the first decade in the century, but became less popular with subsequent governments, especially in the last decade (Cattan et al., 2021). The ECCE study summarised here revealed the negative impact on family outcomes of cuts in resources, and such cuts continued well into the 2020s. A national follow-up study, *Stop Start* (Smith et al., 2018) found widespread closure of CCs, especially in mixed rather than disadvantaged neighbourhoods, and a strong shift away from open access to targeted services for vulnerable families. More CCs survived if they were part of a state-maintained nursery school such as Everton, or a primary school.

KEY ISSUES FOR THE FUTURE

As we have seen, Everton Nursery School and Children's Centre has been affected by progressive cuts in funding, requiring strong, dynamic leadership to continue to provide services leading to positive outcomes for children and families. The ECCE national evaluation shows that the positive effects observed at Everton are not confined to the north-west of England but were found in a wide range of CCs across England. Children from disadvantaged families are behind their more advantaged peers in their development, as early as age two. Regrettably, the gap between children from disadvantaged backgrounds and their more advantaged peers widens with age. One way to ameliorate (but not close) the gap is through locating CCs such as Everton in disadvantaged neighbourhoods to serve a wide range of families. Offering multi-professional services to families under stress requires innovative leadership and secure funding. Unsurprisingly, declining CC budgets resulted in fewer positive effects on the families who use them. As is the case at Everton, with adequate funding CCs can dramatically change lives and should be a political priority for this reason. The ECCE study reached the same conclusion. The new Family Hubs in England (DHSC and DfE, 2022) can only achieve their aims with substantial, secure funding. Transforming the lives of children and families does not require a miracle – we know how it can be done – but it does require strong leadership, vision and effective, multi-professional services, all with a highly qualified, properly remunerated and stable workforce (Nutbrown, 2021) (see Chapters 12 and 13).

Multi-disciplinary early education and care for our youngest children require a future with:

- strong leadership
- clear vision
- multi-professional support services
- intervention programmes attuned to the needs of children and families
- highly qualified, properly remunerated staff
- sustained services for all.

The effectiveness of high-quality services in narrowing the achievement gap has been clearly demonstrated (Lindorff, 2022). Policies aimed at social justice need to offer these services to all, but especially to children and families living in poverty.

QUESTIONS

- Considering the case study of Everton Nursery School and Children's Centre, how might the work of a multi-professional service for children and their families be available to and benefit all?
- Educational outcomes and health are inextricably linked – how can settings foster more interprofessional provision and overcome barriers to it?
- What is the impact on a country's provision and its users if what it offers is targeted solely towards 'vulnerable' families?

FURTHER READING AND RESOURCES

Shuey, E. and Kankaraš, M. (2018) *The Power and Promise of Early Learning*. Education Working Paper No. 186. Paris: OECD Publishing. www.oecd-ilibrary.org/education/the-power-and-promise-of-early-learning_f9b2e53f-en

Synthesis of research demonstrating how early learning is enhanced through ECE, and identifies policy strategies to improve practice.

Sylva, K., Melhuish, E., Sammons, P., Siraj-Blatchford, I. and Taggart, B. (2010) *Early Childhood Matters*. London: Routledge.
Describes the design and findings of the Effective Pre-school and Primary Education Project.

Weinberger, J., Pickstone, C. and Hannon, P. (2005) *Learning from Sure Start: Working with Young Children and their Families*. Maidenhead: Open University Press.
An evaluation of the services for families in one trailblazer Sure Start Children's Centre.

Centre Organisation and Management: https://early-education.org.uk/centenary-book
Early Education – Early years sector provides crucial help to families in poverty (2019): https://early-education.org.uk/early-years-sector-provides-crucial-help-to-families-in-poverty

ACKNOWLEDGEMENTS

The Department for Education in England funded the original ECCE evaluation led by NATCEN and the University of Oxford through grant no. R13706/CN005 from the Department for Education. Pam Sammons led the ECCE impact study and Kathy Sylva led the study of Children's Centre leadership and organisation.

12

THE EARLY YEARS WORKFORCE: ROLES, QUALIFICATIONS AND EXPERIENCE

NATHAN ARCHER AND DAVID YATES

CHAPTER OBJECTIVES

- To explore the configuration of the ECEC workforce
- To consider the roles, qualifications and working conditions of the workforce
- To set an agenda for a sustainable and transformative workforce of the future.

CHAPTER OVERVIEW

When considering the future, looking back at recent changes in the early childhood education and care (ECEC) workforce in the UK, and appraising the current situation can inform what might be. Over the last 100 years, ECEC has evolved enormously; different political administrations have engaged with and intervened in the provision of ECEC to varying degrees. Indeed, the sector has experienced extended periods of policy neglect and substantial investment and policy attention which have shaped provision and practice. As other chapters have demonstrated, devolved education policies across the four UK nations mean fragmentation. In this chapter, we highlight some workforce policy initiatives and draw on the largest data sets and most substantial body of literature relating to England in particular. We consider recent workforce reviews which detail the features and challenges the workforce faces, as we take stock of current roles, initial education and professional development within the sector. We conclude with an essentially bold, ambitious and achievable vision for the future.

INTRODUCTION

In recent years, numerous interventions have aimed to develop the quality and quantity of ECEC provision, with multiple initiatives steering curriculum and pedagogy. In parallel, the nature of early education provision has changed, with a resultant infrastructure that constitutes a market of ECEC offered by the state, private and charitable providers (Lloyd and Penn, 2012). How children access the system and the ways in which children's services are run, differ significantly from the relative uniformity of the school system. While this chapter focuses on the ECEC workforce, it also, necessarily, reflects on the implications of this mixed market model for those who work with young children.

Notably, the employment conditions and work experience of the workforce vary substantially. Those working in Maintained Nursery Schools and primary schools are largely degree-qualified teachers on a national pay scale (with the provision of sick pay and pensions) and are often represented by trade unions. Conversely, educators employed in the private, voluntary and independent (PVI) sectors have variable terms and conditions, qualifications ranging from none to postgraduate level, and often no union representation, and this has implications for quality, not least in pedagogical knowledge. The workforce around the UK is stratified, with resulting differences and inequities in their remuneration, working conditions and opportunities for professional development.

WHO MAKES UP THE EARLY CHILDHOOD EDUCATION AND CARE WORKFORCE?

The 'Systems of early education/care and professionalisation in Europe (seepro.eu) project' provides a comprehensive overview of the professional education and training, and occupational profiles of early childhood personnel in the 27 European Union countries which were EU members at the time of the project, thus including England, Scotland, Northern Ireland and Wales. While much early education policy is devolved to the four nations of the UK, similar models of provision and parallel workforce developments can be discerned.

In England (Department for Education, 2021c), the workforce demographic was overwhelmingly White, female and young, with a reported 97% of paid staff being female and 99% of childminders identifying as female. Despite local and national initiatives to boost the recruitment of men to the sector, this gender imbalance remains unchanged. The DfE (2021c) survey reported 22% of paid staff in PVI settings as being under 25 years old, compared with just 7% of paid staff in schools; further, 15% of staff in PVI settings and 24% in schools were aged 50+. All childminders responding to the survey were 25 or over, and 39% aged 50 or over. The majority of paid staff in the ECEC workforce were reported to be White British; PVI group settings, childminders and schools reported, on average, 83% of staff being White British. For all types of home and group settings, the representation of 'White Other' 'Asian' and 'Black' was under 6% of the workforce.

Taking England as an example, of the lack of diversity is marked; change to workforce composition is necessary to achieve greater workforce diversity across gender, social groups, ethnicity and languages, thus reducing stereotypes, and to offer richer experiences for children (see Chapters 9, 10 and 11). Further, enhanced diversity could increase the number of applicants to the sector from people who, hitherto, have not regarded ECEC as being the field of work for them.

VARIATION IN ROLES AND QUALIFICATIONS

Reviews of the workforce in England (Nutbrown, 2012), Scotland (Siraj and Kingston, 2015) and Wales (Siraj, 2014) all made recommendations on qualification for the early years workforce, particularly to enhance pedagogy and the quality of provision for young children. Unlike the school system, the ECEC sector in England is comprised of multiple roles, with hundreds of possible qualifications which early educators might undertake (Nutbrown, 2012). Though there is less variability in Scotland (Siraj and Kingston, 2015) and Wales (Siraj, 2014), initial education and professional development across the UK seem to be marked by complexity and a lack of parity between subsectors of the workforce.

DIVERSE ROLES

The ECEC workforce is diverse in its types of professional roles, including teachers, educators, assistants and childminders. Some role titles effectively describe specific roles, such as special educational needs co-ordinator or lead practitioner; others are less clear, and there is a lack of agreement about roles and nomenclature which arguably complicates understandings and devalues the nature of the work. This concern remains despite many identifying this as an issue in need of attention (Nutbrown, 2021), and a lack of consistency in the use of job titles makes it difficult to compare roles and responsibilities across setting types.

A RANGE OF QUALIFICATIONS

Several studies have illustrated a strong relationship between the level of staff qualifications and the quality of ECEC (Karemaker et al., 2011; Mathers and Smees, 2014). Yet, despite numerous policy initiatives, qualification levels still vary across the sector (Bonetti, 2019), and important distinctions between staff in different sectors remain, for example between teachers and other members of the ECEC workforce (Bonetti, 2019).

In England, the majority of early years staff employed in schools (82%) and PVI group settings (80%) were reported to be qualified to at least Level 3 (equivalent to A Level) (DfE, 2021c). Almost a third (32%) of staff in schools (34% in those offering nursery provision and 24% in Maintained Nursery Schools) were qualified to degree level (Level 6) in 2021

(DfE, 2021c). Senior managers in group-based settings and Headteachers and early years co-ordinators in schools were more likely than other staff to be qualified to degree level. Among childminders, in 2021 just under three-quarters (74%) were qualified to at least Level 3 and just under one in ten (9%) were qualified to Level 6 (DfE, 2021c).

DEGREE-LEVEL QUALIFICATIONS AND A GRADUATE WORKFORCE

In terms of degree-level study, the DfE (2022d) states that, under the current system, students in England can study for a range of award-bearing qualifications:

- Early Childhood Studies degree (ECS)
- Early Years Teacher Status (EYTS), previously Early Years Professional Status (EYPS)
- Qualified Teacher Status (QTS).

In 2006, the Labour government introduced a new qualification, Early Years Professional Status, and provided a Transformation Fund to develop a graduate-level workforce, later superseded by the Graduate Leader Fund (GLF) established to support private and voluntary settings in recruiting graduates. Bonetti (2020) found that the fund was successful in increasing qualification levels, largely because it was 'evidence based, it was set within a wider and long-term workforce strategy, it was properly funded and provided the right types of incentives for settings to employ high qualified staff' (p. 6). However, this progress was not embedded and improvements in the take-up of higher level qualifications were not sustained after 2013.

Independent reviews of workforce qualifications in England (Nutbrown, 2012), Scotland (Siraj and Kingston, 2015) and Wales (Siraj, 2014) sought to address disparities and weaknesses in the early years initial training frameworks in order to enhance quality, equality, pedagogy and pedagogic leadership. Pedagogical leadership, quality and children's outcomes were a clear focus of the independent reviews in Scotland and Wales, with recommendations for long-term vision and clear responses from governments seeing significant expansion in Scotland (see Chapter 7). In England, the Nutbrown Review examined the make-up of the workforce and how best to strengthen the initial training, qualifications and career pathways in childcare and early learning; to enhance recruitment and retention. It identified the age/gender/ethnicity profiles discussed earlier, and made recommendations for workforce development. Most recommendations were rejected (DfE, 2013b), with the then government instead introducing a new Level 3 Early Years Educator (EYE) qualification and the graduate Early Years Teacher Status (EYTS). However, the unresolved lack of parity in remuneration and career prospects for those with EYTS in comparison to teachers with QTS inhibited take-up for EYE and EYTS qualifications. Enrolment for EYTS has declined, by 2019 to only 354 (DfE, 2019). We turn to this issue in the next section.

COMPLEXITY AND CONDITIONS

The disparity in qualification requirements in England, working conditions and remuneration within the ECEC sector, is marked in comparison with those in schools. This appears to have contributed to the ongoing recruitment and retention challenges.

PAY AND WORKING CONDITIONS

The instability of the English ECEC workforce is related to low pay and poor working conditions (Social Mobility Commission, 2020a). Several studies suggest that pay is a significant factor in a practitioner's decision to leave their employer and/or the ECEC workforce altogether. In 2020 the average wage in the ECEC workforce was £7.42 per hour, compared to the average hourly pay across the female workforce of £11.37 (Social Mobility Commission, 2020a). This was underscored by Bonetti (2019) who found that 44.5% of childcare workers were claiming state benefits or tax credits, highlighting the financial insecurity of many working in the sector. Indeed, some practitioners have reported having to take second jobs, while others described themselves as living on the edge of financial survival (Crellin, 2017). It is little wonder, then, that there is considerable instability in the English workforce. In Scotland, Professor Aline-Wendy Dunlop reviewed relevant statistics in relation to early years teachers in Scotland between 2006 and 2016, reporting a 39% reduction in the number of teachers in the early years but only a 4% decline in children (Summary Statistics for Schools in Scotland No. 6: 2015 edition, 9 December). Further, 12 of Scotland's 32 local authorities are still to employ full-time teachers in every early years setting, with the average nursery teacher–child ratio being 1:94 (EIS, 2016). Dunlop (EIS, 2016: 5) warned that the ambition of the Scottish government will not be realised unless the role of nursery teachers is recognised and invested in.

WORK INTENSIFICATION

The Social Mobility Commission (2020a) also found strong evidence that the instability of the ECEC English workforce is related to high workload, which increased during the COVID-19 pandemic, from March 2020. Hardy et al. (2022) note how COVID-related factors have widened the responsibilities of early years workers and intensified their work. Staff provided more cover for absent colleagues, undertook additional cleaning and some adapted to remote and hybrid learning. The cumulative effect of poor remuneration and working conditions and increasing pressures on the early years workforce, inevitably led people to question whether they wished to work in the sector.

RECRUITMENT CRISES

Recruitment and retention are among the biggest challenges facing the early years sector; one in six (15%) leave their jobs within a year of appointment (Bonetti, 2019). High levels of staff turnover, due to working conditions (Hardy et al., 2022), now exacerbate an existing recruitment crisis which became further intensified at the start of the COVID-19 pandemic in March 2020. By July 2021, over half (55.6%) of nurseries surveyed reported increased difficulty in recruiting new staff, and a quarter (25.6%) reported higher staff turnover than before the pandemic (Hardy et al., 2022). In Scotland, the planned expansion of early learning and childcare has given rise to a different form of recruitment crisis and a subsequent funded recruitment drive (Scottish Government, 2018).

RECENT POLICY DEVELOPMENTS

Internationally, the length of pre-employment education and the minimum level of qualifications for work with young children vary widely (OECD, 2019). This is reflected across the devolved nations of the UK, with varied levels of policy commitment to workforce development. Wales has a workforce strategy (Welsh Government, 2017) and improved coherence in the regulatory framework for the non-maintained sector. Scotland's Skills Investment Plan (Skills Development Scotland, 2017) supported the roll-out of its policy to provide 1,140 free hours of early learning and childcare, and demonstrates commitment to developing a workforce strategy. Meanwhile, in Northern Ireland, following the dissolution of the Northern Ireland Assembly, work was progressing in 2022, on a new early years strategy.

In England, the most recent national early years workforce strategy (DfE, 2017: 4) was deemed 'critical to supporting the sector to continue to grow and deliver high quality provision', but has not resulted in any sustained workforce policy attention or investment. There have been missed opportunities to develop a qualifications infrastructure and associated career pathways, not only providing a supply of future ECEC staff, but also further developing quality provision and thereby improved outcomes for children (Archer and Oppenheim, 2021). The current lack of coherent strategy in England has been critiqued:

> The workforce strategy vacuum is not just about short-term uncertainty ... it undermines confidence, wastes the talents of the existing workforce and, in the absence of a comprehensive career structure, perpetuates the view that working with young children requires fewer skills than working with older children and reduces the likelihood of the brightest and best considering a career in early years in the future. (Hevey, 2018: 1257)

INITIAL TEACHER EDUCATION (ITE) REVIEW

In 2021, Initial Teacher Education (in England) underwent a market review resulting in the DfE requiring re-accreditation of all ITE providers based on new quality requirements (DfE, 2021d). The 'new, rigorous' re-accreditation was planned to run in 'early 2022', with successful providers announced 'before the end of the 2021/22 academic year'. Many raised concerns about this policy, with critics suggesting it would have far-reaching consequences for ITE in England (University of Oxford, 2021). These concerns included the overly centralised control of PGCE programme curriculum content, a risk of squeezing out of university–school partnerships and the costly, time-consuming process of re-accreditation process for ITE providers.

CONTINUING PROFESSIONAL DEVELOPMENT (CPD)

Following a period of substantial investment (2000–10) via LAs, CPD has become more centralised, driven by the Department for Education's priorities. Examples include the recent COVID-19 'catch-up' programmes in response to the COVID-19 pandemic and the development of optional National Professional Qualifications (including for early years). This fragmented series of initiatives has not been responsive to local need, and arguably there is also a lack of a universal, long-term strategy for increasing the skills of the ECEC workforce. Education charities such as Early Education and the Early Years Coalition often fill the CPD gap for practitioners.

While the sector has experienced numerous workforce policy changes in recent years, there remain many opportunities to work in diverse types of settings with children and families. In case study 12.1, David Yates illustrates some of the multiple routes into ECEC, and the many qualifications for working across the early years phase.

CASE STUDY 12.1: A TEACHER'S TALE

David Yates, Nursery Teacher, Tinsley Meadows Primary Academy, Sheffield

Beginnings

My career in the early years sector began following the completion of an undergraduate degree in English language and literature at Sheffield Hallam University in 2006. While studying, I volunteered at a local pre-school, which ignited my interest in young children's play, development and learning. I then discovered the recently developed 'Early Years Professional Status' (EYPS), designed to attract graduates to work with children aged from birth to 5+ years old into the early years sector. I was one of 17 people to study on

(Continued)

the first full-time pathway at Sheffield Hallam University, which also combined EYPS with a Postgraduate Certificate in Early Childhood Studies qualification.

My journey towards becoming an early years professional

My journey towards becoming a 'leader of practice' (Mathers et al., 2011) and catalyst for change, began with the first of three placements in a day nursery (day nurseries provide for children aged 3 months to 5 years and are usually open weekdays between 8.00am and 6.00pm; see www.pacey.org.uk/parents/choosing-great-childcare/types-of-childcare), working with children aged between 6 months and 2 years old. This was the first time I had engaged with such young children, and I realised the complexities of early development, particularly interacting with young children, and how communication and language play an important part in their learning and progress. I also discovered the critical role of observation in making children's development and learning visible through learning stories.

My second placement was in a private, pack-away, full day-care setting and my final placement was in a Children's Centre nursery, which was where the threads of my placement experience came together with the theory, research and pedagogic learning from university. I saw and participated first-hand in multi-professional working, interacting daily with the health visiting and home-visiting teams also based in the building. The Children's Centre and nursery were at the heart of the community, bringing together the true spirit of multi-agency working.

I then worked for a further seven and a half years at the Children's Centre until the eventual closure of the setting in July 2014. During this time, I completed my MA in Early Childhood Education, where I continued to research my interest in using loose parts and open-ended resources to develop children's imaginative language and thinking (see Chapters 1 and 6). The Children's Centre teacher and I developed our practice together – with and for each other and our families. Everyone was incredibly disappointed and frustrated when the setting eventually closed, despite an 'Outstanding' Ofsted inspection report. Government cuts to local authority funding for children's services, ended many years of successful and regularly celebrated practice, including responsive support for children and families (some of whom had child protection plans or received social care services); and a high proportion of children with complex SEND and/or additional needs.

A new beginning...?

Following the closure of the nursery and Children's Centre, I became a senior early years practitioner at the local primary school, based in Reception, an age group I had not worked with before. During my first year in school, I was responsible for a smaller 'mixed' class of Reception-aged children, some of whom I had known since their birth, and two separate groups of nursery-aged children (attending either in the morning or afternoon).

Gradually, I began to reconsider my role as a 'teacher' (without Qualified Teacher Status). I started to become frustrated with government directives and the constant pressure for results and began to feel that some expectations and top-down approaches were developmentally inappropriate for some children, particularly the youngest children I worked with.

I was subsequently offered the opportunity to study for QTS through the Schools Direct route, remaining employed at my school, where I spent my second placement with my own Reception class. I gained a Postgraduate Certificate in Primary Education (3–7) with QTS. This enabled me to gain an insight into the KS1 curriculum and experience teaching in a mixed class of Year 1 and Year 2 children in a contrasting setting to my own school.

Always an early years practitioner at heart

I taught in Reception for a further three years. During this time, it has been my EYPS training and 'early years' philosophy that has shaped the teacher/practitioner I have become, and it is these deep-rooted values and beliefs about children and practice that I constantly return and refer to in my daily interactions with children, families and colleagues. A particular focus of my work with children and families is bridging the gap between home and school, championing developmentally appropriate early maths pedagogy (continuing the work of the two-year Talk for Maths Mastery initiative) (Chilvers, 2022), and celebrating the value of respectful and meaningful partnerships with parents, which I have shared through articles and blogs (Yates, 2018, 2020a, b, c, d). Developmentally appropriate practice and relational pedagogy are now of great significance; I believe in following children's interests and fascinations to support their own unique learning journey, and capturing their learning respectfully in Learning Stories (Carr and Lee, 2012) which we share together.

I am now leading the Nursery Unit with 152 children (part-time), and a separate bespoke space for 2-year-olds. Having seen the difference that the COVID-19 pandemic has made to the lives of the children and families I work with, I continue to support their ever-changing needs and priorities that each day brings. Many more children now begin in the nursery with speech and language delay or require additional support with play or imaginative skills. This continues to present very real and different challenges for us all to face together. Government narratives will no doubt continue to change, but young children and their development will not. I remain committed to doing my very best for them for as long as I work with and for them.

REALISING A VISION FOR THE EARLY YEARS WORKFORCE OF THE FUTURE

Having mapped the current status of the sector, it is important to look ahead to a future sustainable and transformative workforce. Nutbrown (2012) advocated for an education and care system focused on: high-quality care and education experiences for children, whatever the setting; strong professional identity for ECEC professionals; and high-quality ECEC pedagogy led by well-qualified early years practitioners who understand the importance of childhood. Pascal et al. (2020) called anew for this vision to be brought to a reality. We suggest that this means the following:

- *Building a strong and effective early years workforce requires political will to bring about change.* If policy makers believe that early education is indeed foundational, and we are to move beyond the empty rhetoric of 'every child deserves the best possible start in life' (DfE, 2021a), substantial, sustained funding must be committed to meet this vision.

- *Building and sustaining a highly qualified early years workforce requires investment.* Such investment reflects what we value and prioritise as a society, results in positive educational outcomes for children and reaps multiple longer-term social, health and economic benefits.
- *An emphasis on effective and learner-centred pedagogy across the range of qualifications.* If children are to learn in the company of well-educated educators, child-centred and play-based pedagogy must feature in initial and advanced ECEC workforce qualifications.
- *The collaborative action of the sector must be galvanised to influence an ambitious and crucial change agenda.* Given the weight of evidence highlighting the impact of the ECEC workforce on children's outcomes, it is now imperative that the wealth of data and research reviews are drawn together. Multiple stakeholders must work collectively to realise a bold, ambitious vision for early childhood education and care for this twenty-first century. With or without political will, the workforce itself must demand and generate change.

QUESTIONS

- What action might be taken to ensure greater diversity in the workforce?
- What should the priorities be in developing a qualification framework, career structures and professional development?
- What should be the respective roles of government and the ECEC sector in addressing the workforce challenges identified in this chapter?
- How might your setting achieve a more balanced demographic in the workforce?

FURTHER READING AND RESOURCES

Bonetti, S. (2018) *The Early Years Workforce: A Fragmented Picture.* London: Education Policy Institute.

Gives a detailed picture of the ECEC workforce demographics, pay and qualifications in England.

EIS (2016) *Sustain the Ambition: The Contribution of GTCS-Registered Teachers in Early Years.* Edinburgh: The Educational Institute of Scotland and the Child's Curriculum Group. www.eis.org.uk/Content/images/education/Early%20Years/STA-Nursery%20Booklet. pdf (accessed April 2022).

Stresses the importance of teacher qualifications in Scotland for children's early learning.

Social Mobility Commission (2020) *The Stability of the Early Years Workforce in England.* London: Social Mobility Commission.
Highlights the national, regional and organisational barriers to stability in the ECEC workforce.

Scottish Government: Early education and care – www.gov.scot/policies/early-education-and-care/early-learning-and-childcare
The Early Years Coalition is a collaborative of 16 early childhood organisations which, in 2021, published 'Birth to 5 Matters' guidance for educators: www.birthtofive.org.uk

13

LEADERSHIP IN EARLY CHILDHOOD EDUCATION

ELIZABETH WOOD, LOUISE KAY AND JESSICA TRAVERS

CHAPTER OBJECTIVES

- To provide a brief overview of international research on ECE leadership
- To focus on the policy context in England and explore the concept of responsibilisation in the work of Graduate Leaders
- To illustrate the context-specific ways in which leadership is enacted, through a case study of one Graduate Leader of the EYFS in a primary school in London, England
- To propose an agenda for the future development of leadership in ECE which might contribute to raising quality in ways that are sustainable and ethical, specifically in addressing social justice.

CHAPTER OVERVIEW

This chapter draws on international research to indicate how ECE leadership is influenced by national policy frameworks and enacted according to local contexts. Following a brief overview of international research on ECE leadership, we focus on the policy context in England, exploring the concept of responsibilisation in the work of Graduate Leaders, including the ways in which leadership is enacted by one teacher leading a diverse team of practitioners. Finally, we propose an agenda for the future development of leadership in ECE, offering a contrasting understanding of leadership to underpin practice change. We highlight the moral and relational agency of leaders and their role in raising quality in ways that are sustainable and ethical, specifically in addressing social justice.

INTRODUCTION

Over the last 100 years there has been a willingness of governments to invest in ECE and to recognise its importance for young children's learning and development. In the twentieth century, international studies on the effects and effectiveness of ECE informed policy, based on consistent evidence of the benefits of provision for children, families, society and the economy (Children's Commissioner for England, 2020). Policy aspirations to raise quality across the sector drew attention to the urgency of workforce reform, resulting in initiatives to develop national qualification frameworks, enhance professionalism and create distinctive leadership roles (see Chapter 12). The role of ECE leaders is critical to raising quality and improving children's immediate and longer-term outcomes (Nuttall et al., 2014; Nicholson et al., 2018). While the concept of quality is much contested, it nevertheless has significant influence within national policy discourses and strategies (Hunkin, 2018; Kay et al., 2021). Raising quality is associated with social justice – equality of opportunity, anti-discriminatory practice, and inclusion, with a particular focus on children considered to be disadvantaged, vulnerable, marginalised or at risk (see Chapters 8–11). Government investment has also brought new forms of regulation and accountability, so that ECE leaders are responsible for the overall quality of provision, typically evidenced through positive outcomes for children. These outcomes are expected across a sector that is noted for its diversity in types of provision, funding and structures, wide variations in the qualifications of staff, and high staff turnover (Bonetti, 2019). Hence, the work of ECE leaders is multi-faceted, and presents several challenges to their roles and responsibilities.

This chapter draws on international research to indicate how ECE leadership is influenced by national policy frameworks but is enacted according to local contexts. It first provides a brief overview of international research on ECE leadership before taking a specific focus on the policy context in England, to explore the concept of *responsibilisation* in the work of Graduate Leaders. To illustrate the context-specific ways in which leadership is enacted, Jess Travers narrates her experience of being a Graduate Leader of the EYFS in a primary school in London, England (case study 13.1). Jess reflects on the expectations of her leadership of the EYFS in relation to national policies, and the ethos and culture of the school; with examples from practice, she leads within and beyond the age phase to respond to a range of policy expectations. Finally, we draw on empirical work in England and Australia to propose an agenda for the future development of leadership in ECE. We offer a contrasting understanding of leadership to underpin practice change and highlight the moral and relational agency of leaders. We consider how such leadership might contribute to raising quality in ways that are sustainable and ethical, specifically in addressing social justice.

ECE LEADERSHIP: INTERNATIONAL RESEARCH PERSPECTIVES

This section provides a brief overview of key themes in international research, including different ways in which ECE leadership is understood in relation to national policies and professional values. Policies create new discourses and modes of regulation, aiming to influence the conduct of practitioners through the designated role of educational leader. Research indicates how different models of ECE leadership are evolving in country-specific contexts (Kay et al., 2021), but without an agreed definition of what leadership involves in different types of settings. There has been a focus on leaders' roles and tasks, their approaches, and their characteristics and dispositions. Roles and tasks include being leaders of pedagogy and curriculum, leaders of change and professional development, and leaders of people, usually with an overall responsibility for compliance with national inspection and accountability processes. Leadership and management overlap for those with responsibility for administration, managing budgets and employment contracts, and compliance with national standards for training and accreditation (see Chapter 11).

A key theme in research on different approaches to ECE leadership is the contrast between top-down policy influences, and how leaders contextualise their roles locally in relation to their values, ethos and commitments to children, families and communities.

Focusing on ECE leadership in Aotearoa New Zealand, Cooper (2018) challenges the dominant focus on leadership as an individual position to leadership of teaching teams as collective activity, underpinned by core professional values. Bøe and Hognestad (2017) conducted a small-scale study of leaders in Norway, building on the concept of hybrid leadership as a democratic and distributed form of leadership. Hybrid leadership combines individual and collaborative commitments, whereby the educational leader has overall responsibility for the practices within the setting, but deploys strategies such as mentoring, modelling and collaboration. Their findings indicate that the participants combined dialogic and inclusive leadership styles with authoritarian and controlling styles (2017, p. 139). In some contexts, the leaders were able to be 'non-hierarchical' in their interactions with staff, and in others, they had to make solo decisions, for example responding to unforeseen events.

In practice, leaders' roles and tasks are integrated, creating a number of leadership challenges in working with teams. Yang (2019) illustrates this integration in a study of ECE curriculum leadership in China:

> The leaders' roles in motivating and supporting teachers seemed more typical when teachers encountered difficulties in implementing the curriculum. It was the tension between expected innovations and existing barriers that required more guidance from

leaders ... In addition, curriculum leaders would assess the gap between their staff's professional status and the new demands, and then introduce possible training programmes. (2019: 45)

It is perhaps not surprising that distributed, relational, inclusive and democratic approaches have been identified in research on ECE leadership, because a commonality across national contexts is the predominantly female workforce. However, these approaches take different forms. Distributed leadership can be narrowly focused on the distribution of tasks and roles, rather than the genuine distribution of expertise and participation in making decisions about policy and practice. The demands of regulation and accountability, and processes of inspection, may also impose limitations on democratic approaches. The democratic and distributed approaches identified in research contrast with the policy-driven expectations of leaders, specifically what leaders must do to raise quality and to achieve the desired outcomes for children.

Many studies capture the cultural and contextual complexities of different national frameworks, and the top-down influences they exert on leadership practice. Leaders are also described in terms of their characteristics, dispositions and capacities, including their ability to drive systems-level change, practice change and innovation. In the context of mediating national policies at local levels, they are expected to engage in strategic planning, monitoring and compliance, gathering data, reporting to management, and being accountable for overall health, safety and compliance with standards. In relation to colleagues, they support professional development through mentoring, coaching and training, as well as being advocates for ECE. Different approaches to leadership reflect the demands and expectations of national policies, often underpinned by standards and competencies that leaders themselves must demonstrate, and must develop in their colleagues. In addition, the concept of *responsibilisation* (Done and Murphy, 2018) explains how leaders must fulfil those demands and expectations, and achieve other aspirations regarding social justice. As Nuttall et al. (2022) have argued, responsibilisation also shifts the balance of responsibility for quality onto the shoulders of ECE leaders. However, it is important to note that Graduate Leaders are expected to achieve policy goals, regardless of any persistent socio-economic disparities, and of the historic conditions that produce disadvantage and 'under-achievement' for specific groups of children.

In summary, research on ECE leadership indicates a range of structural and systems-level challenges and increasing practice-level expectations, but without adequate funding to improve or sustain quality. Although government policies appear to advocate for the professionalisation of the workforce (see Chapter 12), the mechanisms for achieving these aspirations are not consistent with how professionalism is understood within the field (Martin et al., 2020). While workforce policies focus on the standards to be achieved and demonstrated, situated concepts of professionalism are based on the values embedded within ECE, a broad understanding of what constitutes professional knowledge, and the importance of moral agency in addressing social justice. Situated concepts of professionalism thus acknowledge the complex work of educational leaders, and the significance of context in how their roles are enacted. The next section examines some of these complexities, focusing on the Graduate Leader in England.

THE GRADUATE LEADER IN ENGLAND

As ECE was drawn into wider education reform, policies focused on addressing the diversity of provision, varied levels of qualifications, variations in quality and lack of co-ordination across the sector. Workforce reviews in England, Scotland and Wales (see Chapters 7 and 11) concurred that workforce and workplace reform are central to raising quality and achieving policy aspirations, and highlighted the importance of leadership in ECE. Higher qualifications became associated with positive outcomes for children, which, in England, are measured through baseline assessment at age 4–5 years (Kay et al., 2021). A new graduate-level qualification, Early Years Professional Status, was introduced in 2006, based on a set of professional standards. The Nutbrown Review (Nutbrown, 2012) acknowledged the positive impact of graduate-level leadership and recommended a new early years specialist graduate route to qualified teacher status (QTS). In England, the government response (DfE, 2013b) led to the creation of the graduate-level Early Years Teacher Status, with teaching and leadership roles commensurate with QTS standards and expectations. A significant flaw in EYTS was the lack of parity with the existing graduate-level QTS, specifically the lack of equivalent financial rewards, career progression and professional status. Despite these disparities, all ECE Graduate Leaders (EYTS and QTS) have to work within the same standards and expectations. They take on a wide range of roles, and lead diverse teams, in order to develop practices that will raise quality and improve children's immediate and longer-term outcomes. They must also manage a range of contextual constraints, such as varied levels of staff qualifications, pay and working conditions across the sector, and high staff turnover in some parts of the sector (Social Mobility Commission, 2020b).

In case study 13.1, (parts a–f), we look at how some of these themes play out in the context of Jess's professional history and experience as leader of the EYFS in a large and diverse primary school in London. Although we are focusing on one teacher in one context, this case study illustrates and embodies the leadership challenges that are common across the sector.

CASE STUDY 13.1A: BEING A GRADUATE LEADER OF THE EYFS

Jess Travers, Wingfield Primary School, London

Like many teachers, I knew from a very young age that I wanted to be a primary school teacher. I have vivid memories of myself pretending to be a teacher, taking the register with all of my teddy bears lined up or asking my younger brother to sit through another

(Continued)

storytime! I went to a small primary school that I absolutely loved. The main reason for this was the teachers. I remember them being so kind, fun and caring. They definitely inspired me to want to become a teacher.

I studied Primary Education (BA Hons) with Early Years as a specialist subject at the University of Greenwich, at the same time gaining valuable experience through supply cover for a nursery agency. Having achieved QTS, my early career progression was supported by an inspirational mentor and leader. In my third year of teaching, I became the EYFS Assistant Phase Leader for the school; working closely alongside the EYFS Phase Leader gave me an excellent insight into the EYFS Phase Leader role. The EYFS Phase Leader I worked with was supportive, decisive, knowledgeable and always had the EYFS ethos and the children at the heart of everything that she did. She was an inspirational leader and I learnt an incredible amount from working alongside her. Her style of leadership and passion for the early years have always stuck with me and it really showed me the type of early years leader that I would want to be.

Having taught mostly in nursery and Reception, I became EYFS Phase Leader for Wingfield Primary School in 2019 at a time when a new, larger school was being built within a large-scale community regeneration project. The new mix of private and social housing changed the socio-economic demographic of the school, reflecting the professional/employment status of parents, and families with different ethnicities and heritage. Children's progress has become more stable since these community changes, and around 80% of the children achieve the Good Level of Development (GLD) at the end of the EYFS. There is a strong sense of community, both in the local area and in the school.

The EYFS team is comprised of 14 people, with 142 children in the EYFS: three teachers (one full-time and two part-time nursery teachers), five Early Years Professionals (EYPs), one teaching assistant training to be an EYP, five one-to-one adults for children with complex needs, parent volunteers, and students in Initial Teacher Education.

Consistent with the research literature, Jess has many leadership roles, which include leading within the EYFS, and more widely within the school, as well as her own teaching responsibilities.

CASE STUDY 13.1B: MULTIPLE LEADERSHIP ROLES AND RESPONSIBILITIES

My leadership is underpinned by specialist knowledge of the EYFS, of pedagogy and curriculum, and of children's learning and development. Key aspects of this professional knowledge are demonstrated in:

- *Understanding early years pedagogy,* and really promoting the importance of play. When you have pressures, such as Ofsted looking at early reading – phonics, it is not losing sight of that.

- *Understanding the importance of both transitions* – children coming into EYFS and then moving on to Year 1.
- *Having the assessment knowledge*, based on the observations and the conversations we have as a team about the children's progress.
- Being secure in what a 3-year-old, a 4-year-old or a 5-year-old should be doing, and moving them on in all areas of learning.
- *Getting to know the children really well*, spending time building relationships, carrying out home visits, and having conversations about children's strengths.
- *Planning* – nursery and Reception are quite different. In nursery, we have a mix of adult- and child-initiated activities, so we need to plan time for observations and playing with the children. In Reception, we make more time for direct teaching, including focus groups for literacy and maths, which are differentiated according to children's capabilities. Children who require it receive timetabled individualised support to help them access the whole curriculum. We use playful interventions to support communication skills and learning. We start with the Early Learning Goals in the EYFS as the goals for the end of Reception, then break down what we need to do to get them there. It's important to go at the child's pace and not race ahead. We do phonics assessments to home in on any gaps, along with having day-to-day chats about other skills or areas that need to be targeted, such as self-regulation, and social and emotional skills.

For Jess, team leadership embodies the democratic, relational and distributed approaches identified in research. She describes the importance of positive attributes and practices within a model of collective leadership, but is also firm and decisive when necessary. Building a relationship with parents, children and staff, and working with parents are central to being a good team player. Jess's approach to distributed leadership respects the strengths and knowledge of staff, and building capacity.

CASE STUDY 13.1C: LEADING THE TEAM

As a leader, I work closely with team members and the EYPs have more prominence – their role is very similar to mine. Knowing and celebrating the strengths of staff, and using those, is important. For example, an EYP with Montessori training led an intervention for supporting children in developing their fine motor skills. I showed trust in her to lead the intervention and we evaluated its impact on the children.

I carry out performance appraisals of team members in the form of conversations that inform further development and support distributed expertise. I say, 'what can I do to support you?' and I have arranged for EYPs to do peer observations – they get tips and advice from each other and share resources.

(Continued)

My team leadership extends beyond the EYFS as a member of the school's senior leadership team (SLT). It is important to have that understanding of the wider school because every member of staff will be made aware when changes are made in the EYFS, for example the subject leaders in Key Stages 1 and 2. I am the voice of early years. I am really lucky to be part of an SL team which is aware of the importance of early years. The Headteacher has taught in early years and one SLT member was the early years phase leader before me. The Headteacher is aware that what might work in KS1 and KS2 may not work for us, so he always asks my opinion. This is a two-way process – for example, the way we assess in early years is what the rest of the school is working towards now. It's really nice to be on the SLT where there is an awareness of early years and that it is respected. We have the opportunity to influence practice further up the school.

In the context of a primary school, this ability to influence system-level change is important, not least because of policy intensification in the EYFS, including the influence of Ofsted on practice such as play, phonics and reading, and transitions (Wood, 2019). Jess has an awareness of what is going on in the rest of the school, and can get advice from the Headteacher and other members of the SLT. For example, the focus on the new curriculum in the EYFS (DfE, 2021a) was discussed at SL team meetings, so all staff were up to date and aware of any new changes and adaptations. The Headteacher is really good at giving Jess advice about communicating a difficult message or saying 'no' to the team.

The concept of *responsibilisation* plays out in Jess's moral agency – that is, her responsibilities towards the children, staff and families, and to continuity across the whole school. Inevitably, there are tensions between the democratic, relational approaches that Jess aims to foster, the demands of EYFS policy, and Ofsted.

CASE STUDY 13.1D: WHOLE-SCHOOL CONTINUITY AND RESPONSIBILISATION

It is important to use different strategies to navigate my roles and responsibilities. That can be a tricky part of the role, depending on people's views and prior experiences. I make sure that staff feel listened to if they want to make a change. I need to be clear with messages, following up on where changes have been implemented to ensure that the children are getting the best outcomes possible, and never losing sight of why we are doing this job, with children at the heart of everything we do.

I know my team well – if they have a problem or if there is a change coming up, we have open dialogue and I am always there to listen. I feel like my team do that – if they've got a problem or they're not happy with something, or if they want to make a change, they come to me to talk about it, which is what I've always wanted from the team.

Just having that passion for early years because settings can be so different – play, the children's relationships, their well-being, a focus on the whole child – is at the forefront of everything we do.

The pressures of an Ofsted inspection have an impact in personal and professional ways for me. There is that pressure that you don't want to let anyone down, you don't want to say the wrong thing or be the one who mucks up the lesson observation. There's lots of pressure around Ofsted and schools have to show them what they are looking for.

The current Ofsted focus is early reading. But you also need to keep the needs of the children in mind, get the balance right and make sure that all areas of the curriculum are covered. As I said, children are at the heart of everything we do.

I do understand why we have Ofsted – for that consistency within schools and to ensure that everyone is implementing the EYFS correctly. It's a lot of pressure but the Headteacher is so good at getting us all prepared. Our leadership is outstanding so we all have that mutual trust that things will go well. We always get that message that we know our school is a good school so we do what we usually do every day. We all love early years. I remember saying to my team: 'You are all amazing early years practitioners, you've got nothing to worry about, just do what you do day in, day out.'

MEDIATING POLICY AND PRACTICE

Jess's leadership involves mediating national policies at the level of the school, and the EYFS through a reflective cycle of trying new practices, seeing how they work and then discussing what changes need to be made. Professional dialogue takes place within the EYFS and the SLT. Jess commented: 'We are really lucky to have a Headteacher who is more than happy for you to go to him with ideas about how to change things if you can say, "we think it will work this way" and have the proof to back that up.'

Tensions between policy and practice are evident – for example, at the end of the EYFS as children prepare to make the transition to Key Stage 1 of the National Curriculum (ages 5–7), resulting in some compromises.

CASE STUDY 13.1E: TENSIONS – TARGETS AND PLAY

When we arrive at the summer term, there is that push to get the children to the Good Level of Development so that they are on track for Year 1 and where the government thinks they should be. So they may need extra interventions, but I sometimes think they should still be playing and having that time to develop other skills such as social, emotional and language development. There are pressures to get children to that expected level of development, while we know that, through play, children will get there but at their own pace. It can be difficult to push children to that expected level if they are just not yet ready.

All leaders face challenges in their work and, for Jess, sustaining communication and involvement, and building capacity across the team are key to solving problems and leading practice change.

CASE STUDY 13.1F: CHALLENGE AND CHANGE

Change can be difficult for everyone at first. So, if you're changing something such as the curriculum or planning or feedback, it's important to be on the same page. People react differently to change so it is knowing your team and knowing how they will respond. It is how you deliver that message, and knowing what works for individuals. That can take a lot of time and it's hard to please everybody. So, it's about preparing what you are going to say and pre-empting their reactions so you are ready with a response, and being mindful of people's personal lives.

Consistent with other SLT members, Jess carries out performance appraisals, identifies team and individual needs for support, and identifies courses for or organises internal observations of other members of staff. She makes sure that the team has time to look at the required changes, for example, the revised EYFS (DfE, 2021a), which includes new goals, material and guidance on carrying out assessments. Jess provides feedback from local network meetings and her own professional development activities to build knowledge, capacity and capability across the team. These strategies enable her to lead system-level and practice-level change, within a supportive school culture and ethos, and in collaboration with the SLT.

Reflecting on Jess's leadership experience, and the range of roles and responsibilities she has described, it is perhaps not surprising that Graduate Leaders in the EYFS are identified as 'heroic'. However, the notion of the heroic leader obscures the breadth and nuances of the role, whether Graduate Leaders hold QTS or EYTS, and in whatever setting they are working. Moreover, contextually situated perspectives of professionalism offer a complex understanding of the knowledge that informs their work, and how leaders work to achieve quality, to advocate for ECE and to ensure distributed knowledge and distributed expertise across teams.

KEY ISSUES FOR THE FUTURE

A recent cross-cultural study compared Graduate Leaders in England with the equivalent Educational Leader in Australia (project funded by the Australian Research Council; Discovery Grant No. DP1800100281) (Kay et al., 2021; Martin et al., 2020; Nuttall et al., 2022). There are many consistencies in the policy contexts and in the findings. **Graduate Leaders are agents of change** because they perform a mediational role between national and setting-level policies. As Jess aptly portrays, the mediational work of Graduate Leaders moves between the instrumental policy discourse of 'what works' and 'what works for us', in order to ensure that 'Children are at the heart of everything we do'. Jess exemplifies a key finding of the Australia–England study, notably the capacity of leaders to build a professionalised workforce through their leadership activity (Martin et al., 2020). Consistent with Done and Murphy (2018), **the concept of *responsibilisation* encompasses the leadership and pedagogical roles of Graduate Leaders**, their attention to the wider goals of social justice, and their professional knowledge and values, all of which frame how high-quality provision is designed and experienced. However, it is important to note that Graduate Leaders in England work with the illusion of devolution versus the realities of surveillance and responsibilisation (Kay et al., 2021). **Graduate Leaders are moral agents** because their responsibilities extend towards children, colleagues, families and communities (Martin et al., 2020). **Workforce reform is a necessary condition for raising quality**, and for raising the status of Graduate Leaders. However, there remain significant shortcomings within the workforce, notably variations in the qualifications of staff. In addition, there is a lack of recognition in ECE policy in both England and Australia about the capabilities required for educational leaders, and inadequate resources (human, material and financial) to enable them to sustain their roles. In light of the ongoing crisis of recruitment and retention in ECE in England (and in other countries), and persistent inequities in pay and working conditions (Bonetti, 2020; Nutbrown, 2021), further evidence is needed of how graduate leadership is enacted in different settings. **The mediational roles of leaders require further attention**, along with their important contribution to raising quality and building capacity across teams.

One final point offers further evidence of the contradictions between the powerful rhetoric of workforce reform in England (Kay et al., 2021) and the persistent tensions between policy, practice and quality improvement. In spite of policy attention and investment, there is no requirement for early years settings in England to employ a Graduate Leader. In 2022, and in spite of the pandemic-related concerns over children's learning and development, an erosion of specialist leadership began in Scotland, with nursery schools losing their skilled Headteachers to other leadership roles (see Chapter 7). We have portrayed the highly specialised knowledge and skills of one Graduate Leader, including how Jess influenced systems-level and practice change within and beyond the EYFS. As Bonetti (2020) has argued, workforce reform in England contained the key ingredients for change, but has produced missed opportunities.

How leadership is enacted is likely to vary according to cultural-historical influences on ECE, as well as contemporary policy contexts. Understanding how different models of leadership are enacted in the contexts of practice, what influences the roles and identities that leaders develop, and the ability of leaders to mediate system- and practice-level change within wider policy frameworks, is essential, as is sustainable and ethical leadership, in addressing matters of social justice for children and families.

QUESTIONS

- Thinking about your own leadership – of a setting, a service, of pedagogy – what does the concept of *responsibilisation* mean to your leadership role?
- As a leader, how do you reconcile national policies with your knowledge of the children in your setting, their families and local communities?
- How might the various EY leadership roles contribute to raising quality in ways that are sustainable and ethical, specifically in addressing social justice?

FURTHER READING AND RESOURCES

Done, E.J. and Murphy, M. (2018) The responsibilisation of teachers: A neoliberal solution to the problem of inclusion. *Discourse: Studies in the Cultural Politics of Education, 39*(1), 142–155.
Discusses the responsibilisation of teachers in England and Australia who are constructed as professionals assuming many responsibilities.

Kay, L., Wood, E., Nuttall, J. and Henderson, L. (2021) Problematising policies for workforce reform in early childhood education: A rhetorical analysis of England's Early Years Teacher Status. *Journal of Education Policy, 36*(2), 179–195. DOI: 10.1080/02680939.2019.1637546
Examines ECEC English workforce reform, specifically the implementation of the EYTS qualification.

Martin, J., Nuttall, J., Henderson, L. and Wood, E. (2020) Educational leaders and the project of professionalisation in early childhood education in Australia. *International Journal of Educational Research, 101*: 101559. https://doi.org/10.1016/j.ijer.2020.101559
Reports on how educational leaders in Australian settings interpret and implement their roles.

Nuttall, J., Martin, J., Henderson, L., Wood, E. and Kay, L. (2018–2022) Learning-rich leadership for quality improvement in early childhood education. Australian Research Council Discovery Project No. 180100281.

AN AGENDA FOR THE FUTURE OF EARLY CHILDHOOD EDUCATION

CATHY NUTBROWN AND BEATRICE MERRICK

We bring this book to a close with a consideration of the key issues which have dominated the last 100 years, so that we might anticipate a future of rich possibilities for young children, those who work with them, and their families, in early years settings across the UK. In the Centenary Year of Early Education in 2023, extreme and multiple challenges faced ECE and the wider world. This book has been written at a time of intense global challenge: the COVID-19 pandemic; escalating concerns around global environmental damage; war and conflict in several parts of the world – including Europe; increasing numbers of young children who are homeless, refugees and asylum seekers; many forms of exclusion and discrimination, and rising poverty – with increasing numbers of families relying on food banks. The contributors of this book have offered positive messages of what is needed to ensure high-quality experiences and services for young children around the UK. Building on their conclusions, we offer this agenda for the future of early childhood education.

1. PRIORITISE HIGH-QUALITY PLAY AND PLAY PEDAGOGY IN POLICY AND PRACTICE

The centrality of play must be reaffirmed. Children need opportunities to create their own play, indoors and out, in all early years settings. When policy makers, practitioners and parents respect children's play, and their agency in that play, we can see meaningful engagement and holistic learning. The increasing focus on narrow learning targets for young children in the early years poses a real and present threat to play, and the rich learning possibilities it offers; this leads us to suggest that we might slow a little, to allow children's own motivations and thinking to come to the fore. This means ongoing professional development for educators who – as play pedagogues – know when and how to be watchful supporters of children as they play, and when they might join play to support a child's own purposes.

2. ESTABLISH CHILD-FOCUSED EARLY YEARS CURRICULA

Curricula must see children as central in their world and in their learning. This means respect for individual interests, an awareness of the world today, and of the importance of early years settings regarding children as citizens in an ever-changing global context, with all the difficulty and worry and beauty it holds. The pioneers of early childhood education offered strong, rational and sound practices which modern interpretations can draw on to reimagine ECEC curricula. *Birth to 5 Matters* (EYC, 2021) demonstrates how settings can bring together policy requirements with priorities for children, reaffirming 'core principles', focusing on: a unique child, positive relationships, enabling environments, and learning and development. Recent understandings of the importance of what children bring to their learning can be maximised by highly skilled educators who work flexibly and bring their professional knowledge of: children's funds of knowledge, equity, sustainability, children's rights, twenty-first century skills, and professional judgement, to established national policies and children's own immediate concerns and curiosities.

3. PRIORITISE ASSESSMENT FOR LEARNING OVER ASSESSMENT FOR ACCOUNTABILITY

What children *can do* must be recognised and understood, with the primary purpose of assessment being to support children's learning, over systemic accountability. Formalised universal assessments such as the Reception Baseline Assessment do not support children's learning or help practitioners to plan. We need policy to support understanding of children's strengths and recognise their uniqueness across the UK; building on the best examples in the country, which home in on children's fascinations and identify their points of learning in free play, rather than through standardised formal assessments at the age of 4.

4. ENSURE EARLY CHILDHOOD EDUCATION DEVELOPS CULTURES OF SUSTAINABILITY AND OUTDOOR LEARNING

There are many examples in this book, from all countries of the UK, which show the success – and sheer joy – of playing and learning sustainably, and outdoors. It is our duty to work imaginatively and creatively to move to a future unfettered by narrow objectives, where playing in and caring for nature brings a slowness to pedagogical practice. Such ways of working stimulate children's explorations around real-life problems, leading them to engage with persistence, in self-identified challenges and meaningful learning. ECEC policy must be attuned to international priorities around rights and the environment. Developing cultures of sustainability is possible and requires: a trust in children; a commitment to sustainable pedagogy; collaboration with parents and communities; and creativity of mind. The outdoors has always played a key part in the development of early years pedagogy, and the COVID-19 pandemic saw many settings that remained open, moving towards increased use of the outdoors as the safest way to engage with others, and effectively promote learning. We know that the outdoors is crucial for well-being and health, yet some settings have no outdoor space, nor do they access green spaces for play. We need a coming together of policy makers (who listen to practitioners), local planners (who provide green spaces), practitioners (with time to develop their outdoor pedagogy), and financial and material resources.

5. RECOGNISE FAMILIES AS PARTNERS IN YOUNG CHILDREN'S LEARNING

Parents have long been regarded as central to young children's learning and development. Yet, how settings support parents in their role as facilitators of children's learning is not sufficiently recognised. Policy should support work to help parents learn more about their central role as educators, informally in their homes and communities. With policy recognition and funding for essential family learning work, practitioners can share their professional knowledge about playful learning in children's earliest years. Initial training and ongoing CPD are essential if practitioners are successfully to involve and support parents as their children's first teachers. Parents are also key in supporting children as they move from one setting to the next, and effort is needed to ensure practitioners can fully support parents' understanding of the processes and their role as children leave the familiar and begin in unknown spaces. This requires funded support for practitioners to develop their knowledge, and skills to enable work with families on young children's learning and on effective, holistic transition experiences.

6. END DISCRIMINATORY PRACTICES AND PRIORITISE MEANINGFUL INCLUSION

Discrimination means that we all suffer. We need a renewed commitment to putting the legislation of policy into meaningful day-to-day practice. Despite the illegality of discrimination, there is no doubt that it continues, whether through unconscious bias or intention. Issues relating to SEN/D, racism and LGBTQ+ identities are still in need of work, and concern over the unequal outcomes of white, working-class boys shows that we cannot overlook issues of class and poverty. Media reports of the exclusion of Traveller families, families who have become refugees, and families who do not conform to the expected 'norm' of a group or society, still shock. Individuals may face multiple intersectional discrimination in relation to different facets of their identity, and economic exclusion is rampant and entrenched, as measures of social mobility show.

It is essential, without further delay, that *all* children experience early education and care which ably meet their needs, celebrates their identities and achievements and challenges inequalities. This is an issue of rights. All children, parents and practitioners must be protected from discrimination of all kinds, and anti-discriminatory policies and practices must be promoted and supported. Discrimination and exclusion can be overt or subtle, affecting children, parents and practitioners. Therefore, ongoing, funded support and CPD are essential to promote inclusive attitudes and approaches, while refusing to tolerate any form of discrimination and exclusion. ECEC is often promoted as a force to create greater equality of opportunity, but it can only do so much – governments must also commit to greater social and economic equality in all aspects of national life.

7. SUPPORT, PROMOTE AND FUND STRONG LEADERSHIP OF SETTINGS AND SERVICES

We know that children from disadvantaged families can, as young as age 2, do less well developmentally than their more advantaged peers, and the gap between them widens with age. We know, too, that high-quality nursery education such as integrated Children's Centres and Maintained Nursery Schools can go some way towards ameliorating this, especially in disadvantaged neighbourhoods, given strong leadership and secure funding. But, in much of the UK, the number of MNSs is being steadily eroded, and Children's Centres struggle for funding.

Strong leadership forms part of a social justice agenda whereby high-quality services known to make a difference can be offered to all, and especially to children and families struggling in the misery of poverty. To this end, Graduate Leaders are essential, and investment in the workforce to realise this remains a pressing need, but regrettably, in many cases, is not a government priority. Governments show little willingness to invest to remove the discrepancy in quality, qualifications, pay and conditions between the maintained and private/voluntary sectors. Strong leadership, including confidently informed pedagogical leadership, is essential to raising quality, building individual and team capacity, and changing children's lives; every child should be entitled to high-quality experiences.

8. A LONG-TERM STRATEGY FOR ECEC

The challenges in the ECEC system are neither small nor easy to solve and will only be addressed by an ambitious long-term plan. A consistently high-quality system needs a stable, well-qualified workforce, which requires better status, pay and conditions. Increasing investment in the workforce while reducing costs for parents requires governments to invest more, and more intelligently. Return on investment needs to be measured in long-term social impact, not in children's test scores. Such a strategy should not only be based on economic returns, but also on the rights of children and families – and should exemplify the way that we value childhood and children.

This book has demonstrated that early childhood education settings and services around the UK have some high-quality practices which can be shared across the whole country. We have also seen how enabling policies truly enhance learning, and where policy is found to cut across meaningful pedagogy and children's rights and interests, there are examples from our neighbouring countries in the UK which can assist and be built on.

Since the organisation was established in 1923, members of Early Education have played a strong role in lobbying for policy change. Our first president, Margaret McMillan, lobbied for free school meals for young children; in our centenary year of 2023, many children are still hungry, and many settings continue to work to mitigate the very present daily effects of poverty. The eight points above inform an *agenda for action* for Early Education. Realising these changes will require persistent argument and take political will.

The lobbying continues.

REFERENCES

Aboud, F.E. (2008) A social-cognitive developmental theory of prejudice. In S.M. Quintana and C. McKown (eds), *Handbook of Race, Racism, and the Developing Child*. Hoboken, NJ: John Wiley & Sons, pp. 55–71.

Allegretti, A. (2019) Esther McVey under fire for defending parents pulling children out of same-sex relationship classes. *Sky News*. https://news.sky.com/story/esther-mcvey-under-fire-for-defending-parents-pulling-children-out-of-same-sex-relationship-classes-11731759 (accessed April 2022).

Allen G. (2011) *Early Intervention: The Next Steps*. London: Cabinet Office.

Amanti, C., Neff, D. and Gonzalez, N. (1992) Funds of knowledge for teaching: Using a qualitative approach to connect homes and classrooms. *Theory into Practice, 31*(2), 132–141.

Amnesty International UK (2022) *UK government's teaching guidance will have 'chilling effect'*. www.amnesty.org.uk/press-releases/uk-governments-teaching-guidance-will-have-chilling-effect (accessed March 2022).

Apperly, E. (2019) Why Europe's Far Right Is targeting gender studies. *The Atlantic*. www.theatlantic.com/international/archive/2019/06/europe-far-right-target-gender-studies/591208 (accessed April 2022).

Archer, N. and Oppenheim, C. (2021) *The Role of Early Childhood Education and Care in Shaping Life Chances*. London: Nuffield Foundation. www.nuffieldfoundation.org/publications/early-childhood-education-care-shaping-life-chances (accessed April 2022).

Association Montessori Internationale (2022) Glossary of terms, Glossary of Montessori Terms | Association Montessori Internationale (https://montessori-ami.org) (accessed April 2022).

Athey, C. (2007) Extending Thought in Young Children: A Parent–Teacher Partnership, 2nd edition. London: Paul Chapman Publishing.

Bates, L. (2014) *Everyday Sexism*. London: Simon & Schuster.

Beauvoir, S.D. (1956) *The Second Sex*. London: Jonathan Cape.

Belsky, J., Melhuish, E. and Barnes, J. (2008) Research and policy in developing an early years' initiative: The case of Sure Start. *International Journal of Child Care and Education Policy, 2*(2), 1–13.

Bergan, V., Krempig, I.W., Utsi, T.A. and Boe, K.W. (2021) 'I want to participate': Communities of practice in foraging and gardening projects as a contribution to social and cultural sustainability in early childhood education. *Sustainability*, *13*, 4368. www.mdpi.com/2071-1050/13/8/4368/htm (accessed March 2022).

Berk, L.E., Mann, T.D. and Ogan, A.T. (2006) Make-believe play: Wellspring for development of self-regulation. In D.G. Singer, R.M. Golinkoff and K. Hirsh-Pasek (eds), *Play = Learning: How Play Motivates and Enhances Children's Cognitive and Social-Emotional Growth*. Oxford: Oxford University Press, pp. 74–100. https://doi.org/10.1093/acprof:oso/9780195304381.001.0001

Bernstein, B.B. (2000) *Pedagogy, Symbolic Control, and Identity: Theory, Research, Critique* (revised edition). Oxford: Rowman and Littlefield.

Bøe, M. and Hognestad, K. (2017) Directing and facilitating distributed pedagogical leadership: Best practices in early childhood education. *International Journal of Leadership in Education, 20*(2): 133–148. DOI: 10.1080/13603124.2015.1059488

Bonetti, S. (2019) *The Early Years Workforce in England*. London: Education Policy Institute.

Bonetti, S. (2020) *Early Years Workforce Development in England: Key Ingredients and Missed Opportunities*. London: Education Policy Institute.

Bourdieu, P. (1990) Rites of institution. In *Language and Symbolic Power* (trans. P. Collier). Cambridge: Polity Press, and Cambridge, MA: Harvard University Press (1990, orig. 1982), pp. 117–127.

Boyd, D.J. (2017) Early Childhood Education for Sustainable Development Framework (ECEfS). Liverpool John Moore's University.

Boyd, D.J. (2018) Early childhood education for sustainability and the legacies of two pioneering giants. *Early Years: An International Research Journal*, Special Issue, *38*(2), 227–239.

Briggs, N., Kurtz, A. and Paull, G. (2012) *Evaluation of Children's Centres in England (ECCE) Strand 5: Case Studies on the Costs of Centres in the Most Deprived Areas*. London: Department for Education.

Brodin, J., Kruythoff, K., Goodwin, J. and Knell, G. (2018) *Value of Play Report*. The Real Play Coalition. www.ikea.com/ca/en/files/pdf/bb/2f/bb2f0627/the-real-play-coalition_value-of-play-report_a.pdf

Bronfenbrenner, U. (1977) Toward an experimental ecology of human development. *American Psychologist, 32*(7), 513.

Bronfenbrenner, U. and Evans, G.W. (2000) Developmental science in the 21st century: Emerging questions, theoretical models, research designs and empirical findings. *Social Development, 9*(1), 115–125.

Browne, N. (1986) 'Do the gentlemen in Whitehall know best?' An historical perspective of pre-school provision in Britain. In N. Browne and P. France (eds), *Untying the Apron Strings: Anti-sexist provision for the under fives*. Milton Keynes: Open University Press.

Bruner, J.S. (1996) *The Culture of Education*. Cambridge, MA: Harvard University Press.

Butler, J.S. (1993) *Bodies That Matter: On the Discursive Limits of 'Sex'*. London: Routledge.

Button, J. and Wilde, A. (2019) Exploring practitioners' perceptions of risk when delivering Forest School for 3- to 5-year-old children. *International Journal of Play*, 8(1), 25–38. DOI: 10.1080/21594937.2019.1580334

Campbell-Barr, V. and Georgeson, J. (2021) 'Child Centred Competences for Early Childhood Education and Care, Early Education: Child Centred Competences for Early Childhood Education and Care1' (https://yumpu.com) (accessed October 2022).

Campbell-Barr, V. and Nygård, M. (2014) Losing sight of the child? Human capital theory and its role for early childhood education and care policies in Finland and England since the mid-1990s. *Contemporary Issues in Early Childhood*, 15(4), 346–359.

Campbell-Barr, V., Georgeson, J., Adams, H. and Short, E. (2018) *Child-Centredness in Practice Report on Output 2*. Plymouth: Plymouth University. www.plymouth.ac.uk/uploads/production/document/path/11/11819/Report_O2_Analysis_of_Observations_of_Child-Centred_Practice_in_European_Early_Childhood_Education_and_Care.pdf

Care Inspectorate (2016) *My World Outdoors: Sharing good practice in how early years services can provide play and learning wholly or partially outdoors.* https://hub.careinspectorate.com/how-we-support-improvement/care-inspectorate-programmes-and-publications/my-world-outdoors

Care Inspectorate (2017) *Space to Grow: Design guidance for early learning and childcare and out of school care settings.* https://hub.careinspectorate.com/media/1623/space-to-grow.pdf (accessed April 2022).

Care Inspectorate: Zero Tolerance (2019) *Gender equal play in early learning and childcare.* https://hub.careinspectorate.com/how-we-support-improvement/care-inspectorate-programmes-and-publications/gender-equal-play-in-early-learning-and-childcare (accessed April 2022).

Carr, M. and Lee, W. (2012) *Learning Stories: Constructing Learner Identities in Early Education*. London: Sage.

Cattan, S., Conti, G., Farquharson, C., Ginja, R. and Pecher, M. (2021) *The Health Effects of Universal Early Childhood Interventions: Evidence from Sure Start*. IFS Working Paper 21/25, Institute for Fiscal Studies.

Centre for Social Justice (2014) *Closing the Divide: Tackling educational inequality.* www.centreforsocialjustice.org.uk/library/closing-the-divide-tackling-educational-inequality-in-england (accessed April 2022).

Chambers, B., Cheung, A.C.K., Slavin, R.E., Smith, D. and Laurenzano, M. (2010) *Effective Early Childhood Education Programs: A Systematic Review*. CfBT Education Trust. https://files.eric.ed.gov/fulltext/ED527643.pdf (accessed April 2022).

Chesworth, E.A. (2019) Theorising young children's interests: Making connections and in-the-moment happenings. *Learning, Culture and Social Interaction*, 23: 100263. https://eprints.whiterose.ac.uk/139677/1/Chesworth%20Theorising%20young%20children%27s%20interests%20final%20authors%20copy.pdf (accessed April 2022).

Children's Commissioner for England (2020) *Best beginnings in the early years.* https:// childrenscommissioner.gov.uk/reports (accessed October 2021).

Chilvers, D. (ed.) (2022) *How to Recognise and Support Mathematical Mastery in Young Children's Play: Learning from the 'Talk for Maths Mastery' Initiative.* Abingdon: Routledge.

Chung, S. and Walsh, D.J. (2000) Unpacking child-centredness: A history of meanings. *Journal of Curriculum Studies, 32*(2), 215–234.

Connell, R. and Pearse, R. (2014) *Gender: In World Perspective.* Cambridge: Polity Press.

Connell, R.W. (2005) *Masculinities,* 2nd edition. Berkeley, CA: University of California Press.

Cooper, M.R. (2018) *Shifting the lens: Everyday collective leadership activity in education.* Unpublished thesis submitted in fulfilment of the requirements for the degree of Doctor of Philosophy in Education, University of Auckland.

Crellin, N. (2017) *An exploration into early years practitioners' work experiences in private day nurseries and voluntary sector pre-schools in England.* Doctoral dissertation, University of Southampton.

Csíkszentmihályi, M. (2000) *Finding Flow: The Psychology of Engagement with Everyday Life.* New York: Basic Books.

Cumming, F. and Nash, M. (2015) An Australian perspective of a forest school: Shaping a sense of place to support learning. *Journal of Adventure Education and Outdoor Learning, 15*(4), 296–309. DOI:10.1080/14729679.2015.1010071

Curriculum Review Group (2004) *A Curriculum for Excellence.* Edinburgh: Scottish Executive.

Curtis, L. (2002) *Case Study One – Everton Early Childhood Centre, Liverpool.* NAHT Primary Leadership Paper No. 5, Spring, 6–10. Developing the Foundation Stage, Haywards Heath, West Sussex.

Curtis, L. (2007a) An integrated life: Distributed leadership in a children's centre. *Early Education Integrate, 9,* July, p. 9.

Curtis, L. (2007b) Everton Children and Family Centre celebrating 75 years, 1932–2007. *Early Childhood Practice: The Journal for Multi-Professional Partnership, 9*(2), 35–37.

Curtis, L. and Burton, D. (2009) Naïve change agent or canny political collaborator? The change in leadership role from nursery school to Children's Centre. *Education 3–13, 37*(3), 287–299.

Dayal, H.C. and Tiko, L. (2020) 'When are we going to have the real school?' A case study of early childhood education and care teachers' experiences surrounding education during the COVID-19 pandemic. *Australasian Journal of Early Childhood, 45*(4): 336–347. https://doi.org/10.1177/1836939120966085

Demir-Lira Ö, Applebaum LR, Goldin-Meadow S, Levine SC. (2019) Parents' early book reading to children: Relation to children's later language and literacy outcomes controlling for other parent language input. *Developmental Science 22*(3):e12764. https:// doi.org/10.1111/desc.12764.

DePalma, R. and Atkinson, E. (2009) 'No outsiders': Moving beyond a discourse of tolerance to challenge heteronormativity in primary schools. *British Educational Research Journal, 35*(6), 837–855. https://doi.org/10.1177/1836939120966085

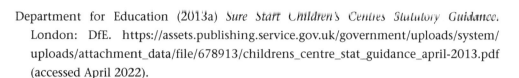

Department for Education (2013a) *Sure Start Children's Centres Statutory Guidance.* London: DfE. https://assets.publishing.service.gov.uk/government/uploads/system/uploads/attachment_data/file/678913/childrens_centre_stat_guidance_april-2013.pdf (accessed April 2022).

Department for Education (2013b) *More Great Childcare.* London: DfE.

Department for Education (2017) *Early Years Workforce Strategy.* London: DfE. https://assets.publishing.service.gov.uk/government/uploads/system/uploads/attachment_data/file/596884/Workforce_strategy_02-03-2017.pdf (accessed March 2022).

Department for Education (2019) *Initial Teacher Training Census for 2019–2020, England.* London: DfE. https://assets.publishing.service.gov.uk/government/uploads/system/uploads/attachment_data/file/848851/ITT_Census_201920_Main_Text_final.pdf (accessed March 2022).

Department for Education (2020) *Development Matters: Non-statutory Curriculum Guidance for the Early Years Foundation Stage.* https://assets.publishing.service.gov.uk/government/uploads/system/uploads/attachment_data/file/1007446/6.7534_DfE_Development_Matters_Report_and_illustrations_web__2_.pdf (accessed April 2022).

Department for Education (2021a) *Statutory Framework for the Early Years Foundation Stage: Setting the standards for learning, development and care for children from birth to five.* https://assets.publishing.service.gov.uk/government/uploads/system/uploads/attachment_data/file/974907/EYFS_framework_-_March_2021.pdf (accessed April 2022).

Department for Education (DfE) (2021b) *Sustainability and Climate Change: A draft strategy for the education and children's services systems.* https://assets.publishing.service.gov.uk/government/uploads/system/uploads/attachment_data/file/1031454/SCC_DRAFT_Strategy.pdf (accessed March 2022).

Department for Education (2021c) *Childcare and early years providers survey: 2021.* www.gov.uk/government/statistics/childcare-and-early-years-providers-survey-2021 (accessed March 2022).

Department for Education (2021d) *Initial teacher training (ITT): Accreditation.* www.gov.uk/guidance/initial-teacher-training-itt-accreditation (accessed March 2022).

Department for Education (DfE) (2022a) *Early Years Foundation Stage Profile 2022 Handbook.* London: DfE. https://assets.publishing.service.gov.uk/government/uploads/system/uploads/attachment_data/file/1024319/Early_years_foundation_stage_profile_handbook_2022.pdf (accessed April 2022).

Department for Education (DfE) (2022b) *Opportunity for all: Strong schools with great teachers for your child.* White Paper. London: HMSO. https://assets.publishing.service.gov.uk/government/uploads/system/uploads/attachment_data/file/1063602/Opportunity_for_all_strong_schools_with_great_teachers_for_your_child__print_version_.pdf (accessed April 2022).

Department for Education (DfE) (2022c) *SEND review: Right support, right place, right time.* www.gov.uk/government/consultations/send-review-right-support-right-place-right-time

Department for Education (DfE) (2022d) *Guidance: Pathway into early years education.* www.gov.uk/government/publications/pathway-into-early-years-education/pathway-into-early-years-education (accessed March 2022).

Department for Education (DfE) (2022e) *Political impartiality in schools.* www.gov.uk/government/publications/political-impartiality-in-schools/political-impartiality-in-schools (accessed April 2022).

Department of Education Northern Ireland (DENI) (2013) *Learning to Learn: A Framework for Early Years Education and Learning.* Belfast: DENI. www.education-ni.gov.uk/sites/default/files/publications/de/a-framework-for-ey-education-and-learning-2013.pdf (accessed May 2022).

Department of Education Northern Ireland (DENI) (2018) *Curricular Guidance for Pre-School Education.* Belfast: Council for the Curriculum, Examinations and Assessment. https://ccea.org.uk/downloads/docs/ccea-asset/Curriculum/Curricular%20Guidance%20for%20Pre-School%20Education.pdf

Department of Education and Science (DES) (1990) *Starting with Quality: The (Rumbold) Report of the Committee of Inquiry into the Quality of the Educational Experience offered to 3- and 4-year-olds.* London: HMSO.

Department for Health and Social Care (DHSC)/Department for Education (DfE) (2022) *Family Hubs and Start for Life* Programme guide. https://assets.publishing.service.gov.uk/government/uploads/system/uploads/attachment_data/file/1096786/Family_Hubs_and_Start_for_Life_programme_guide.pdf (accessed November 2022)

Done, E.J. and Murphy, M. (2018) The responsibilisation of teachers: A neoliberal solution to the problem of inclusion. *Discourse: Studies in the Cultural Politics of Education, 39*(1), 142–155. DOI: 10.1080/01596306.2016.1243517

Donaldson, G. (2015) *Successful Futures – Independent Review of Curriculum and Assessment Arrangement in Wales.* OGL. https://gov.wales/sites/default/files/publications/2018-03/successful-futures.pdf (accessed September 2022).

Dunlop, A-W. (2018a) The child's curriculum as a gift. In C. Trevarthen, J. Delafield-Butt and A-W. Dunlop (eds), *The Child's Curriculum.* Oxford: Oxford University Press.

Dunlop, A-W. (2018b) Transitions in early childhood education. In A. Hynds (ed.), *Oxford Bibliographies in Education.* New York: Oxford University Press.

Dunlop, A-W. Peters, S. and Kagan, S.L. (2022) *The Bloomsbury Handbook of Early Childhood Transitions.* London and New York: Bloomsbury Academic Press.

Dunlop, A-W., Burns, M. and McNair, L. (2020) Raising the status of the early years workforce and what this means for children's experience. In S. Palmer (ed.), *Play is the Way: Child Development, Early Years and the Future of Scottish Education.* Paisley: CCWB Press.

Duran, A. and Ömeroğlu, E. (2022) How parents spent time at home with their preschool-aged children during the COVID-19 pandemic of 2020. *Journal of Early Childhood Research, 20*(1), 13–26. https://doi.org/10.1177/1476718X211059906

Early Years Coalition (EYC) (2021) *Birth to 5 Matters: Non-statutory Guidance for the Early Years Foundation Stage*. St Albans: Early Education. www.birthto5matters.org.uk (accessed 22 March 2022).

Education Endowment Foundation (EEF) (2022) Working with Parents to Support Children's Learning: Guidance Report. https://d2tic4wvo1iusb.cloudfront.net/eef-guidance-reports/supporting-parents/EEF_Parental_Engagement_Guidance_Report.pdf (accessedJanuary 2022).

Education Scotland (2015) *How Good is Our School?* 4th edition. https://education.gov.scot/improvement/documents/frameworks_selfevaluation/frwk2_nihedithgios/frwk2_hgios4.pdf (accessed September 2022).

Education Scotland (2016) *How Good is Our Early Learning and Childcare?* https://education.gov.scot/improvement/documents/frameworks_selfevaluation/frwk1_niheditself-evaluationhgielc/hgioelc020316revised.pdf (accessed September 2022).

Education Scotland (2020a) *Realising the Ambition: Being me.* https://education.gov.scot/media/3bjpr3wa/realisingtheambition.pdf (accessed April 2022).

Education Scotland (2020b) *Early Level Play Pedagogy Toolkit.* https://education.gov.scot/improvement/learning-resources/early-level-play-pedagogy-toolkit (accessed April 2022).

Educational Institute of Scotland (EIS) (2016) *Sustain the Ambition: The Contribution of GTCS-Registered Teachers in Early Years*. Edinburgh: The Educational Institute of Scotland and the Child's Curriculum Group. www.eis.org.uk/Content/images/education/Early%20Years/STA-Nursery%20Booklet.pdf (accessed April 2022).

Eisenstadt, N. (2011) *Providing a Sure Start: How Government Discovered Early Childhood.* Bristol: Policy Press.

Eisenstadt, N. and Oppenheim, C. (2019) *Parents, Poverty and the State: 20 Years of Evolving Family Policy*. Bristol: Policy Press.

Ellis, C., Beauchamp, G., Sarwar, S., Tyrie, J., Adams, D., Dumitrescu, S. and Haughton, C. (2021) 'Oh no, the stick keeps falling!': An analytical framework for conceptualising young children's interactions during free play in a woodland setting. *Journal of Early Childhood Research*, 19(3), 337–354. https://doi.org/10.1177/1476718X20983861

Ephgrave, A. (2018) *Planning in the Moment with Young Children*. Abingdon: Routledge.

Eugene, F. and Provenzo, J. (2009) Friedrich Froebel's gifts connecting the spiritual and aesthetic to the real world of play and learning. *American Journal of Play*, 2(10), 85–99.

Evangelou, M., Coxon, K., Sylva, K., Smith, S. & Chan, L.S. (2013) 'Seeking to engage 'hard-to-reach' families: towards a transferable model of intervention. *Children and Society*, 27(2): 127–138.

Evangelou, M., Goff, J., Hall, J., Sylva, K., Eisenstadt, N., Paget, C., Parkin, T., Tracz, R., Davis, S., Sammons, P. and Smith, T. (2014) *Evaluation of Children's Centres in England (ECCE) Strand 3: Parenting Services in Children's Centres Research Report*. London: DfE.

Evangelou, M., Goff, J., Sylva, K., Sammons, P., Smith, T., Hall, J. and Eisenstadt, N. (2017) Children's Centres: an English Intervention for Families Living in Disadvantaged Communities in the Handbook on Positive Development of Minority Children. In Natasha J. Cabrera and Birgit Leyendecker (Eds) Chapter Part VI, 5, (pp. 455–470). Netherlands: Springer.

Fausto-Sterling, A. (2000) *Sexing the Body*. New York: Basic Books.

Fawcett Society (2020) Unlimited Potential: Report of the Commission on Gender Stereotypes in Early Childhood. www.fawcettsociety.org.uk/event/unlimited-potential-report-of-the-commission-on-gender-stereotypes-in-early-childhood (accessed April 2022).

Faye, S. (2021) *The Transgender Issue*. London: Allen Lane.

Fleet, A. and Patterson, C. (2001) Professional growth reconceptualized: Early childhood staff searching for meaning. *Early Childhood Research and Practice*, *3*(2). https://ecrp.illinois.edu/v3n2/fleet.html (accessed September 2022).

Fleet, A., De Gioia, K., Madden, L. and Semann, A. (2018) Evaluating innovation and navigating unseen boundaries: Systems, processes and people. *European Early Childhood Research Journal*, *26*(1), 66–79. DOI:10.1080/1350293X.2018.1414012

Freire, P. (1972) Education: Domestication or liberation? *Prospects*, *2*, 173–181.

Freire, P. (1992) *Pedagogy of the City*. New York: Continuum.

Freire, P. (2005) *Pedagogy of the Oppressed*, 30th anniversary edition. Trans. M.B. Ramos. New York: Continuum.

Friedman, S., Imrie, S., Fink, E., Gedikoglu, M. and Hughes, C. (2022) Understanding changes to children's connections to nature during the COVID-19 pandemic and implications for child well-being. *People and Nature*, *4*(1), 155–165. DOI:10.1002/pan3.102

Froebel, F. (1826) *The Education of Man*. New York: Lovell and Co.

Gabriel, N. (2017) *The Sociology of Early Childhood: Critical Perspectives*. London: Sage.

General Teaching Council for Scotland (GTCS) (2021) *The Standard for Full Registration: Mandatory Requirements for Registration with the General Teaching Council for Scotland*. www.gtcs.org.uk/professional-standards/professional-standards-for-teachers

Giardiello, P. (2014) *Pioneers in Early Childhood Education*. London: Routledge.

Gill, T. (2014) The benefits of children's engagement with nature: A systematic literature review. *Children, Youth and Environments*, *24*(2), 10–34.

Ginsburg, K. (2007) The importance of play in promoting healthy child development and maintaining strong parent–child bonds. *Pediatrics*, *119*(1), 182–191.

Given, B.K. (2002) *Teaching to the Brain's Natural Learning Systems*. Alexandria, VA: Association for Supervision and Curriculum Development.

Gleave, J. and Cole-Hamilton, I. (2012) *A World Without Play: A Literature Review*. Play England and British Toy and Hobby Association.

Goble, P. and Pianta, R.C. (2017) Teacher–child interactions in free choice and teacher-directed activity settings: Prediction to school readiness. *Early Education and Development*, *28*(8), 1035–1051.

Goff, J., Hall, J., Sylva, K., Smith, T., Smith, G., Eisenstadt, N., Sammons, P., Evangelou, M., Smees, R. and Chu, K. (2013) *Evaluation of Children's Centres in England (ECCE) – Strand 3: Delivery of Family Services by Children's Centres Research Report*. DfE Research Report No. DFE-RR297. London: DfE.

Greenberg, S. (1978) *Right from the Start: A Guide to Nonsexist Child Rearing*. Boston: Houghton Mifflin Company.

Greene, M. (1995) *Releasing the Imagination Essays on Education, the Arts, and Social Change*. New York: Wiley.

Hà, T.A. (2022) Pretend play and early language development – relationships and impacts: A comprehensive literature review. *Journal of Education*, 202(1), 122–130. DOI: 10.1177/0022057420966761.

Hall, J., Eisenstadt, N., Sylva, K., Smith, T., Sammons, P., Smith, G. and Hussey, D. (2015) A review of the services offered by English Sure Start Children's Centres in 2011 and 2012. *Oxford Review of Education*, 41(1), 89–104.

Hannon, P., Nutbrown, C. and Morgan, A. (2020) Effects of extending disadvantaged families' teaching of emergent literacy. *Research Papers in Education*, 35(3), 310–336. DOI: 10.1080/02671522.2019.1568531

Hardy, K., Tomlinson, J., Cruz, K. Norman, H., Whittaker, X. and Archer, N. (2022) *Essential but undervalued: Early years care and education during COVID-19*. University of Leeds/ESRC/UKRI.

Hardy, L. (1913) *The Diary of a Free Kindergarten*. London: Gay and Hancock.

Hayashi, A. and Tobin, J. (2015) *Teaching Embodied: Cultural Practices in Japanese Preschools*. Chicago: University of Chicago Press.

Hayes, N., Berthelsen, D.C., Nicholson, J.M. and Walker, S. (2018) Trajectories of parental involvement in home learning activities across the early years: Associations with socio-demographic characteristics and children's learning outcomes. *Early Child Development and Care*, 188(10), 1405–1418. https://doi.org/10.1080/03004430.2016.1262362

Heckman, J.J. (2011) The economics of inequality. *The Education Digest*, 77(4), 4–11.

Hevey, D. (2018) United Kingdom – ECEC Workforce Profile. In P. Oberhuemer and I. Schreyer (eds), *Early Childhood Workforce Profiles in 30 Countries with Key Contextual Data*. Munich: Staatsinstitut für Frühpädagogik, pp. 1192–1264. www.seepro.eu/ISBN-publication.pdf (accessed April 2022).

Hillman, J. and Williams, T. (2015) *Early years education and childcare: lessons from evidence and future priorities*. London: Nuffield Foundation. www.nuffieldfoundation.org/sites/default/files/files/Early_years_education_and_childcare_Nuffield_FINAL.pdf (accessed April 2022).

Hirschfeld, L.A. (2008) Children's developing conceptions of race. In S.M. Quintana and C. McKown (eds), *Handbook of Race, Racism, and the Developing Child*. Hoboken, NJ: John Wiley & Sons, pp. 37–54.

Hirsh-Pasek, K. (ed.) (2009) *A Mandate for Playful Learning in Preschool: Presenting the Evidence*. London: Oxford University Press.

Hirst, N. (2020) Early childhood and education for sustainability – it's not all about saving the planet. *Nursery News*. Huddersfield: NDNA, pp. 12–13.

Hoff, E. (2006) How social contexts support and shape language development. *Developmental Review*, *26*(1), 55–88. https://doi.org/10.1016/j.dr.2005.11.002

Hughes, C., Daly, I., Foley, S., White, N. and Devine, R.T. (2015) Measuring the foundations of school readiness: Introducing a new questionnaire for teachers – The Brief Early Skills and Support Index (BESSI). *British Journal of Educational Psychology*, *85*(3), 332–356.

Hunkin, E. (2018) Whose quality? The (mis)uses of quality reform in early childhood and education policy. *Journal of Education Policy*, *33*(4), 443–456. doi:10.1080/02680939.2017.1352032.

Hutchings, J, Griffith, N, Bywater, T.jJ. and Williams, M. (2017) Evaluating the Incredible Years Toddler Parenting Programme with parents of toddlers in disadvantaged (Flying Start) areas of Wales. *Child: Care, Health & Development*. *43*(1), 104-113. https://doi.org/10.1111/cch.12415

Hyun, E. and Marshall, J.D. (2003) Teachable-moment-oriented curriculum practice in early childhood education. *Journal of Curriculum Studies*, *35*(1), 111–127. DOI: 10.1080/00220270210125583

Improving Gender Balance Scotland (2017) *An Action Guide for Early Learning and Childcare Practitioners*. Improving Gender Balance Scotland.

Inspiring Scotland (2018) *Scotland's National Outdoor Play and Learning Position Statement*. www.inspiringscotland.org.uk/wp-content/uploads/2021/03/National-Position-Statement-Dec-2020.pdf

Isaacs, S. (1937) *The Educational Value of the Nursery School*. London: The British Association for Early Childhood Education.

Isaacs, S. (1929, 1968) *The Nursery Years*. New York: Shocken.

Jackson, S. (1999) *Heterosexuality in Question*. London: Sage.

Jaffe, S. (2018) The collective power of #MeToo. *Dissent*, *65*(2), 80–87.

Jagose, A. (1997) *Queer Theory: An Introduction*. New York: New York University Press.

Jarvis, P., Swiniarski, L. and Holland, W. (2017) *Early Years Pioneers in Context: Their Lives, Lasting Influence and Impact on Practice Today*. Oxon: Routledge.

Jordan, R. (2001) *Autism with Severe Learning Difficulties*. London: Souvenir Press.

Josephidou, J., Kemp, N. and Durrant, I. (2021) Outdoor provision for babies and toddlers: Exploring the practice/policy/research nexus in English ECEC settings. *European Early Childhood Education Research Journal*, *29*(6), 925–941. DOI:10.1080/1350293X.2021.1985555

Justice, L.M., Jiang, H., Bates, R. and Koury, A. (2020) Language disparities related to maternal education emerge by two years in a low-income sample. *Maternal and Child Health Journal*, *24*(11), 1419–1427.

Kalpogianni, D.E. (2019) Why are the children not outdoors? Factors supporting and hindering outdoor play in Greek public day-care centres. *International Journal of Play*, *8*(2), 155–173. DOI:10.1080/21594937.2019.1643979.

Kania, J., Kramer, M. and Senge, P. (2018) The water of systems change. www.fsg.org/publications/water_of_systems_change

Karemaker, A.M., Mathers, S., Hall, J., Sylva, K. and Clemens, S. (2011) *Evaluation of Graduate Leader Fund: Factors Relating to Quality*. London: DfE.

Katz, P.A. (2003) Racists or tolerant multiculturalists? How do they begin? *American Psychologist*, 58(11), 897–909. https://doi.org/10.1037/0003-066X.58.11.897b

Kay, L., Wood, E., Nuttall, J. and Henderson, L. (2021) Problematising policies for workforce reform in early childhood education: A rhetorical analysis of England's Early Years Teacher Status. *Journal of Education Policy*, 36(2), 179–195. DOI: 10.1080/02680939.2019.1637546

Kelly, D.J., Quinn, P.C., Slater, A.M., Lee, K., Gibson, A., Smith, M., Ge, L. and Pascalis, O. (2005) Three-month-olds, but not newborns, prefer own-race faces. *Developmental Science*, 8(6), F31–F36. https://doi.org/10.1111/j.1467-7687.2005.0434a.x

Kim, J. (2020) Learning and teaching online during Covid-19: Experiences of student teachers in an early childhood education practicum. *International Journal of Early Childhood*, 52, 145–158. https://doi.org/10.1007/s13158-020-00272-6

Kinzler, K.D. (2016) How kids learn prejudice. *New York Times*, 21 October. www.nytimes.com/2016/10/23/opinion/sunday/how-kids-learn-prejudice.html (accessed September 2022).

Kudryavtsev, A., Krasny, A. and Stedman, R.C. (2012) The impact of environmental education on sense of place among urban youth. *Ecosphere*, 3(4), 1–15.

Laevers, F. (2000) Forward to basics! Deep-level learning and the experiential approach. *Early Years*, 20(2), 20–29.

LGBTQIA+ Working Group (2021) *LGBTQIA+ Early Years magazine*. https://lgbtqearly-years.org/product/lgbtqia-early-years-magazine-downloadable-copy.

Liebovich, B. (2019) Margaret McMillan's contributions to cultures of childhood. *Genealogy*, 3(43), 1–13.

Lindorff, A., Sammons, P. and Hall, J. (2020) International perspectives in educational effectiveness research: A historical overview. In J. Hall, A. Lindorff and P. Sammons (eds), *International Perspectives in Educational Effectiveness Research*. New York: Springer, pp. 9–31.

Lindström, B. and Eriksson, M. (2005) Salutogenesis. *Journal of Epidemiology and Community Health*, 59, 440–442. DOI:10.1136/jech.2005.034777

Lingham, G., Yazar, S. and Lucas, R.M. (2021) Time spent outdoors in childhood is associated with reduced risk of myopia as an adult. *Scientific Reports*, 11, 6337. www.nature.com/articles/s41598-021-85825-y

Lloyd, E. and Penn, H. (eds) (2012) *Childcare Markets: Can they Deliver an Equitable Service?* Bristol: Policy Press.

Lorber, J. (1994) *Paradoxes of Gender*. New Haven, CT: Yale University Press.

Louis, S. and Betteridge, H. (2020) 'Unconscious Bias in the Observation, Assessment and Planning Process'. The Foundation Stage forum. https://eyfs.info/articles.html/general/unconscious-bias-in-the-observation-assessment-and-planning-process-r338 (accessed April 2022).

Louv, R. (2013) *Last Child in the Woods: Saving our Children from Nature Deficit Disorder.* New York: Atlantic Books.

Love, J. (2018) *Julián is a Mermaid.* https://jesslove.format.com/julian-is-a-mermaid (accessed April 2022).

Lukoff, K. (2022) *When Aidan Became a Brother.* NY: Lee and Low Books www.leeandlow.com/books/when-aidan-became-a-brother (accessed April 2022).

Lynch, J. and Prins, E. (2022) *Teaching and Learning about Family Literacy and Family Literacy Programmes.* New York: Routledge.

MacNaughton, G. (2000) *Rethinking Gender in Early Childhood Education.* Australia: Allen & Unwin.

Manning-Morton, J. (2013) *Exploring Well-being in the Early Years.* Maidenhead: Open University Press.

Marmot, M., Allen, J., Goldblatt, P., Boyce, T., McNeish, D., Grady, M. and Geddes, I. (2010) *Fair Society, Healthy Lives* (The Marmot Review). Institute of Health Equity.

Martin, J., Nuttall, J., Henderson, L. and Wood, E. (2020) Educational leaders and the project of professionalisation in early childhood education in Australia. *International Journal of Educational Research, 101*: 101559.

Mathers, S., Ranns, H., Karemaker, A., Moody, A., Sylva, K., Graham, J.,and Siraj-Blatchford, I. (2011) Research Brief: Evaluation of the Graduate Leader Fund Final report DFE-RB144 ISBN 978-1-84775-963-4 July 2011 https://assets.publishing.service.gov.uk/government/uploads/system/uploads/attachment_data/file/197418/DFE-RB144.pdf

Mathers, S. and Smees, R. (2014) *Quality and inequality: Do three- and four-year-olds in deprived areas experience lower quality early years provision?* London: Nuffield Foundation. www.nuffieldfoundation.org/about/publications/quality-and-inequality-do-three-and-four-year-olds-in-deprived-areas-experience-lower-quality-early-years-provision (accessed April 2022).

Mathias, S., Daigle, P., Dancause, K.N. and Gadais, T. (2020) Forest bathing: A narrative review of the effects on health for outdoor and environmental education use in Canada. *Journal of Outdoor and Environmental Education, 23*, 309–321. DOI:10.1007/s42322-020-00058-3

McClelland, M.M., Acock, A.C., Piccinin, A., Rhea, S.A. and Stallings, M.C. (2013) Relations between preschool attention span-persistence and age 25 educational outcomes. *Early Childhood Research Quarterly, 28*(2), 314–324.

McMillan, M. (1919) *The Nursery School.* London: J. M. Dent and Sons.

McMillan, M. (1930) *The Nursery School.* London: J. M. Dent and Sons.

McMillan, M and Roberts, E. (1917) Education of an imperial race to-morrow. *The Sociological Review, 9*(2), 68–78.

McMurray, B. (2012) *The New Goldilocks and the Three Bears: Mama Bear, Mommy Bear and Baby Bear/Papa Bear, Daddy Bear and Baby Bear.* Scotts Valley, CA: CreateSpace.

McNair, L. and Cerdan, C. (2022) *Nurturing Self-regulation: A Froebelian Approach.* London. The Froebel Trust. www.froebel.org.uk/uploads/images/Nurturing-self-regulation---A-Froebelian-approach.pdf (accessed April 2022).

Melhuish, E.C., Sylva, K., Sammons, P., Siraj-Blatchford, I., Taggart, B. and Phan, M. (2008) Effects of the Home Learning Environment and preschool center experience upon literacy and numeracy development in early primary school. *Journal of Social Issues, 64*(1), 95–11.

Miles, L. (2022) Marxism, moral panic and the war on trans people. *International Socialism: A Quarterly Review of Socialist Theory*, 173. http://isj.org.uk/war-on-trans (accessed September 2022).

Montessori, M. (1965) *Dr Montessori's Own Handbook.* New York: Schocken Books.

Montessori, M. (1912) *The Montessori Method.* New York: Frederick Stokes Company.

Moore, T., Ryan, R.M., Fauth, R.C. and Brooks-Gunn, J. (2019) Low-income and young children. In O. Saracho and B. Spodek (eds), *Handbook of Research on the Education of Young Children*, 4th edition. New York: Routledge.

Morgan, A., Nutbrown, C. and Hannon, P. (2009) 'Fathers' involvement in young children's literacy development: implications for family literacy programmes' *British Educational Research Journal 35*(2), 167–185.

Moss, P. (2006) From a childcare to a pedagogical discourse – or putting care in its place. Chapter 8, in J. Lewis (ed.), *Children, Changing Families and Welfare States*. Cheltenham: Edward Elgar, pp. 154–172.

Moss, S. (2012) *Natural Childhood.* Swindon: The National Trust. https://nt.global.ssl.fastly.net/documents/read-our-natural-childhood-report.pdf (accessed April 2022).

Murdock, G.P. (1949) *Social Structure.* New York: Macmillan.

Murray, J. (2020) In a time of COVID-19 and beyond, the world needs early childhood educators. *International Journal of Early Years Education, 28*(4), 299–302. DOI: 10.1080/09669760.2020.1839830

National Education Union (2022) *Political Impartiality in Schools.* https://neu.org.uk/press-releases/political-impartiality-schools (accessed March 2022).

National Literacy Trust (NLT) and DfE (2018) *Improving the Home Learning Environment: A behaviour change approach.* London: HM Government and The National Literacy Trust. https://assets.publishing.service.gov.uk/government/uploads/system/uploads/attachment_data/file/919363/Improving_the_home_learning_environment.pdf (accessed April 2022).

Neary, A. (2018) New transvisibilities: Working the limits and possibilities of gender at school. *Sex Education, 18*(4), 435–448.

Neary, A. (2021) Trans children and the necessity to complicate gender in primary schools. *Gender and Education, 33*(8), 1073–1089, DOI: 10.1080/09540253.2021.1884200.

NHS Digital (2018) *Mental Health of Children and Young People in England 2017: Summary of key findings.* https://files.digital.nhs.uk/A6/EA7D58/MHCYP%202017%20Summary.pdf

NHS Digital (2021) *National Child Measurement Programme: England 2020–2021 school year.* https://digital.nhs.uk/data-and-information/publications/statistical/national-child-measurement-programme/2020-21-school-year#summary

Nicholson, J., Kuhl, K., Maniates, H., Lin, B. and Bonetti, S. (2018) A review of the literature on leadership in early childhood: Examining epistemological foundations and considerations of social justice. *Early Child Development and Care, 127*(1), 1–32. doi:10.1080/03004430.2018.1455036.

Nind, M. and Hewitt, D. (2005) *Access to Communication: Developing Communication with People who have Severe Learning Difficulties.* London: David Fulton.

Nutbrown, C., Hannon, P. and Morgan, A. (2005) *Early Literacy Work with Families: Research, policy and practice.* London: Sage.

Nutbrown, C. (2012) *Foundations for Quality: The Independent Review of Early Education and Childcare Qualifications Final Report.* Cheshire: Department for Education. https://assets.publishing.service.gov.uk/government/uploads/system/uploads/attachment_data/file/175463/Nutbrown-Review.pdf (accessed March 2022).

Nutbrown, C. (2021) Early childhood educators' qualifications: A framework for change. *International Journal of Early Years Education, 29*(3), 236–249.

Nutbrown, C., Clough, P., Davies., K. and Hannon, P. (2022) *Home Learning Environments for Young Children.* London: Sage.

Nuttall, J., Henderson, Wood, E. and Trippestad, T.A. (2022) Policy rhetorics and responsibilization in the formation of early childhood educational leaders in Australia. *Journal of Education Policy, 37*(1), 17–38. DOI: 10.1080/02680939.2020.1739340

Nuttall, J., Thomas, L. and Wood, E. (2014) Travelling policy reforms reconfiguring the work of early childhood educators in Australia. *Globalisation, Societies and Education, 12*(3), 358–372.

OECD (2019) 'Good Practice for Good Jobs in Early Childhood Education and Care: Eight policy measures from OECD countries', https://oe.cd/pub/ecec2019.

Office for Standards in Education (Ofsted) (2019) *Education Inspection Framework*, updated 23 July 2021. www.gov.uk/government/publications/education-inspection-framework/education-inspection-framework

Office for Standards in Education (Ofsted) (2020) *Official Statistics: Childcare Providers and Inspections as at 31 March 2019 – Main findings.* London: Ofsted. www.gov.uk/government/statistics/childcare-providers-and-inspections-as-at-31-march-2019/childcare-providers-and-inspec-tions-as-at-31-march-2019-main-findings#registers-and-places

Office for Standards in Education (Ofsted) (2021) *Early Years Inspection Handbook for Ofsted-registered Provision.* www.gov.uk/government/publications/early-years-inspection-handbook-eif/early-years-inspection-handbook-for-ofsted-registered-provision-for-september-2021#grade-descriptors (accessed January 2022).

Osgood, J. and Robinson, K. (2019) Re-turns and dis/continuities of feminist thought in childhood research: Indebtedness and entanglements. In J. Osgood and K. Robinson (eds), *Feminists Researching Gendered Childhoods: Generative Entanglements*. London. Bloomsbury.

Pacini-Ketchabaw, V., Kind, S. and Kocher, L.L.M. (2017) *Encounters with Materials in Early Childhood Education*. London: Routledge.

Parke, C. (2018) Hungary bans gender studies because it is 'an ideology not a science'. *Fox News*. www.foxnews.com/world/hungary-bans-gender-studies (accessed November 2019).

Parker-Rees, R. (2015) Concepts of childhood: Meeting with difference. In R. Parker-Rees and C. Leeson (eds), *Early Childhood Studies: An Introduction to the Study of Children's Lives and Children's Worlds*, 4th edition. London: Sage.

Pascal, C., Bertram, T. and Cole-Albäck, A. (2020) *Early Years Workforce Review: Revisiting the Nutbrown Review – Policy and impact*. August. London: Sutton Trust. www.suttontrust.com/wp-content/uploads/2020/08/Early-Years-Workforce-Review.pdf (accessed March 2022).

Pasifikus, R., Wijaya, C., Novianti Bunga, B. and Kiling, I.J. (2022) Socio-emotional struggles of young children during COVID-19 pandemic: Social isolation and increased use of technologies. *Journal of Early Childhood Research*, 20(1), 113–127.

Phipps, A. (2021) White tears, white rage: Victimhood and (as) violence in mainstream feminism. *European Journal of Cultural Studies*, 24(1), 81–93.

Pretty, J., Angus, C., Bain, M., Barton, J., Gladwell, V., Hine, R., Pilgrim, S., Sandercock, G. and Sellens, M. (2009) Nature, childhood, health and life pathways. *Interdisciplinary Centre for Environment and Society*. Occasional Paper, University of Essex, UK.

Rae, L. (2017) *Getting Started: Celebrating difference and challenging gender stereotypes in the Early Years Foundation Stage*. Stonewall. www.stonewall.org.uk/resources/getting-started-toolkit-early-years

Rich, A. (1980) Compulsory heterosexuality and lesbian existence. *Signs*, 5(4), 631–660.

Richardson, M. and McEwan, K. (2018) 30 days wild and the relationships between engagement with nature's beauty, nature connectedness and well-being. *Frontiers in Psychology*, 9, 1500. DOI: 10.3389/fpsyg.2018.01500

Ridgeway, C.L. and Smith-Lovin, L. (1999) The gender system and interaction. *Annual Review of Sociology*, 25, 191–216.

Rietveld, E. and Kiverstein, J. (2014) A rich landscape of affordances. *Ecological Psychology*, 26(4), 325–352, DOI:10.1080/10407413.2014.958035 .

Rippon, G. (2019) *The Gendered Brain: The New Neuroscience that Shatters the Myth of the Female Brain*. London: Random House.

Roberts-Holmes, G. (2021) School readiness, governance and early years ability grouping. *Contemporary Issues in Early Childhood*, 22(3), 244–253.

Robinson, K. (2013) *Innocence, Knowledge and the Construction of Childhood*. London: Routledge.

Rochford, D. (2016) *Rochford Review: Final report, 19 October 2016*. https://dera.ioe.ac.uk/27776 (accessed March 2022).

Sameroff, A. (ed.) (2009) *The Transactional Model of Development: How Children and Contexts Shape Each Other*. Washington, DC: American Psychological Association.

Sammons, P., Sylva, K., Hall, J., Evangelou, M. and Smees, R. (under review) Promoting equity in the early years: The impact and legacy of Children's Centres in England.

Sammons, P., Hall, J., Smees, R., Goff, J., Sylva, K., Smith, T., et al. (2015a) *Evaluation of Children's Centres in England (ECCE). Strand 4: The Impact of Children's Centres – Studying the effects of Children's Centres in promoting better outcomes for young children and their families*. Research Report DFE-RR495. London: Department for Education.

Sammons, P., Toth, K., Sylva, K., Melhuish, E., Siraj, I. and Taggart, B.L. (2015b) The long-term role of the home learning environment in shaping students' academic attainment in secondary school. *Journal of Children's Services*, 10(3), 189–201. DOI 10.1108/JCS-02-2015-0007

Sandseter, E.B.H., Cordovil, R., Hagen, T.L. and Lopes, F. (2020) Barriers for outdoor play in early childhood education and care (ECEC) institutions: Perception of risk in children's play among European parents and ECEC practitioners. *Child Care in Practice*, 26(2), 111–129. DOI: 10.1080/13575279.2019.1685461

Sandwell MCB (2020) *Big Plans for a Great Place ... for the People of Sandwell: The Sandwell Plan, 2020–2025*. www.sandwell.gov.uk/downloads/file/29963/corporate_plan_-_big_plans_for_a_great_place_for_the_people_of_sandwell (accessed 25 January 2022).

Schiebinger, L.L. (2000) *Feminism and the Body*. New York: Oxford University Press.

Scottish Early Childhood, Children and Families Transitions Position Statement (2019, updated 2022) https://education.gov.scot/improvement/self-evaluation/scottish-early-childhood-and-families-transitions-statement/#:~:text=%E2%80%8BThe%20Scottish%20Children%20and,local%20policy%20and%20transitions%20practice (accessed 18 September 2022).

Scottish Government (2012) *Learning for Sustainability: The report of the One Planet Schools working group*. www.education.gov.scot/media/l50b5bco/one-planet-schools-report-learning-for-sustainability.pdf

Scottish Government (2017) *Health and Social Care Standards: My support, my life*. https://hub.careinspectorate.com/media/2544/sg-health-and-social-care-standards.pdf

Scottish Government (2018) *A Blueprint for 2020: The expansion of early learning and childcare in Scotland – Delivery support for early learning and childcare providers*. www.gov.scot/binaries/content/documents/govscot/publications/strategy-plan/2018/12/delivery-support-plan-early-learning-childcare-providers/documents/00544556-pdf/00544556-pdf/govscot%3Adocument/00544556.pdf

Scottish Government (2019) *Out to Play: Practical guidance for creating outdoor play experiences in early learning and childcare*. www.gov.scot/publications/out-play-practical-guidance-creating-outdoor-play-experiences-children/documents

Scottish Government (2020) *Realising the Ambition: Being me*. https://education.gov.scot/media/3bjpr3wa/realisingtheambition.pdf

Seavey, C.A., Katz, P.A. and Zalk, S.R. (1975) Baby X: The effect of gender labels on adult responses to infants. *Sex Roles*, 1(2), 103–109.

Segal, L. (ed.) (1997) *New Sexual Agendas*. Basingstoke: Palgrave Macmillan.

Seidman, S. (2015) *The Social Construction of Sexuality*, 3rd edition. New York: W.W. Norton & Co.

Sen, A. (1999) *Development as Freedom*. Oxford: Oxford University Press.

Singer, D.G., Golinkoff, R.M. and Hirsh-Pasek, K. (eds) (2006) *Play = Learning: How Play Motivates and Enhances Children's Cognitive and Social-Emotional Growth*. Oxford: Oxford University Press.

Siraj, I. (2014) *An Independent Stocktake of the Foundation Phase in Wales: Final Report, September 2013–March 2014*. London: IOE. https://dera.ioe.ac.uk/20340/1/140519-independent-stocktake-of-the-foundation-phase-in-wales-en.pdf (accessed April 2022).

Siraj, I. and Kingston, D. (2015) *An Independent Review of the Scottish Early Learning and Childcare (ELC) Workforce and Out of School Care (OSC) Workforce*. London: UCL IoE (accessed April 2022).

Siraj-Blatchford, J., Smith, K.C and Pramling Samuelsson, P. (2010) *Education for Sustainable Development in the Early Years*. Organisation Mondiale pour L´Eduation Prescolaire (OMEP). https://omepworld.org/wp-content/uploads/2021/02/Education_for_Sustainabl_Early_Years.pdf

Skene, K., O'Farrelly, C.M., Byrne, E.M., Kirby, N., Stevens, E.C. and Ramchandani, P.G. (2022) Can guidance during play enhance children's learning and development in educational contexts? A systematic review and meta-analysis. *Child Development*, 93(4), 1162–1180.

Skills Development Scotland (2017) *Skills Development Plan*. www.skillsdevelopmentscotland.co.uk/media/43127/early-learning-and-childcare-sip-digital.pdf (accessed March 2022).

Smith, G., Sylva, K., Smith, T., Sammons, P. and Omonigho, A. (2018) *Stop Start: Survival, Decline or Closure – Children's centres in England*. London: The Sutton Trust.

Sobel, D. (2013) *Place-based Education: Connecting Classrooms and Communities*. Gt Barrington, MA: Orion.

Social Mobility Commission (2020a) *The Stability of the Early Years Workforce in England: An examination of national, regional and organisational barriers*. Research Report August 2020. National Centre for Social Research. https://assets.publishing.service.gov.uk/government/uploads/system/uploads/attachment_data/file/906906/The_stability_of_the_early_years_workforce_in_England.pdf (accessed March 2022).

Social Mobility Commission (2020b) *Monitoring Social Mobility: Is the government delivering on our recommendations?* London: The Social Mobility Commission. Monitoring Report 2013 to 2020. www.gov.uk/government/publications/monitoring-social-mobility-2013-to-2020/monitoring-social-mobility-2013-to-2020 (accessed March 2022).

Standards and Testing Agency (2020) *The Engagement Model Guidance for Maintained Schools, Academies (Including Free Schools) and Local Authorities*. https://assets.publishing.service.gov.uk/government/uploads/system/uploads/attachment_data/file/903458/Engagement_Model_Guidance_2020.pdf

Stockton, K.B. (2009) *The Queer Child, or Growing Sideways in the Twentieth Century*. Series Q. Durham, NC: Duke University Press.

Sutton Trust and Social Mobility Commission (2019) *Elitist Britain: The educational backgrounds of Britain's leading people*. www.suttontrust.com/wp-content/uploads/2019/12/Elitist-Britain-2019.pdf

Sylva, K. (2014) The role of families and pre-school in educational disadvantage. *Oxford Review of Education, 40*(6), 680–695. DOI: 10.1080/03054985.2014.979581

Sylva, K., Chan, L., Good, J. and Sammons, P. (2012) *Children's Centre Leadership and Management Rating Scale: CCLMRS*. Oxford: Department of Education and National College for School Leadership. www.researchconnections.org/childcare/resources/26223

Sylva, K., Goff, J., Eisenstadt. E., Smith, T., Hall, J., Evangelou, M., Smith, G. and Sammons, P. (2015) *Evaluation of Children's Centres in England (ECCE). Strand 3: Organisation, services and reach of Children's Centres*. London: Department for Education.

Sylva, K., Melhuish, E., Sammons, P., Siraj-Blatchford, I. and Taggart, B. (2010) *Early Childhood Matters*. London: Routledge.

Taggart, B., Sylva, K., Melhuish, E., Sammons, P. and Siraj, I. (2015) *Effective Pre-school, Primary and Secondary Education Project (EPPSE 3–16+), 50*. https://assets.publishing.service.gov.uk/government/uploads/system/uploads/attachment_data/file/455670/RB455_Effective_pre- school_primary_and_secondary_education_project.pdf.pdf

Tembo, S. (2021) 'More work to do': Thinking through equalities with young children in Scotland. In S. Palmer (ed.), *Play is the Way*, 2nd edition. Paisley: CCWB Press, pp. 186–196.

Trevarthen, C., Delafield-Butt, J. and Dunlop, A-W. (eds) (2018) *The Child's Curriculum: Working with the Natural Values of Young Children*. Oxford: Oxford University Press.

United Nations (1989) *Convention on the Rights of the Child*. New York: United Nations. www.unicef.org.uk/rights-respecting-schools/wp-content/uploads/sites/4/2017/01/UNCRC-in-full.pdf (accessed January 2022).

University of Oxford (2021) *Initial Teacher Training Market Review Response*. www.education.ox.ac.uk/initial-teacher-training-market-review-response (accessed March 2022).

Van Gennep, A. (1981 [1909]) *Les rites de passage*. Paris: Picard.

Van Manen, M. (2015) *Pedagogical Tact: Knowing What to Do When You Don't Know What to Do*. London: Routledge.

Veitch, J., Bagley, S., Ball, K., Salmon, J. (2006) Where do children usually play? A qualitative study of parents' perceptions of influences on children's active free-play, Health & Place, *12*(4), 383–393, https://doi.org/10.1016/j.healthplace.2005.02.009.

Warin, J. and Price, D. (2019) Transgender awareness in early years education (EYE): 'We haven't got any of those here'. *Early Years, 40*(1), 140–154. DOI: 10.1080/09575146.2019.1703174

Warner, M. (ed.) (1993) *Fear of a Queer Planet: Queer Politics and Social Theory.* Minneapolis, MN: University of Minnesota Press.

Weeks, J. (2016) *What is Sexual History?* Cambridge: Polity Press.

Weiner, G. (2006) Education and the Sex Discrimination Act. *Educational Research, 20*(3), 163–173.

Welsh Government (2015) *Curriculum for Wales: Foundation stage framework.* https://hwb.gov.wales/api/storage/d5d8e39c-b534-40cb-a3f5-7e2e126d8077/foundation-phase-framework.pdf

Welsh Government (2017) *Early Years Workforce Plan* https://gov.wales/sites/default/files/publications/2019-07/early-years-workforce-plan.pdf (accessed March 2022).

Welsh Government (2020) *Curriculum for Wales Guidance.* https://hwb.gov.wales/api/storage/afca43eb-5c50-4846-9c2d-0d56fbffba09/curriculum-for-wales-guidance-120320.pdf

Welsh Government (2022) *A Curriculum for Funded Non-maintained Nursery Settings.* https://hwb.gov.wales/api/storage/3e89a21c-60fb-416c-99dd-6e1af3982409/a-curriculum-for-funded-non-maintained-nursery-settings2.pdf (accessed April 2022).

Whitebread, D. (2015) Young children learning and early years teaching. In D. Whitebread and P. Coltman (eds), *Teaching and Learning in the Early Years,* 4th edition. London: Routledge.

Whitebread, D., Basilio, M., Kuvalja, M. and Verma, M. (2012) *The Importance of Play: A report on the value of children's play with a series of policy recommendations.* Toy Industries of Europe.

Wilson, E.O. (1984) *Biophilia.* Cambridge, MA: Harvard University Press.

Women and Equalities Select Committee (2016) *Transgender Equality: First report of session 2015–16.* https://publications.parliament.uk/pa/cm201516/cmselect/cmwomeq/390/390.pdf (accessed April 2022).

Woods, A. (2016) *Elemental Play and Outdoor Learning- Young children's playful connections with people, places and things.* London: Routledge.

Wood, E., and Hedges, H. (2016) 'Curriculum in early childhood education: critical questions about content, coherence, and control', *The Curriculum Journal, 24*(3), 387–405, https://doi.org/10.1080/09585176.2015.1129981

Wood, E. (2019) Unbalanced and unbalancing acts in the Early Years Foundation Stage: A critical discourse analysis of policy-led evidence on teaching and play from the Office for Standards in Education in England (Ofsted). *Education 3–13, 47*(7), 784–795.

Wood, E. (2020) Learning, development, and the early childhood curriculum: A critical discourse analysis of the Early Years Foundation Stage. *Journal of Early Childhood Research, 18*(3), 321–336.

Yang, W. (2019) Moving from imitation to innovation: Exploring a Chinese model of early childhood curriculum leadership. *Contemporary Issues in Early Childhood, 20*(1), 35–52.

Yates, D. (2018) Making their mathematical mark. *Early Years Educator, 20*(5), 38–44.

Yates, D. (2020a) Bringing literacy to life. *Early Years Educator, 20*(4), 36–39.

Yates, D. (2020b) Capturing conversations. *Early Years Educator, 20*(3), 37–39.

Yates, D. (2020c) Let children be the teachers. *Early Years Educator, 21*(10), 29–31.

Yates, D. (2020d) Sharing home learning at a distance: Loving home learning in lockdown. *Early Education: Pedagogic resources.* https://early-education.org.uk/sharing-home-learning-at-a-distance-loving-home-learning-in-lockdown (accessed May 2021).

Yelland, N. (ed.) (1998) *Gender in Early Childhood.* London: Routledge.

Young, I. M. (1980) Throwing like a girl: A phenomenology of feminine body comportment motility and spatiality. *Human Studies, 3,* 137–156. DOI:10.1093/0195161920.003.0003

Zosh, J., Hirsh-Pasek, K., Hopkins, E., Jensen, H., Liu, C., Neale, D., Solis, S.L. and Whitebread, D. (2018) Accessing the inaccessible: Redefining play as a spectrum. *Frontiers in Psychology, 9,* article no. 1124.

Zosh, J., Hopkins, E., Jensen, H., Liu, C., Neale, D., Hirsh-Pasek, K., Lynneth, S. and Whitebread, D. (2017) *Learning through Play: A review of the evidence.* The Lego Foundation. http://dx.doi.org/10.13140/RG.2.2.16823.01447

AUTHOR INDEX

SUBJECT INDEX